YOUTH UNEMPLOYMENT AND SOCIAL EXCLUSION IN EUROPE

A comparative

Edited

The POLICY

P P

P R E S S

First published in Great Britain in July 2003 by

The Policy Press
University of Bristol
Fourth Floor, Beacon House
Queen's Road
Bristol BS8 1QU
UK

Tel +44 (0)117 331 4054
Fax +44 (0)117 331 4093
e-mail tpp-info@bristol.ac.uk
www.policypress.org.uk

British Library Cataloguing in Publication Data

A catalogue record for this book is available from the British Library

ISBN 1 86134 368 X paperback

A hardcover version of this book is also available

Torild Hammer is the coordinator of the EU-funded research project on which the book is based. She is a Senior Research Fellow at Norwegian Social Research (NOVA), Norway.

Cover design by Qube Design Associates, Bristol.
Printed and bound in Great Britain by Hobbs the Printers Ltd, Southampton.

Contents

List of tables and figures

Tables

Figures

Notes on contributors

José Luis Álvaro is Professor at the Faculty of Political Science, Compultense University, Madrid, Spain.

Jan Carle is Assistant Professor and Director of Studies at the Department of Sociology, Göteborg University, Sweden.

Floro Ernesto Caroleo is Professor at the Department of Economic and Statistical Sciences, University of Salerno, Italy.

Fred Cartmel is Researcher at the Department of Sociology, University of Glasgow, UK.

Hans Dietrich is at the Institute for Employment Research, Germany.

Andy Furlong is Professor of Sociology and Head of the Department of Sociology and Anthropology, University of Glasgow, UK.

Alicia Garrido is Associate Professor at the Faculty of Political Science, Compultense University, Madrid, Spain.

Torild Hammer is Senior Research Fellow at Norwegian Social Research (NOVA), Oslo, Norway.

Ivan Harsløf is Research Fellow at Norwegian Social Research (NOVA), Oslo, Norway.

Ilse Julkunen is Associate Professor at the Swedish School of Social Science, University of Helsinki, Finland.

Ira Malmberg-Heimonen is Researcher in Economics at the Swedish School of Social Science, University of Helsinki, Finland.

Francesco Pastore is Researcher in Economics at the Department of Theoretical and Applied Economics, University of Naples, Italy.

Isabelle Recotillet is Researcher at the Department of Industrial Relations, LEST-CNRS, University of Aix-en-Provence, France.

Patrick Werquin is at the Organisation for Economic Co-operation and Development, Directorate of Education. At the time of the first draft, he was with GREQAM-EHESS, Marseilles, France.

ONE

Introduction

Torild Hammer

This book is based on data from a new comparative study of Youth Unemployment and Social Exclusion in Europe (YUSE) data. Representative samples of unemployed youth were interviewed one year after they were registered as unemployed in 10 countries: Denmark, Finland, France, Germany, Iceland, Italy, Norway, Scotland, Spain and Sweden. The various chapters analyse the situation of unemployed youth (aged 18- to 24-years-old) and their risk of social exclusion.

Throughout Europe, unemployment rates are higher among young people than among the general population and as a result there is a serious risk of their marginalisation and exclusion (EC, 1994a). In 2000, the rate of youth unemployment within the European Union (EU) was around 16%, more than twice the unemployment rate experienced by adults (7%). About 40% of the unemployed were younger than 25 years, although this age group comprises only 20% of the labour force. The increase in youth unemployment over the

Table 1.1: Unemployment rate, labour force participation and employment/population ratio: 15- to 24-year-olds

	Unemployment rate	Labour force participation	Employment/ population ratio
Denmark (1997)	8.1	74.2	68.2
Finland (1997)	25.3	44.6	33.3
France (2000)	20.7	29.5	23.3
Germany (2000)	7.7	52.5	48.4
Iceland (1997)	7.7	60.3	55.7
Italy (2000)	31.5	38.1	26.1
Norway (1997)	10.6	61.6	55.1
Spain (2000)	25.5	48.2	35.9
Sweden (1997)	21.0	50.2	39.6
UK (1998)	12.3	69.5	61.0
European Union (2000)	15.6	48.3	40.8

Note: The year given for each country is the year of data collection. At the time of the survey, Campania's unemployment was at 23.7%, youth unemployment was at 62.6% and the long-term unemployment rate at 17.7%. In Veneto, the average unemployment rate was 4.5%, the rate for the young unemployed was 11.7% and the long-term rate of unemployment 1.3%.

Source: OECD (2001)

past decade has occurred despite a demographic decrease in youth and an increased level of education within most member states. European Union countries have seven million young unemployed people, and 40% of them are long-term unemployed, that is, unemployed for more than one year (OECD, 2001).

The unemployment rate has dropped since 2000 in most western European countries. However, both the unemployment rates for young people and the proportion of long-term unemployed are still very high in some countries. Italy, Spain and Finland have the highest youth unemployment and Italy in particular has a very high proportion of long-term unemployment. Sweden and France are in the middle, while Denmark, Germany and Norway have the lowest levels, in particular as regards long-term unemployment. Different countries have handled these problems in different ways, both regarding labour market measures and welfare policies. How do different welfare arrangements and labour market policies influence the situation of unemployed youth and their risk of social exclusion?

Defining social exclusion

The introduction of the concept of 'social exclusion' was initially adopted by the EU in order to avoid discussions about poverty. As Berghman wrote: "The concept was introduced by politicians in the European Commission and not by researchers. The reason seems to have been that the Member States expressed reservations about the word 'poverty' when applied to their respective countries. 'Social exclusion' would then be a more adequate and less accusatory expression to designate the existing problems and definition" (Berghman, 1997, p 5). Although the term was originally utilised in a political setting, Berghman argues that the comprehensiveness and dynamic character of social exclusion renders it useful for researchers. Gallie (1999) claims that a focus on social exclusion reflects a shift in theory. Poverty studies have indeed been increasingly extended from a narrow focus on financial deprivation to a concern for the general capacity of people to share in the quality of life and to participate in the social activities that characterise their societies. The concept of social exclusion maintains a sharper focus on the significance of the non-financial aspects of life, particularly the problem of social isolation.

Paugam (1996) claims that extreme forms of marginalisation occur when prolonged unemployment is coupled with a disintegration of the social networks that bind the individual to the community. In his view, social exclusion represents the end of a process of cumulative disadvantage. Less stable family relations may create isolation and vulnerability.

At the same time, the decline of class solidarity, which previously gave the less privileged a sense of belonging to an identifiable social group, may have encouraged a tendency for people to withdraw into themselves (Gallie, 1999).

In modern society, employment is a central feature of daily life and the main source of financial independence, status, prestige, identity and social participation.

Labour market changes have undermined employment stability as a source of social integration.

In terms of theory, it is important to differentiate between unemployment, poverty, deprivation, marginalisation and social exclusion. An unemployed person may experience poverty and deprivation – but not necessarily social exclusion. Social exclusion can also be described as the process of becoming detached from the moral order or from prevailing norms in society (Room, 1995). In accordance with previous studies, social exclusion may be described as a dynamic and multidimensional concept (Berghman, 1995). Employment promotes social integration, but unemployment may not necessarily imply social isolation.

Some authors (for example, Room, 1995) also suggest that social exclusion should be used as a structural concept to identify structures in society that promote individual marginalisation. Within this perspective, social exclusion can be defined as the failure of one or more of the following sub-systems:

- the demographic and legal system, which promotes civic integration;
- the labour market, which promotes economic integration;
- the welfare system, promoting social integration;
- the family and community system, which promotes interpersonal integration.

In practice, however, system failures are admittedly difficult to separate. The labour market promotes economic integration, but also social and interpersonal integration, and the welfare system promotes economic integration as well as social integration. Yet another perspective regards social exclusion as a process in which dominant groups exclude outsiders in order to protect their own position (Jordan, 1996). Room (1995) links exclusion to lack of resources, which results in "inadequate social participation, lack of social protection, lack of social integration and lack of power" (p 53). In his writing, social exclusion is used to highlight dynamic linkages between material situations on the one hand and attitudes and values on the other, which may reinforce a situation of disadvantage. Social exclusion underlines the ways in which disadvantage in one dimension of life can result in a new and more debilitating set of disadvantages.

The concept of marginalisation has been used to characterise an intermediate position somewhere between full integration and social exclusion. The concept describes risk for social exclusion in different dimensions. Groups of people may be financially integrated, but politically or socially marginalised. They may be culturally integrated (as is the case, for example, with some ethnic groups), but socially marginalised. Young unemployed people are in a marginalised position, but may or may not be excluded from the labour market for a certain period. The concept is useful because the situation of young people can often be characterised as an intermediate position in which we know little about the final outcome. A period of unemployment does not necessarily constitute a problem and may even be a necessary step in obtaining a good adjustment in the labour market.

Presenting the different chapters

The different chapters in the book are based on a common dataset from surveys in 10 countries of nearly 17,000 young unemployed people. In Chapter Two, Jan Carle and Torild Hammer describe the method and research design and discuss some of the methodological problems in the project. In the Appendix a more detailed description of samples and attrition of the surveys in each country is given.

In Chapter Three Andy Furlong and Fred Cartmel describe the social background of the respondents and their families. Furlong and Cartmel (2001) claim that, when addressing issues of social exclusion among young people, it is necessary to acknowledge that paid work has traditionally been regarded as central to the process of social integration. However, it is also necessary to recognise a range of subjective factors, such as attitudes and values, which are not simply outcomes of labour market processes, but which can mediate patterns of exclusion. One important research question addressed by Furlong and Cartmel therefore relates to the extent to which unemployment is associated with social exclusion among young people. For young people who become unemployed, poverty is not necessarily linked to political, cultural, or social exclusion (Room, 1995). Furlong and Cartmel analyse in Chapter Three whether different dimensions of social exclusion are related to each other. First, they examined the relationship between labour market marginalisation and social background. Then, using cluster analysis, they identified different careers and investigated the ways in which such trajectories were related to the subjective dimension of marginalisation. These dimensions include: work commitment, financial deprivation, wellbeing and sociability. They found that Finnish youth experienced more long-term unemployment and more financial deprivation than in Sweden and Spain.

The difficult situation among Scottish and Finnish youth can also be found using other subjective dimensions of social exclusion such as subjective wellbeing. In Finland and Scotland labour market experience was most heavily dominated by unemployment, and Scottish youth in particular also faced problems trying to escape unemployment. Furlong and Cartmel conclude that inadequate benefits can be counterproductive, in that they may reinforce social exclusion.

How strong is the link between a return to employment and social integration? Perhaps the link is not automatic and depends on the nature of work contracts. In countries like Spain and southern Italy, precarious employment is common, and does not necessarily provide the means for integration (Eurostat, 1997a). In Spain, for example, 34% of the labour force is in temporary employment (INEM, 1997a).

Work in the illegal economy is also more frequent in southern Europe than in northern European countries. Indeed, some people have argued that the subterranean economy represents a 'Mediterranean solution' to economic crises and high unemployment (Lemkow, 1987). According to a report on the Italian labour market prepared for the European Commission, 'non-institutional' economic activities involve some 15% of Italian resident employment positions (Brodolini, 1996). In Spain, the hidden economy affects between 18% and 25% of the labour force. It has been estimated that nearly 40% of such irregular work is performed by young people between 18 and 25 years old (Comisiones Obreras, 1994). The hidden economy is less influential in the Nordic countries, although the results of our comparative analyses indicate that 22% of unemployed Icelandic men reported experience with 'moonlight jobs' (Julkunen, 2002).

There are several problems with this type of employment, including low pay, non-existent unemployment benefits or health insurance, and dangerous working conditions. Unemployed youth who work in the hidden economy can end up in dead-end jobs with few prospects for the future. Thus, an important research question relates to the way in which work in the informal economy influences working careers and affects the risk of social exclusion.

Chapter Four by Ivan Harsløf analyses the impact of precarious work among previously unemployed youth. He studies the prevalence of temporary employment and occasional/irregular work among those who had entered employment by the time of the survey. How does such precarious work facilitate the integration of young people into the labour market? Does non-standard labour force participation, such as temporary work or work in the informal economy, represent a step towards social exclusion and labour force marginalisation? Or should it rather be regarded as a step towards a permanent work career? These questions were addressed by evaluating different dimensions of the job quality of these types of jobs. He uses data from Finland, Norway, Scotland and Spain – countries with very different youth labour markets – and analyses the probability of being underemployed according to one's own preferences, receiving formal training as part of the job, and the perceived risk of being unemployed one year later.

His findings are that in countries like Spain and Finland, where there is high unemployment, the majority of unemployed youth receive only temporary or irregular work contracts. In Spain and Italy in particular, many young people in occasional work worked without a contract, which constitutes irregular employment. Many of these young people expected to be unemployed again one year later. Temporary contracts also reduced the probability of the individual receiving on-the-job training, because employers have little reason to invest in employees hired on a temporary basis. The result is that many young people end up in dead-end jobs with few prospects for the future. The conclusion is that temporary employment does not provide sufficient integration into the labour market.

In France, recurrent periods of unemployment are more common among males than among females, but longer among females and members of ethnic minorities (Drew et al, 1992; Werquin, 1997). High levels of labour market mobility among young people, including movements between the job market and education, can be an expression of voluntary behaviour, indicating increased options and individual choices in a modern society where career patterns and transitions to adulthood have become more individualised and destandardised (Banks et al, 1992; Furlong and Cartmel, 1997).

Isabelle Recotillet and Patrick Werquin (Chapter Five) analyse such occurrence dependence in the labour markets of France, Sweden and Spain. The transition from school to work often includes short spells of work interspersed with periods of unemployment. The recurrence of unemployment can be interpreted either as a positive phenomenon or as a depreciation of human capital. According to job-matching theory, switching between jobs and unemployment may be necessary to reach an optimal match. However, according to signalling theory, successive periods of unemployment may also have negative effects, given that employers sort job seekers on the basis of individual characteristics and the number of previous employers. From this point of view, the probability of obtaining a permanent job decreases the greater the number of previous employers. Successive periods of unemployment may also be due to selection effects or state dependence.

The transition from school to work is accompanied by spells of unemployment for many young people. Recotillet and Werquin analyse the probability of successive periods of unemployment in France, Germany and Sweden by asking respondents to provide them with diaries of their main occupations every six months over a five-year period. They found a higher probability of successive periods of unemployment in countries with a high level of unemployment, independent of educational level. However, education did have a significant effect. Young people with lower levels of education had a higher probability of undergoing successive periods of unemployment, even when the authors controlled for unobserved heterogeneity. Moreover, the younger the individual at the time of the first spell of unemployment, the higher the probability of being unemployed again. The authors also calculated the average duration of unemployment, and found that the shorter the average duration, the higher the risk of being unemployed again. Of course several periods of unemployment require that several periods of work occur between them, and recurring unemployment is a different phenomenon than long-term unemployment. This difference is particularly noticeable in France, where many spells of unemployment do not necessarily mean that the respondent has a longer cumulated duration of unemployment. However, the situation in France is different from that of Sweden and Germany, where those who experience several spells of unemployment also face a longer cumulated duration of unemployment. These national differences may be explained by the higher rate of youth unemployment in France, with its higher proportion of long-term unemployment. Compared with Germany and Sweden, it is more difficult to find work in France, and however long each period of unemployment may be, spells of both work and unemployment occur less frequently.

The success of activation policies?

An important question regarding policy to combat youth unemployment concerns the effect of active labour market policies. At one extreme, Denmark spends almost 1.8% of its GDP on active measures, whereas the UK spends just 0.5% (EC, 1994c), Italy 0.90% and France 0.98% (UNEDIC, 1995) of their GNP on comparable measures. In France, about 700,000 people were participating in a range of labour market schemes in 1994 (DARES, 1996). Two French measures seem to be more successful than others: *Contrat d'adaption* and *Contrat de qualification* (DARES, 1997). However, for all measures, the probability and the degree of success are strongly correlated to initial educational level (Demazière and Verdier, 1994). In Italy, trainee contracts provide tax incentives to firms that hire and train young workers (age 16-32), which has become the usual method of smoothing the entry of young people into the labour market. Trainee contracts have been more successful in the north than in the south of Italy (Venturini, 1995). There are also special mobility programmes, as well as so-called 'socially useful projects' (characterised by their social purpose), which provide employment for workers on special short-time compensation with fixed-time contracts. In Italian labour market policy there is, however, a lack of evaluation of the effectiveness of different programmes (Brodolini, 1996).

A great deal of work has been undertaken on evaluations of different national training schemes for unemployed youth in the other countries (see Breen, 1991; O'Connell and Lyons, 1994; Ingerslev, 1994 for a review from the Nordic countries and TemaNord, 1994; in Spain, Comunidad Autonóma de Madrid, 1997). However, there are obvious advantages associated with comparative analyses of different countries, as these measures are developed differently and within a different context in each country. From our project, analysis of data from the Nordic countries has shown that training schemes based on subsidised employment (especially in Sweden) increases job opportunities among unemployed youth (Carle and Julkunen, 1998). Sweden has developed training schemes with the purpose of integrating the young unemployed in ordinary employment. The results are in accordance with Raffe (1987), who argues that the training 'content' of the schemes is less important than the 'context' in which training was provided. Indeed, the key to success centres on the degree to which the schemes supplied the participants with informal contacts with potential employers.

Longitudinal research in Scotland has also highlighted the ways in which policy initiatives that were introduced to help alleviate the consequences of high levels of youth unemployment have provided an institutional framework for the reproduction of inequalities. Whereas youth training schemes provide increasing numbers of people with valuable skills and work experience, those who fail to find full-time employment immediately after completing their schemes tend to be especially vulnerable to long-term unemployment (Furlong, 1993). It has also been noted that young black people are often concentrated in schemes with the poorest employment prospects (Drew et al, 1992; Roberts 1995). It is also important to evaluate training schemes not only as labour market measures, but also as a type of social policy measure that may help young people to cope with problems related to unemployment and prevent social exclusion. Furthermore, increased educational motivation and a return to education are important outcomes (Carle and Julkunen, 1998).

One of the aims of this project has been to describe young people's experience with different activation measures and to examine the extent to which such measures increase job opportunities or education.

Chapter Six by Hans Dietrich analyses active labour market policy in nine European countries. The questions address the recruitment of long-term unemployed youth and attempt to identify those who are recruited to activation schemes. Furthermore, he has estimated the probability of employment after participation in labour market training schemes and possible effects on income.

Dietrich found in his study that in all 10 countries, a total of 40% of unemployed young people had ever participated in a training scheme. The results showed that participation in training schemes now seems to be an institutionalised pattern in the school-to-work transition. However, scheme participation varied significantly across countries. In Italy, only 11% had participated compared with 60% in Sweden. The Nordic countries and Germany have developed an elaborate system of schemes, while Italy and Scotland (before the New Deal) offered only weak support for long-term unemployed people. In all countries, females had a higher participation rate than males. Females are a recognised target group for labour market policy. Individual characteristics, like own children or ethnic minority background, reduced scheme participation in most countries, while young people with health problems or disabilities gained access to labour market training schemes more often than average. In Scotland, Denmark and Germany the best qualified got access to the schemes, whereas the opposite was the case in the Nordic countries. However, in all countries both the number of unemployment spells and accumulated duration of unemployment increased the probability of scheme participation. Duration of unemployment and scheme participation seemed to reduce the probability of entering employment in nearly all countries. However, these results should be interpreted with care because of methodological problems. The findings indicate different mechanisms between getting a job and job outcome, measured as gross hourly income of employed respondents. If the threshold of re-employment is successfully conquered, income depends much more on 'classical human capital'-based indicators, such as qualifications and type of qualifications. The opposite appeared to be the case when considering duration of unemployment, which reduced income. It can therefore be concluded that scheme-based labour market policy had some effect, and supported integration only had an impact to a certain degree.

Floro Ernesto Caroleo and Fransesco Pastore (Chapter Seven) have also evaluated the impact of training on the employability of the young (aged 18-24) long-term unemployed. Here they have focused on three countries that represent different educational and training systems. Spain is an example of a rigid sequential system and Sweden an example of a flexible one, with training taking place when education is completed or interrupted. Germany is an example of a dual educational and training system.

Sweden experienced increased unemployment in the early 1990s, as a consequence of the deepest economic crisis in the post-Second World War period. Unemployment has remained high, despite the large-scale implementation of training programmes, reaching a peak of about 3% of GDP in 1994. Features of the Spanish labour market include high unemployment, widespread temporary employment, and a strong role played by the family, as opposed to public welfare. Germany has also seen unemployment increase since unification in 1991, and has recently introduced labour market measures on a large scale as an alternative to unemployment benefits.

Caroleo and Pastore have focused on the effect of training on labour market participation of a specific group, controlling for individual characteristics, human and social capital endowment, the reservation wage and unemployment duration. They assume that the effectiveness of the activation measures implemented depends on the overall working of the market and on education, training and employment schemes. This approach is novel, as previous literature has focused on a programme-oriented approach to policy evaluation. Multinomial Logit estimates of the probability of belonging to one of five different labour market statuses – unemployment, employment, training, education and inactivity – provide a vivid picture of the features of youth labour market participation in the three countries considered. The authors have evaluated the outcome of training schemes and the probability of employment in countries with such different educational systems.

Comparing Spain, Sweden and Germany, it has been found that such measures seem to have had a weak positive effect only in Sweden. The authors argue that educational reforms may be better than training schemes as a way of qualifying young people for the labour market.

The public/private mix of youth unemployment protection

A main difference between the north and south of Europe, with implications for our study, concerns the mix of public and private support received by unemployed youth. Nordic welfare states provide relatively generous benefits, whereas in southern Europe few young people are entitled to either insurance benefits or social assistance. For example, according to Eurostat Labour Force data, only 20% of the unemployed in Italy are entitled to unemployment benefits compared with an average of 40% in the EU as a whole (Eurostat, 1997a). In Spain, only 17% of the registered unemployed, less than 25 years of age, are entitled to benefits (INEM, 1997b); in France this figure is 36% (UNEDIC, 1995). In the Nordic countries, the proportion of young unemployed receiving benefits varies between 60% and 75% (with the exception of Finland, at 25%) (Carle and Julkunen, 1998). However, the compensation levels of benefits also vary greatly among countries. Denmark has a compensation level of 90% (up to £1,150 per month), whereas in Italy the amount has just recently been raised to 40% (up to £575 per month for ordinary benefits). However, in Italy income support does not depend directly upon previous earnings as it does in the other countries, but on the characteristics of the job lost (sector, size of firms, type of employment relation). Workers in small firms and in most service firms are eligible only for ordinary benefits, whereas workers from medium-sized or large industrial and commercial firms are the most favoured. According to a recent study on living conditions and inequalities in Europe (Vogel, 1997), there are three distinct geographical clusters with three distinct welfare delivery strategies:

- a Nordic (or northern) cluster of advanced institutional welfare states (Nordic countries);
- a southern cluster of family welfare states relying on the traditional family as the prime welfare delivery strategy (Spain and Italy);
- an intermediate central European cluster with moderate institutional and family arrangements in combination with corporate social protection strategies (France, Scotland, Ireland) corresponding to Esping-Andersen's (1990) typologies.

However, in most countries unemployed youth will also be entitled to some type of public support, even if the level of support and degree of coverage varies considerably across countries. Gallie and Paugam (2000) have developed a typology of welfare regimes based on different protection systems for the unemployed in Europe:

- The *sub-protective* model is dominant in southern Europe and provides incomplete coverage and low levels of support – virtually nonexistent, in fact, for unemployed youth. Spain is somewhat more generous in this regard than is Italy. In 1999, 12.5% of unemployed 16- to 24-year-olds received unemployment benefits and an additional 10% received welfare benefits (Álvaro, 2000).
- The *liberal/minimal* model provides an incomplete coverage and low level of support. The UK is an example. Unemployed Scottish youth are entitled to a flat-rate benefit, Jobseeker's Allowance.
- The *employment-centred* model dominant in France and Germany provides a higher level of support than does the *liberal/minimal* model, but exclusively for those established in the labour market. In this way the protection system is divided into insiders and outsiders, which adversley affects unemployed youth with little or no work experience.
- The *universalistic* model, with its high levels of support, high degrees of coverage and an active labour market policy, is the system that dominates in Scandinavia.

An important question here relates to the ways in which different welfare strategies affect unemployment careers and the probability of re-employment.

Obviously, the consequences of unemployment among young people will be related to their financial situation. In Denmark, with a generous insurance system, young people are able to leave their parental home even when unemployed. However, both Spain and Italy have highly family-orientated cultures. A comparative study based upon EC surveys showed that in Italy, 95% of young people in the 16-24 age group were still living in their parental home; this figure compares with 45% in Denmark (Heath and Miret, 1996) and 52% in France (Barailler and Werquin, 1997). Moreover, there is evidence that the young unemployed (especially males) stay much longer with their parents in northern Europe (Wallace, 1986; Hammer, 1996) and in Spain (Navarro, 1994; Bahr et al, 1995) than they do in the other countries. This type of parental dependency may represent barriers against geographical mobility. For instance, the labour force survey in Spain showed that only 38% of the unemployed were willing to move to another area. Furthermore, parental dependency may strengthen the process of inter-generational transmission of poverty in deprived areas. At the same time, parental support may be essential to the prevention of poverty among unemployed youth and may also lessen homelessness and social exclusion, especially in southern Europe (Vogel, 1997). The prolonging of youth as a phase in the life cycle, which can be observed in most European societies, also gives rise to many general problems, especially in southern Europe, where it is not unusual for young people to remain in the parental home until their mid-30s even in areas with higher rates of employment (Cavalli, 1996).

A generous unemployment insurance system may also reduce the incentives for jobsearch activities, thereby reducing job opportunities. Yet evidence from Spain indicates that unemployment benefits do not exert a clear negative influence on jobsearch behaviour or on re-employment (Cebrian et al, 1996). Analyses thus far undertaken in this project based on data from the Nordic countries have revealed that a high compensation level reduces job opportunities. At the same time, economic problems seem to have a negative impact on the chances of employment (Hammer, 1997b).

Another aim of the project was to examine combinations of public and private support and the ways in which such support is related to job opportunities among unemployed youth. In Chapter Eight Torild Hammer and Ilse Julkunen analyse the relationship in six countries between unemployment careers on the one hand and risk of financial deprivation and sources of income on the other. To what extent do different welfare regimes offer economic protection to the young unemployed? There is a need for comparative knowledge from different countries that can identify contrasting policies and outcomes of different welfare models in Europe. An aim of this study, therefore, was to compare the financial circumstances of young unemployed people in Denmark, Finland, Norway, Scotland, Spain and Italy and to study the ways in which different welfare arrangements influence the risk of financial marginalisation among unemployed youth. They found that the level of deprivation was highest in Scotland and Finland, and higher among women than among men.

The young unemployed in Scotland and Finland seem to fall between two categories. Many of them are not entitled to public support and they are not well supported by their parents as young unemployed people in Italy so often are.

In Italy and Spain most young unemployed people live with their parents. The different timing of transition is important. It is reasonable to expect more problems among young people in their thirties when they leave home and establish families of their own.

Both public and private support may have intended or unintended consequences, depending on the individual's coping strategies. Theoretically, it is important to differentiate between coping strategies as 'problem solving' (for example, economic strategies and activities in the informal economy) and strategies related to 'emotional coping' (to maintain self-esteem and deal with emotional problems such as anxiety and depression). Previous research has documented higher levels of anxiety and depression among unemployed youth than among youth in employment or education (Feather and O'Brien, 1986; Warr et al, 1988; Winefield et al, 1988; Hammer, 1993; Álvaro and Frazer, 1994). Some studies indicate that mental health problems among unemployed youth are also related to their work ethic or work involvement. According to the World Value Study, there are strong differences among European countries between work involvement and intrinsic work commitment. Work involvement is high in Scotland and in the Nordic countries (except Denmark), and relatively low in Spain (Ashford and Timms, 1992; Marsh and Álvaro, 1990). Obviously, work commitment is also an expression of work motivation, which in turn influences job opportunities among unemployed youth (Hammer, 1997b; Gallie and Vogler, 1994). Thus the relationships between mental health, work involvement and jobsearch creates important research questions in this study.

In Chapter Nine Ilse Julkunen and Ira Malmberg-Heimonen analyse the ways in which welfare regimes are related to different breadwinner models from a gender perspective. They identify how different predictors and buffers influence mental health in different countries. One can argue that in countries like Spain and Germany, which operate with a male breadwinner model, the domestic role will act more as a buffer than it does in countries like Sweden and Finland, with a dual-breadwinner model. Julkenen and Malmberg-Heimonen also assess the extent to which work commitment, financial dependency and jobsearch influence mental health in countries with different gender systems. They found that the highest level of depression was among young women who reported financial dependency. Among women in male-breadwinner societies such as Spain and Germany, having children acted as a buffer against mental health problems. This was not the case in dual-breadwinner societies such as Finland and Sweden, however; unemployed women in those countries who reported a strong work commitment also reported higher levels of depression. The social network apparently formed an important buffer against depression in Spain and Germany, but not in Scandinavia.

These results are in accordance with other research from this project. Hammer and Russell (2003: forthcoming) found that unemployed women with children tend to withdraw from the labour market in Spain and Germany, but not in the dual-breadwinner societies of Finland and Sweden. The family and social network is more important for women in male-breadwinner societies, where their more traditional social role acts as a buffer against mental health problems.

José Luis Álvaro and Alicia Garrido (Chapter Ten) also analyse the relationship between mental health and social integration. Unemployed young people do not form a homogenous group. How they cope with unemployment depends on the social and cultural context, and differences among countries can highlight the ways in which such cultural differences have an impact on mental health. Utilising the welfare regimes developed by Gallie and Paugam (2000), the authors examine different outcomes in different countries. The overall result was that financial deprivation was strongly related to mental health problems. Unemployed youth in Spain and Italy reported fewer financial problems and higher levels of social support from their parents. This serves to moderate the problems related to the experience of unemployment. By contrast, the young unemployed in northern Europe, particularly in Scandinavia, leave home much earlier and consequently face different problems. However, the results showed diverse situations within the Scandinavian countries. Danish unemployed youth enjoyed the best situation: even those who had left home tended to receive substantial instrumental support from their parents. Finnish and Norwegian youth reported less social support. More mental health problems were found among youth in Spain, the Nordic countries and Scotland than in the other countries. The Spanish situation is particularly interesting; 78% of unemployed youth live with their parents, so their financial situation is generally good. Yet they report an intermediate level of mental health, primarily because the overall average of mental health problems is raised because of the high incidence of mental health problems among those who do leave home and face difficult situations often leading to financial deprivation.

Yet another question relates to the political exclusion of unemployed youth. To what extent do they participate in politics? What are their political attitudes? Being detached from the political process may be part of a broader disenchantment with traditional values, including the work ethic. An important research question concerns the need to chart young people's social and political orientation and values and their social participation. A recent publication from the ECHP survey (European Community Household Panel) shows that homemakers, people in poor households, immigrants and the unemployed are less active in social and political organisations (Vogel, 1997). However, there are large differences among countries; Scandinavian countries display a culture of membership, compared with much lower participation in southern Europe. Political marginalisation may be a response to unemployment.

Chapter Eleven by Jan Carle looks at political attitudes and political participation among unemployed youth, and the author explores how welfare regimes may influence political activity and attitudes. Political marginalisation is an important dimension of social exclusion.

Levels of political activity were lower among the long-term unemployed compared with short-term unemployed in this study. Carle also found that the activity level was related to different welfare regimes. Young unemployed people in employment-centred regimes were more reluctant to participate in politics than were those in liberal/minimal welfare regimes. However, he did not find that young people in the universalistic welfare regime were involved in greater political activity than were the young people in the other countries. Levels of political activity among Finnish and Scottish youth were clearly lower than for young people in the other countries. However, because previous research has found that young people in these two countries generally tend to be politically passive, it is difficult to blame unemployment for political passivity. On the other hand, political withdrawal was higher among the long-term unemployed than among those with short-term unemployment or those in employment or education, suggesting that unemployment may, in fact, have a politically debilitating effect in the long run.

Some caution is necessary when interpreting the findings of this study. The survey included only unemployed youth with permanent residences; we were unable to contact unemployed young people who had no permanent place to live – the most severely excluded of European youth. Further, our data did not allow us to examine more closely such particularly vulnerable groups as ethnic minorities. Such analyses require stratified samples, and our data yielded so few members of different ethnic minorities that it was not possible to subject them to separate analyses. To obtain better data on the situation facing different ethnic minorities among unemployed youth is an important topic for future research.

References and further reading

Álvaro, J.L. (2000) 'Background report for Spain', Unpublished Working Paper.

Álvaro, J.L. and Marsh, C. (1993) 'Cultural mediation of political responses to unemployment: a comparison of Spain and the UK', *International Journal of Sociology and Social Policy*, vol 13, no 3/4, pp 77-106.

Álvaro, J.L. and Frazer, C. (1994) 'The psychological impact of unemployment in Spain', *International Journal of Sociology and Social Policy*, vol 14, no 9, pp 1-19.

Andress, H.J. (1989) 'Recurrent unemployment, the West German experience: an exploratory analysis using count data models with panel data', *European Sociological Review*, vol 5, no 3, pp 275-97.

Ashford, S. and Timms, N. (1992) *What Europe thinks: A study of European values*, London: Dartmouth Publishers.

Bahr, H.M., Déchaux, J.H. and Stiehr, K. (1995) 'Evolución de los vínculos familiares: padres e hijos adultos', in S. Langlois and S. Del Campo (eds) *Convergencia o Divergencia*, Bilbao: BBV.

Banks, M.H. and Ullah, P. (1988) *Youth unemployment in the 1980s: Its psychological effects*, London and Sydney: Croom Helm.

Banks, M. et al (1992) *Career and identity*, Buckingham: Open University Press.

Barailler, C. and Werquin, P. (1997) *School to work transitions: What can be learned from ECHP?*, Working paper of the European Research Network on Transition in Youth, Dublin: ESRI.

Beck-Jorgensen, B. (1991) 'What are they doing when they seem to do nothing?', in J. Ehrnroot and L. Siurala (ed) *Construction of youth*, Finnish Youth Research Society, Helsinki: Vapk-publishing.

Berghman, J. (1995) 'Social exclusion in Europe: policy context and analytical framework', in G. Room (ed) *Beyond the threshold: The measurement and analysis of social exclusion*, Bristol: The Policy Press.

Berghman, J. (1997) 'The resurgence of poverty and the struggle against exclusion: a new challenge for social security in Europe?', *International Social Security Review*, no 50, pp 3-21.

Borzaga, C. (1991) 'The Italian non-profit sector: An overview of an undervalued reality', *Annals of Public and Cooperative Economics*, no 62.

Breen, R. (1991) *Education, employment and training in the youth labour market*, ESRI General Research Series Paper No 152, Dublin: ESRI.

Brodolini, F.G. (1996) *Labour market studies, Italy*, Report prepared for the use of the European Commission, Directorate-General for Employment, Industrial Relations and Social Affairs.

Carle, J. (1987) 'Youth unemployment – individual and societal consequences, and research approaches', *Social Science and Medicine*, vol 25, no 2, pp 147-52.

Carle, J. (1997) 'Politisk aktivitet bland langtidsarbetsløsa ungdomar i Norden', ('Political activity among long-term unemployed youth in the Nordic countries'), Paper presented at the 1997 Nordic Sociology Congress, Copenhagen, 13-15 June.

Carle, J. and Julkunen, I. (eds) (1998) *Young and unemployed in Scandinavia – A Nordic comparative study*, Nord, No 14, Copenhagen: The Nordic Council of Ministeries.

Caroleo, F.E. and Mazzotta, F. (1997) *Youth unemployment and youth employment policies in Italy*, Working Paper, Genève: ILO.

Cavalli, A. (1996) 'The delayed entry into adulthood: is it good or bad for society', Paper prepared for the international conference 'Growing Up Between Centre and Periphery', Lisbon, 2-4 May.

Cebrian, I., Garcia, C., Muro, J., Toharia, L. and Villagomez, E. (1996) 'The influence of unemployment benefits on unemployment duration: evidence from Spain', *Labour*, vol 10, no 2, pp 239-67.

Comisiones Obreras (1994) *Economía sumergida*, Madrid: GPS.

Comunidad Autonóma de Madrid (1997) *La formación para el empleo en la Comunidad de Madrid*, Madrid: CAM.

DARES (1996) *Quatorze ans de politique d'emploi*, Labour Market Ministry.

DARES (1997) *La politique de l'emploi*, Labour Market Ministry.

Demazière D. and Verdier E. (1994) *Evaluation des aides publiques à l'insertion et à la réinsertion*, CEREQ IFRESI.

Dodds, S., Furlong, A. and Croxford, L. (1989) 'Quality and quantity: tackling non-contact attrition in a longitudinal survey', *Sociology*, vol 23, no 2, pp 275-84.

Drew, D., Gray, J. and Sime, N. (1992) *Against the odds: The education and labour market experiences of black young people*, Sheffield: Employment Service.

EC (European Commission) (1994a) *European social policy*, White Paper COM(94) 333, 27 July.

EC (1994b) *Growth, competitiveness, employment: The challenges and ways forward into the 21st century*, White Paper.

EC (1994c) *Employment in Europe*, White Paper COM(94) 381.

Esping-Andersen, G. (1990) *The three worlds of welfare capitalism*, New York, NY/Cambridge: Polity Press.

Eurostat (1997a) *Labour force survey*, Principal results 1996.

Eurostat (1997b) 'Unemployment in the European Union: Theme 3, Population and social conditions', Eurostat monthly short-term statistics, May.

Feather, N.T. and O'Brien, G.E. (1986) 'A longitudinal analysis of the effect of different patterns of employment and unemployment on school-leavers', *British Journal of Psychology*, vol 6, no 77, pp 459-79.

Franklin, M., Mackie, T., Valen, H. et al (1992) *Electoral change: Responses to evolving social and attitudinal structures in Western countries*, Cambridge: Cambridge University Press.

Furlong, A. (1992) *Growing up in a classless society? School to work transitions*, Edinburgh: Edinburgh University Press.

Furlong, A. (1993) 'The youth transition, unemployment and labour market disadvantage', *Youth and Policy*, no 31, pp 24-35.

Furlong, A. and Cartmel, F. (1997) *Young people and social change: Individualisation and risk in the age of high modernity*, Buckingham: Open University Press.

Furlong, A. and Cartmel, F. (2001) 'Does long-term youth unemployment lead to social and economic exclusion? Evidence from six European countries', in B. Furaker (ed) *Employment and unemployment and marginalisation: Studies in contemporary labour markets*, Gothenburg: Gothenburg University Press.

Gallie, D. (1999) 'Unemployment and social exclusion in the European Union', *European Societies*, vol 1, no 2, pp 139-67.

Gallie, D. and Paugam, S. (eds) (2000) *Welfare regimes and the experience of unemployment in Europe*, Oxford/New York: Oxford University Press.

Gallie, D. and Vogler, C. (1994) 'Unemployment and attitudes to work', in D. Gallie, C. Marsh and C. Vogler (eds) *Social change and the experience of unemployment*, Oxford: Oxford University Press.

Goffman, E. (1963) *Stigma: Notes on the management of spoiled identity*, Place?, NJ: Penguin Books.

Hammer, T. (1993) 'Unemployment and mental health among young people: a longitudinal study', *Journal of Adolescence*, vol 16, pp 407-20.

Hammer, T. (1996) 'Consequences of unemployment from youth to adulthood in a life course perspective', *Youth and Society*, vol 27, no 4, pp 450-68.

Hammer, T. (1997a) 'History dependence in youth unemployment', *European Sociological Review*, vol 13, no 1, pp 17-33.

Hammer, T. (1997b) 'The influence of different compensation levels of unemployment benefits upon job chances among unemployed youth: a comparative study of the Nordic countries', *Acta Sociologica*, vol 42, no 2, pp 123-37.

Hammer, T. and Russell, H. (2003: forthcoming) 'Gender differences in work commitment among unemployed youth in Europe', in D. Gallie (ed) *Resisting marginalisation*, Oxford: Oxford University Press.

Hannan, D. and O'Riain, S. (1993) *Pathways to adulthood in Ireland: Causes and consequences of success and failure in transitions amongst Irish youth*, ESRI general research series paper No 161, Dublin: ESRI.

Heath, S. and Miret, P. (1996) *Living in and out of the parental home in Spain and Great Britain: A comparative approach*, Cambridge Group for the History of Population and Social Structure, Working Paper Series: 2/96, Manchester: Department of Sociology, University of Manchester.

INEM (Instituto Nacional de Empleo) (1997a) *Official statistics.*

INEM (1997b) *Encuesta de población activa.*

Ingerslev, O. (1994) *Arbejde, uddannelse eller ledighed? Effekter af den kommunale beskæftigelsesinnsats i 1991 og 1992*, Copenhagen: AKF Forlaget.

Inglehart, R. (1990) *Cultural change: The impact of economic and socialpolitical change on economics, society and politics in advanced industrial society*, Princeton, NJ: Princeton University Press.

Jordan, B. (1996) *A theory of poverty and social exclusion in the European Union*, London: Polity Press.

Julkunen, I. (2002) 'Social and material deprivation among unemployed youth in Northern Europe', *Social Policy and Administration*, vol 36, no 3, pp 235-53.

Julkunen, I. and Hammer, T. (1997) 'Ung och arbetslos i Norden', ('Young and unemployed in the Nordic countries') *Nordisk Sosialt Arbeid*, vol 17, no 2, pp 75-8.

Julkunen, I. and Malmber, I. (1998) *The encounter of high unemployment among youth in the Nordic countries*, Helsinki: The Labour Ministry.

Lane, J.E. and Ersson, S. (1987) *Politics and society in Western Europe*, London: Sage Publications.

Lemkow, L. (1987) 'The employed unemployed: the subterranean economy in Spain', *Social Science in Medicine*, vol 25, no 2, pp 111-13.

Main, B. (1990) 'The effect of the youth training schemes on employment probability', in A. Furlong, D. Raffe and B. Main (eds) *Young people's routes into and within the labour market*, Edinburgh: Industry Department for Scotland.

Malmberg, I. (1997) *Ung, modern och arbetslös (Young, modern and unemployed)*, SSKH meddelande 45, Helsinki.

Marsh, C. and Álvaro, J.L. (1990) 'A cross-cultural perspective on the social and psychological distress caused by unemployment: a comparison of Spain and the United Kingdom', *European Sociological Review*, vol 6, no 3, pp 237-55.

Navarro, M. (1994) 'Relaciones de parentesco', in S. del Campo (ed) *Tendencias Sociales en España*, vol 1, pp 151-9.

O'Connell, P.J. and Lyons, M. (1994) 'Schemes for success? Individual characteristics and the effects of active labour market programmes on employment in Ireland: a preliminary analysis', Paper presented to the European Science Foundation/Consortium for Sociological Research Conference on 'European Society', Espinho, Portugal, October.

O'Connell, P.J. and Sexton, J.J. (1994) 'Labour market developments in Ireland: 1971-1993', in S. Cantillon, J. Curtis and J. Fitzgerald (eds) *Economic perspectives for the medium term*, Dublin: ESRI.

OECD (Organisation for Economic Co-operation and Development) (1996) *Education at a glance: OECD indicators*, Centre for Educational Research and Innovation, Paris: OECD.

OECD (2001) *Employment Outlook*, Paris: OECD.

Pedersen, P.J. and Westgard-Nielsen, N. (1993) 'Unemployment: a review of the evidence from panel data', *OECD Economic Studies*, No 20, Paris: OECD.

Paugam, S. (1996) 'Poverty and social disqualification: a comparative analysis of cumulative social disadvantage in Europe', *Journal of European Social Policy*, vol 6, no 4, pp 287-303.

Raffe, D. (1987) 'The context of the youth training scheme: an analysis of its strategy and development', *British Journal of Education and Work*, vol 1, no 1, pp 1-31.

Ranci, C. (1994) 'The role of the third sector in welfare policies in Italy', in I. Vidal (ed) *Delivering welfare: Repositioning non-profit and co-operative action in Western European welfare state*, Barcelona: Centre d'Initiatives de l'Economie Social.

Roberts, K. (1995) *Youth and employment in modern Britain*, Oxford: Oxford University Press.

Room, G. (ed) (1995) *Beyond the threshold: The measurement and analysis of social exclusion*, Bristol: The Policy Press.

Rosvold, E.O. and Hammer, T. (1991) 'Arbeidslcshet og psykisk helse: en longitudinell studie', *Tidsskrift for Samfunnsforskning*, vol 32, no 2, pp 121-42.

Samek, M. (1997) 'Active and passive labour market policy in Italy', *Trends, Employment Observatory*, no 28, pp 40-6.

Siurala, L. (1994) *Nuorisi-ongelmat modernisaatioperspektiivissa*, Helsinki: Helsingin kaupungin tietokeskuksen tutkimuksia.

Svedberg, L. (1995) *On marginality*, Lund.

TemaNord (1994) *Ungdomsarbetslösheten i de nordiska länderna*, Report 1994:557 Copenhagen: The Nordic Council.

Togeby, L. (1989) *Ens og Forskellig: Gresrodeltagelse i Norden*, Århus: Århus University Press.

Ullah, P., Banks, M. and Warr, P. (1985) 'Social support, social pressure and psychological distress among unemployment', *Psychological Medicine*, no 15, pp 283-95.

UNEDIC (1995) *Bulletin de liaison* (Official Statistics).

Venturini, A. (1995) 'Youth unemployment policies: causes and effects: contrasting the Italian case with the French and the Spanish ones', Paper prepared for the SISDEM seminar.

Vogel, J. (1997) *Living conditions and inequality in the European Union 1997*, Eurostat Working Papers: Population and Social Conditions, E/1997-3.

Wallace, C. (1986) 'From girls and boys to women and men: the social reproduction of gender roles in the transition from school to (un)employment', in S. Walker and L. Barton (eds) *Youth, unemployment and schooling*, Milton Keynes: Open University Press.

Warr, P., Jackson, P. and Banks, M.H. (1988) 'Psychological effects of unemployment', *Journal of Social Issues*, vol 44, no 4.

Werquin, P. (1997) '1986-1996: Dix ans d'intervention publique sur le marché du travail', *Economie et Statistiques*, nos 304-305, pp 121-36.

Winefield, A.H., Tiggemann, M. and Goldney, R.D. (1988) 'Psychological concomitance of satisfactory employment and unemployment in young people', *Social Psychiatry and Psychiatric Epidemiology*, vol 23, pp 149-57.

Xiberras, M. (1994) *Les theories de l'exclusion*, Paris: Meridiens.

TWO

Method and research design

Jan Carle and Torild Hammer

Marginalisation is the leading concept in this study. The main research question addresses the degree to which labour market position correlates with other social circumstances in the lives of young people.

Different aspects of marginalisation in relation to youth unemployment are highlighted and analysed in the study. The following dimensions of marginalisation and integration were chosen:

* employment;
* family situation;
* living conditions;
* social network;
* politics and society;
* education.

The study is cross-sectional. At one point, a group of young people, who had been at least three months continuously unemployed during the first half of the year, was selected as a sample. Thus, the authors chose to study a group that, according to marginalisation theories, had a problematic relationship with one central area: employment. The crucial question, then, concerns the extent to which this position is interpreted as problematic in relation to other domains. To what extent does labour market position covary with access to other resources and with the individual capacities of the young people involved?

The research design can be illustrated as follows:

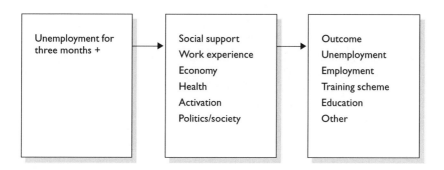

At the time of the samples being drawn, all of the young people in the study were unemployed. Approximately six to 12 months later, when they were interviewed, the situation had changed. What factors could have influenced this outcome? A certain number of variables problematic to this relationship were chosen, as follows:

- social support;
- work experience and education;
- unemployment experiences;
- financial situation;
- health situation;
- experiences of labour market schemes;
- political attitudes.

From an analytical perspective, however, it is not evident how these variables should be regarded. Do they reflect circumstances that can be influenced by an outcome, or are they more permanently structured? To deal with the time dimension, different time perspectives were included in the questions, under the assumption that certain variables are stable enough to be regarded as having the capacity to influence employment outcome.

This research strategy was chosen in order to shed light on the ways in which different degrees of marginalisation, or, to be more specific, different levels of integration into the labour market, may be related to other circumstances in the lives of the young people in our study. The aim was also to be able to form an opinion on the processes of marginalisation in terms of the relationship between the outcome of unemployment and differences in the life situations of young people.

In countries with different labour market and educational policies, unemployed youth can end up in work, education, employment schemes, or permanent unemployment. This research investigates the outcome of long-term unemployment among youth.

In all countries except Italy and Scotland, representative samples were drawn from national unemployment registers, with eligible respondents defined as young people between the ages of 18 and 24 who had been unemployed for a period of at least three months during the previous six months. They were interviewed one year later. No national unemployment register provides this information in Italy, however, so Italian unemployed young people in this age group were contacted through the local employment offices ($n = 6,000$). The researchers then drew a stratified sample of the north ($n = 500$) and the south ($n = 1,000$) of Italy, and members of this sample were interviewed one year later. In Scotland, researchers were denied access to the unemployment register and used a sampling procedure in much the same way as in Italy ($n = 1,500$). In this way, Scotland and Italy managed to use the same sample design as the other countries.

The total sample in all countries thus consists of young unemployed people with a variety of work histories who, at the time of the interviews, were located in a wide range of positions inside and outside of the labour market. This survey design is conducive to a comparison of young people with unemployment experience, some of whom have managed to acquire positions in the full-time labour market; some of whom have resumed full-time study; and others who have remained unemployed, have withdrawn from the labour market, or have become marginalised in some other way.

In the Nordic countries, the surveys were conducted in 1996. The surveys were initially based on postal questionnaires with additional strategies employed to minimise bias due to skewed response rates. Those who failed to respond to the initial questionnaire after having been sent a reminder were interviewed by telephone. Attrition analyses based on register data in Norway showed no skewed attrition as a function of educational level, duration of unemployment, work experience, proportion without relevant work experience or education, proportion receiving unemployment benefits, age, gender, or county. In Sweden, Norway and Finland, register data did not show any skewed attrition. In the other countries permission that would allow the researchers to couple the survey with register data was not obtained. However, country-specific attrition analyses have found the data to be representative. In Denmark, the sample was drawn from insured unemployed young people in the same age group (about 80% of the young unemployed are insured in Denmark). However, analyses of the differences between insured and uninsured unemployed youth in Norway, Sweden, Finland and Denmark show that the differences are basically the same in all countries (Ulldal-Poulsen, 2000). In other words, we can control for the biased sample in Denmark, by comparing with all other countries, only those unemployed youth who are insured, and additionally, with the use of multivariate analysis, by controlling for insured versus uninsured.

In Scotland, data collection was conducted in 1997/98. Analyses of attrition found the sample to be representative. Length of unemployment did not affect response rates. However, there were more non-respondents living in poorer urban areas than in rural areas, although this effect was not statistically significant.

Data collection in Italy, Spain, France and Germany was conducted in 1999/ 2000. As in the Scandinavian countries, postal questionnaires were used in Spain and Scotland, whereas telephone interviews were employed in France and Germany. In summary, the study draws on comparative surveys in 10 European countries among representative samples of 18- to 24-year-olds who had been unemployed for at least three months continuously, and who were interviewed six to 12 months later.

The samples and response rates were: Denmark, 76% of $n = 1,540$; Finland, 73% of $n = 2,386$; France, 51% of $n = 4,000$; Germany, 65% of $n = 3,000$; Iceland, 63% of $n = 2,280$; Italy net sample, $n = 1,421$ 89% of $= 1,590$; Norway, 56% of $n = 1,997$; Scotland, 56% of $n = 1,500$; Spain, 52% of $n = 5,000$; Sweden, 63% of $n = 3,998$.

The fact that data collection was conducted in different years presents a problem, because of changes in the business cycle in the period 1996 to 2000.

After a review of the economic literature, the research group decided to solve this problem by controlling in the multivariate analyses for some economic indicators for the year of data collection (Lancaster and Imbens, 1994; Van den Berg and Van der Klaauw, 1999). The measurements used for each of the variables are explained and described in the various chapters of this book.

Collecting the survey data

The questionnaire was addressed to unemployed young people aged 18-24 years. The following criterion was decided on in our sample: *at least three months of continuous unemployment during the first half year before the time of sampling.* It would have been both interesting and fruitful to include a randomly selected group of young people as a reference group to see if there were marked differences between the chosen group and a randomly selected sample of the entire youth population. It was thought possible that comparisons could be made on the basis of existing register data. Yet it was decided not to include a control group, primarily because a first-hand comparison of the unemployment situation in the countries was desired. It was expected that, even within the group we had selected, a considerable number of young people would be employed at the time of the interviews, and that this situation would guarantee variations within the group. It was thus possible to focus on the question of which groups remained unemployed and which groups gained employment or re-entered the educational system after the sample had been chosen.

More detailed descriptions of sample and attrition in the countries are given in the Appendix.

Measurements

The questionnaire is based upon the use of different measures and indices in previous research. In order to allow the reader to evaluate the results presented in the following chapter, some of the main variables are briefly described:

- *Unemployment* was measured through self-reports: during the week prior to the interview, was the respondent employed or not? The respondent could choose between 20 occupational categories and select more than one option. Thus one person could be unemployed and a housewife. The data were coded hierarchically, so that unemployment status took precedence over all other categories. Those who were employed and in education were coded under education. Apprentices were also coded as being in education.
- *Unemployment* was also measured by the total number of spells of unemployment that the respondent had experienced: (1) total months of unemployment experience, and (2) duration of the longest spell of unemployment.
- *Jobsearch* was measured with seven questions about applied jobsearch strategies. Respondents who did not apply for a job were also asked why.

- *Education* was measured according to the Casmin Scale, which was developed in previous comparative research and has been applied in a number of comparative studies (for a short description, see W. Mueller: www.nuff.ox.ac.uk). The Casmin Education classification is based upon two primary classification criteria: (1) the differentiation of a hierarchy of educational levels, and (2) the difference between 'general education' and 'vocationally oriented education'.
- *Financial deprivation* was measured with an 11-item scale that addressed both material and cultural deprivation and had been used in several comparative studies, including Fridberg, 1993. The question was: during the last 12 months, which of the following have you had to give up due to lack of money:
  - warm meals;
  - essential clothes for yourself or your family;
  - paying rent and bills on time;
  - visiting the cinema, theatre or concerts;
  - inviting friends to your home;
  - visiting relatives or friends living in other towns;
  - buying birthday or Christmas presents;
  - holidays away;
  - newspapers, hobbies, or other recreational activities;
  - visiting pubs or restaurants.

Each item was scored from 1 (often) to 3 (never), and an additive index included all questions.

- *Work commitment* was determined by a scale developed by Warr et al (1979). It required respondents to agree or disagree with six statements:
  - 'It is very important to me to have a job.'
  - 'If I won a lot of money I would want to work.'
  - 'I hate being unemployed.'
  - 'I feel restless if I do not have a job.'
  - 'Work is one of the most important things in my life.'
  - 'I would prefer to work even if unemployment benefits were generous.'

The response categories for each item were: 'strongly agree', 'agree', 'neither agree nor disagree', 'disagree' and 'strongly disagree'. Higher scores indicate greater work commitment.

- *Mental health* was measured with 10 questions from Hopkins Symptoms Checklist (HSCL) (Derogatis et al, 1974) that focused on anxiety and depression. These items were selected as the result of a factor analysis of a health survey of the same age group (CBS, 1991). We have used the mean score of the 10 items, which were scored from 1 = 'no problems' to 4 = 'heavy problems' (range = 1.00 to 4.00).

- *Coping with unemployment* was constructed as an index based on seven items used previously in the Level of Living Surveys (CBS, 1991):
  - 'I have more time for family and friends.'
  - 'I do not accomplish anything.'
  - 'I have problems planning for the future.'
  - 'I am financially dependent on others.'
  - 'I can use my time as I please.'
  - 'I have more time for my hobbies.'

The response categories for each item were: 'strongly agree', 'agree', 'neither', 'disagree' and 'strongly disagree', the negative items being reversed for coding. The scores ranged from 1 to 5, with higher scores indicating greater coping problems.

Conclusions about the sample and attrition in the countries

With the exception of Iceland, the sample was based on a criterion of at least three months of continuous unemployment during the period 1 January to 30 June 1995. For several reasons, Iceland used two months as a criterion. Because of the small population of Iceland, the number of young unemployed people would have been too small if a requirement of three months of unemployment had been instituted. Furthermore, it was decided to conduct a total study on all the unemployed young people in Iceland, and a criterion of two months yielded a large enough population to make this possible.

The Danish sample did not include non-insured young people. It can be assumed that the non-insured young unemployed people differ with regard to experiences of both unemployment and employment, financial resources, living and family conditions, and political and social attitudes. If differences between the countries involved in the study are to be found, the question arises as to whether they are due to the divergent sampling frame or to real differences in unemployment situations among the countries. One way to examine the importance of a divergent sample is to try to compare the national samples to see if there would have been differences if the non-insured were excluded. Another way is to compare the insured in the respective countries and to analyse differences and similarities within these groups. Statistically this can be controlled in multivariate analyses.

The time variations in the realisation of the survey also created some problems. These problems have been noted and analyses that concern the aspect of time have therefore been cautious. The data material was coded in a way that enabled tendency analysis of response differences between the postal questionnaire rounds and the telephone interviews. Information is available on 6,006 individuals (77% of the respondents – Denmark is not included) on whether they responded without a reminder; to the first, second, or third reminder; or through the telephone interview. Certain tendencies were observed in the responses of those who responded without reminders and those who responded after the reminders:

- women responded to a greater extent to the first mailing;
- those in the 20- to 22-year-old group were more likely to respond to the first mailing;
- people in Finland were those most likely to respond to the first mailing, followed by those in Norway, Sweden and Iceland;
- those with less experience of unemployment responded to a greater extent to the first mailing;
- those with higher education responded to a greater extent to the first mailing;
- those who did not feel that people looked down on the unemployed responded to a greater extent to the first mailing;
- those who did not feel isolated or unhealthy, and who had not lost confidence, responded to a greater extent to the first mailing;
- those who self-reported more mental problems, such as anxiety and feelings of hopelessness and nervousness, were more likely to respond to the first mailing and the telephone interview;
- those who reported being more to the political left were more likely to respond to the first mailing.

According to one hypothesis, the tendency of the attrition follows the tendency of the reminders. If this is the case, it seems that the questionnaire was less likely to reach the young people with longer experiences of unemployment, with a lower educational background, or with self-reported feelings of isolation. The differences were small, but taken together they point to a tendency in the material. This is not a surprising finding; the opposite finding, in fact, would be amazing. However, there is evidence from previous research of a process of gradual passivity and coping. What is interesting in this study is the implication that there was a group of people who were worried about their situation, some of whom responded rapidly and some after several reminders. This could indicate that people new to the unemployment process worry about their situation and want to tell others about their experiences, whereas those who have become more passive during a long process of unemployment need to be nudged into response through reminder notices.

It is obvious that there are various methodological problems in comparative research. However, the attrition analyses conducted for the countries involved showed that, all in all, the material is well balanced and that there is no need to correct skewness. However, the Scottish and Italian cluster samples are difficult to evaluate because they are not representative samples.

References

CBS (Statistics Norway) (1991) *The Norwegian level of living survey*, Oslo: Statistics Norway.

Derogatis, L.R., Lipman, R.S., Uhlenhut, E.H. and Covi, L. (1974) 'The Hopkins Sympton Checklist: a self-report symptom inventory, *Behavioural Sciences*, vol 19, pp 1-15.

Fridberg, T. (ed) (1993) *On social assistance in the Nordic capitals*, Copenhagen: The Danish National Institute of Social Research.

Lancaster, A. and Ibens, G. (1994) 'Combining micro and macro data in microeconometrics models', *Review of Economic Studies*, no 2, pp 23-34.

Uldall-Poulsen, H. (2000) 'Differences between unemployment insurance benefit claimants and social assistance benefit claimants in the Nordic countries', in A. Furlong and T. Hammer (eds) *Youth unemployment and marginalisation in Northern Europe*, Oslo: Norwegian Social Research 18/2000, pp 109-29.

Van den Berg, G.J. and Van der Klaauw, B. (1999) 'Combining micro and macro unemployment duration data', Working Paper, Amsterdam: University of Amsterdam.

Warr, P., Cook, J. and Wall, T. (1979) 'Scales for the measurement of some work attitudes and aspects of psychological well-being', *Journal of Occupational Psychology*, vol 52, pp 129-48.

THREE

Unemployment, integration and marginalisation: a comparative perspective on 18- to 24-year-olds in Finland, Sweden, Scotland and Spain

Andy Furlong and Fred Cartmel

Introduction

In modern industrial societies, it is not uncommon for young people to experience a period of unemployment and, in many ways, it can be argued that unemployment has become a normal part of youth transitions. In the four countries studied here, many young people will encounter a period of unemployment at some stage between leaving education and obtaining their first full-time jobs. For many, unemployment can be regarded as a temporary stage in an otherwise smooth and predictable transition. Others, however, find it extremely difficult to escape from unemployment and gain a secure foothold in the labour market. In this chapter, the experiences of young adults who faced a recent period of unemployment of a duration of at least three months in Finland, Sweden, Scotland and Spain are examined. The main objective is to identify patterns of labour market integration and marginalisation in societies with a range of different rates of overall unemployment and to explore the links between labour market transitions and more subjective and social manifestations of unemployment that are often regarded as components of social exclusion (Silver, 1995; Strobel, 1996). We view social exclusion as a dynamic process and argue that long-term unemployment frequently leads to marginalisation but does not necessarily result in exclusion.

The chapter begins with a discussion of the concept of social exclusion before moving on to examine structural differences in experiences of unemployment in the four countries, highlighting routes out of unemployment and emerging patterns of marginalisation. Finally, variations in subjective responses to unemployment are examined and the significance of factors that mediate the relationship between structures of unemployment and subjective experiences and therefore serve to reduce the likelihood of social exclusion are explored.

With origins in French sociology, in recent years the term 'social exclusion' has become established in many countries as a key sociological concept. However, its theoretical underpinnings are not always clear. As Silver acknowledges, social exclusion is an "essentially contested concept" (Silver, 1995, p 7); it involves economic position as well as cultures and value systems that are linked to life chances. Exclusion is not simply linked to a prevailing situation of an individual or group, but is also linked to future prospects and draws on past experience. Indeed, Atkinson argues that "people are excluded not just because they are currently without a job or income, but because they have few prospects for the future" (Atkinson, 1998, p 6). In this sense, exclusion is also related to past labour market experiences that may leave "people feeling that they lack control of their lives" (O'Brien, 1986, p 23). In other words, the concept of social exclusion is used to highlight *dynamic* linkages between material situations and attitudes and values that may be seen as reinforcing a situation of disadvantage. It underlines the ways in which disadvantage in one dimension of life can result in a new and more debilitating set of disadvantages. This relationship is explored in this chapter.

In any discussion of social exclusion among young people it is necessary to acknowledge that paid work has traditionally been regarded as central to the process of social integration (Levitas, 1998). At the same time, it is important to acknowledge that there are a range of subjective factors (such as attitudes and values) that are not simply outcomes of labour market processes but can themselves mediate patterns of exclusion (Furlong et al, 2003). Long-term unemployment, for example, may in some circumstances lead to social exclusion, yet high levels of social or financial support may reduce the chances of exclusion. Agency must also be regarded as a key component of an individual's resource base and can smooth processes of integration even when structural resources are weak (Furlong et al, 2003).

In terms of young people's experiences, the model below (Table 3.1) highlights ideal types of exclusion and integration. While neither position necessarily involves all of the factors listed, there is an extent to which objective and subjective factors have been regarded as mutually reinforcing. The proposition developed in this chapter is that the relationship between subjective and objective dimensions of exclusion is complex and mediated by nationally specific aspects of the unemployment experience.

Table 3.1: Integration versus exclusion: ideal types

Social integration	Social exclusion
Employment/sporadic unemployment	Long-term unemployment
High employment commitment	Low employment commitment
Financial security	Financial insecurity
Optimism	Pessimism
Life satisfaction	Life dissatisfaction
High social support	Low social support
Active lifestyle	Passive lifestyle

Patterns of unemployment: national variations

The unemployment experiences of young people in the four countries are strongly influenced by welfare regimes and levels of state support available during a period of unemployment. The four countries selected for this chapter illustrate the contrasting welfare regimes described by Gallie and Paugam (2000). At one extreme we have the 'sub-protective' regime of Spain, and at the other the 'universalistic' regime of Sweden.

Gallie and Paugam (2000) describe a sub-protective regime as one that provides the unemployed with very minimal protection at a level that is unlikely to meet subsistence requirements. Many unemployed people receive no benefits whatsoever. A liberal/minimal regime is slightly more comprehensive in its coverage, but levels of compensation remain low and there is a risk of poverty. In such regimes, higher levels of compensation tend to be regarded as something that may remove the incentive to work and disrupt the equilibrium of the labour market. In employment-centred regimes, benefit eligibility tends to depend on previous labour market involvement. As such, the risk of poverty tends to be concentrated among those with limited recent labour market involvement, especially the long-term unemployed. Gallie and Paugam identify a universalistic regime as being the only type that provides comprehensive benefit coverage and a relatively high level of financial recompense, usually irrespective of the income of other members of the household.

Levels of all-age unemployment in the four countries in 1995 show that Finland (17%) had the highest rate, followed by Spain (15.4%), Sweden (8.7%) and Scotland (8.6%). As would be expected, experience of unemployment among the sample of young people was affected by the overall levels of unemployment within each of the countries, although it has been noted that in the EU rates of youth unemployment tend to be around twice as high as among the adult population (European Commission, 1997). A slightly different pattern emerges, in relation to long-term unemployment among young people, which was most common in Scotland and Spain (Table 3.2). It also shows that males tended to have longer continuous periods of unemployment in all countries except Spain.

Table 3.2: Longest continuous period of unemployment, by country (mean months)

	Male	Female
Finland	14.6	12.8
Sweden	9.6	9.2
Scotland	16.4	13.7
Spain	16.5	18.8
All	13.4	12.9

Anova $f = 122.625$ $p < 0.001$

While a comparison of the longest periods of time for which young people had been unemployed provides an indication of those countries in which long-term youth unemployment is most common, here it provides an incomplete picture of labour market prospects. Given that the chance of long-term unemployment among the sample is affected by time spent in the labour market (which varies between samples as a result of age differences and variations in average school-leaving ages), a calculation was made of mean number of months spent employed for each month of unemployment (Table 3.3). Here we find that males and females in Spain had spent five months employed for every one month they had spent unemployed. At the other end of the scale, the labour market histories of young Finns were clearly dominated by unemployment: on average they had spent less than two months employed for every month of unemployment. Although overall differences were relatively small, unemployment figured slightly more prominently in the labour market histories of males.

Patterns of unemployment: accounting for personal and family characteristics

National differences in the unemployment experiences of young people are affected by personal and social characteristics. In a highly educated and culturally homogenous society, unemployment may be widely distributed between social groups, whereas in a society characterised by strong inequalities, unemployment may be heavily concentrated among the least advantaged. Sociologically, it would have been interesting to compare the impact of social class on patterns of unemployment in the different countries, but unfortunately the data from Sweden and Finland do not contain information about parents' social class. Among the full sample, the best available proxy for social class is parental education and here there are quite large variations between the countries. Young people in Finland and Scotland were most likely to have parents educated to university level, while the Spanish were least likely to have parents who had received a university education. In Finland, for example, 16% of the sample had fathers educated to university level and 12% had mothers with university degrees. In Spain, far fewer parents had received a university education (3% of fathers and 1% of mothers). In Spain and Scotland, relatively high proportions

Table 3.3: Mean number of months spent employed for each month of unemployment, by country

	Male	Female
Finland	1.5	1.8
Sweden	3.6	4.9
Scotland	2.7	2.9
Spain	5.2	5.1
All	3.1	4.0

Figure 3.1: Highest educational level of respondents' parents, by country

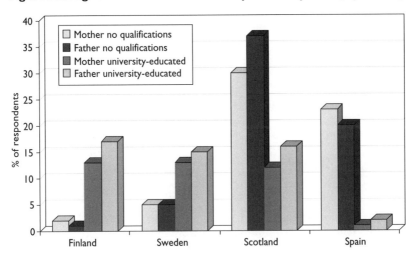

had fathers who had left education with no qualifications (37% and 20% respectively), while three in 10 young Scots (30%) and nearly one in four young Spaniards (23%) had mothers who had left without qualifications (Figure 3.1).

While parental education provides some indication of cultural capital, family experience of unemployment (especially long-term unemployment) provides a better indication of economic hardship within the family and may also reflect low levels of opportunity in the local labour market. Looking at the proportions of young people with parents who had been unemployed for six months or more out of the past 12 months (Figure 3.2), two countries stand out as having

Figure 3.2: Long-term unemployment among respondents' family, by country

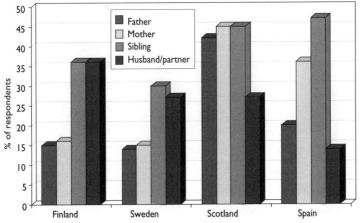

high levels of inter-generational unemployment: Scotland and Spain. Levels of long-term sibling unemployment were also high in Scotland and Spain, suggesting that in these countries a substantial proportion of the sample came from families in which unemployment was common. With both of these countries having weak welfare regimes, the risk of social exclusion is high.

With the sample being drawn from those who have recently experienced unemployment, we would expect the qualification profile of the group to be somewhat below that of the age range in general. Educational attainments are difficult to compare, but if we take those who have minimal education (those who have not been educated beyond the level of compulsory schooling), some sharp differences emerge (Figure 3.3). Notably, young people from Scotland tend to be far less qualified than those from the other countries. However, a different picture emerges when we compare those who have completed university. The highest proportion of graduates are found in Scotland (12%) and Sweden (7%), while there are very few graduates in Finland (2%). In part, these differences reflect institutional structures and sampling procedures: the high number of Scottish graduates, for example, is a partly a consequence of a relatively short degree course.

Unemployment and labour market integration

With some young people having ended their spell of unemployment between the sample date and interview, it is necessary to put the discussion of processes of labour market marginalisation into perspective by looking at patterns of

Figure 3.3: Educational level of respondents, by country

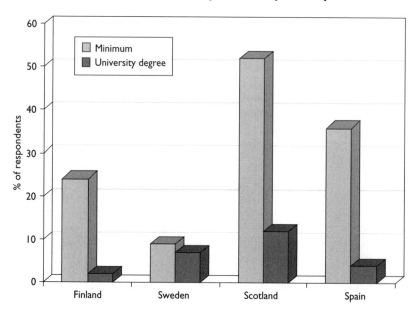

integration. In each country, among both males and females, it was a minority of young people who had managed to obtain permanent full-time employment six months after a period of unemployment (15% overall). For both males and females, the Finns had been least successful while young people in Scotland had been most successful (Figure 3.4). In all countries except Scotland, males were most likely to have obtained stable employment.

Analysis was undertaken to trace unemployment outflows across 10 consecutive six-monthly time periods in order to highlight variations in routes out of unemployment and the degree to which unemployment careers become entrenched (Table 3.4). The outflow figures were drawn from a diary question which asked for information on respondents' *main* activity during a series of six-month periods (entry into short term-jobs, training, or further brief spells of unemployment *within* these periods are therefore hidden). Analysis of these outflows show that a large proportion of those who were mainly unemployed in any one six-monthly period remained unemployed in the next period.

Continuity in unemployment was greatest in Scotland and Spain where, over the period covered by the diaries, an average of over 70% remained unemployed from one time period to the next. Finland and Sweden had lower levels of unemployment continuity (47% and 37% respectively). Levels of unemployment continuity are particularly significant given that researchers in a number of countries have shown that long-term unemployment tends to be associated with a decline in the chances of finding paid employment, partly due to a process of stigmatisation (Jensen, 1987).

Average levels of outflow from unemployment to employment across the time periods were relatively low in Scotland and Spain (both 19%). However, it is important to recognise that the quality of jobs entered and the security of these jobs is also likely to vary strongly between countries and between genders. We are unable to address this issue from existing data. Relatively few young people moved between unemployment and education in any of the countries,

Figure 3.4: Young people who have gained permanent employment, by country

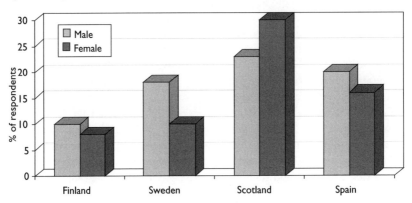

Table 3.4: Destinations six months after a period of unemployment: country averages over 10 six-monthly time periods (5 years) (%)

Unemployment to: (all)	Finland	Sweden	Scotland	Spain
Unemployment	47	37	72	71
Employment	21	26	19	19
Training	7	15	5	2
Education	15	12	3	4
Other	10	9	1	3
Total	(100)	(99)	(100)	(99)
Unemployment to: (males)	**Finland**	**Sweden**	**Scotland**	**Spain**
Unemployment	49	38	74	68
Employment	18	27	17	20
Training	6	15	5	2
Education	11	11	2	4
Other	13	8	1	6
Total	(99)	(99)	(99)	(100)
Unemployment to: (females)	**Finland**	**Sweden**	**Scotland**	**Spain**
Unemployment	43	35	65	74
Employment	26	24	26	19
Training	7	15	3	1
Education	21	14	4	5
Other	3	10	2	1
Total	(99)	(99)	(99)	(100)

although the situation was better in Finland and Sweden than in Scotland and Spain. Average rates of movement between unemployment and education tended to be somewhat higher for females, especially in Finland. Training routes also tend to be underdeveloped with relatively few young people ending their unemployment through training. While an average of 15% of young people in Sweden moved from unemployment to training, in all other countries less than one in 10 went into training (ranging from 7% in Finland to 2% in Spain).

In order to gain further insights into variations in labour market histories, cluster analysis was used to identify the four main typologies of experience among the sample. Information from the diary question on all nine possible destinations at each of the 12 time points was entered and the K-Means classification method used to construct groups. The four groups identified were:

- *Education-dominant:* those whose diaries were dominated by educational participation, with the remainder of the time being fairly equally divided between work and unemployment. This group accounted for 25% of the sample.
- *Mixed experience:* although work and unemployment dominate labour market histories, education and training are also significant. This group accounted for around 19% of the sample.

- *Employment-dominant:* among this group, work was clearly the dominant experience. More than one in four members of the sample fell into this group (27%).
- *Unemployment-dominant:* the recent experiences of this group had been heavily dominated by unemployment. This heavily disadvantaged group represented around 28% of the sample and, by a very small margin, was the largest group.

Looking at the variation of dominant experiences by country (Table 3.5), it is clear that the Finns and Scots (males and females) were most likely to have labour market histories dominated by unemployment, although in both of these countries, males were more likely to have followed such routes. The employment-dominant route was also strong in Sweden and Scotland among males and the mixed route most common in Sweden (with little gender variation). The education-dominant route was most common in Spain (males and females).

Table 3.5: Clusters of labour market experiences, by gender and country (%)

Male	Education-dominant	Mixed	Employment-dominant	Unemployment-dominant
Finland	13	18	18	52
Sweden	20	23	34	23
Scotland	20	9	34	37
Spain	43	14	23	33
All	22	18	27	33
p<0.001				
Female				
Finland	22	18	27	40
Sweden	23	20	28	16
Scotland	30	19	27	25
Spain	45	14	25	19
All	29	19	27	23
p<0.001				

Subjective dimensions

The analysis of patterns of youth unemployment within the four countries provides some indication of the extent to which young people face the risk of labour market marginalisation. However, it is important to recognise that young people's interpretation of their own situations may be at odds with patterns that are viewed from a structural perspective. Du Bois Reymond (1998), for example, draws attention to what she refers to as the 'trendsetters' who move constantly between unemployment and temporary, part-time or low-skill service jobs as part of a process of self-actualisation and exploration. For du Bois Reymond, the process of modernisation is seen as linked to the emergence of 'choice biographies' in which unemployment may no longer be linked to processes of pessimism and despair. However, in many respects, the concepts of biography and choice biography have emerged from the more affluent European societies in which levels of unemployment have been relatively low and social security benefits relatively high.

In this section we examine the links between labour market routes and the subjective responses of young people living within societies characterised by different opportunity structures, cultures and support networks. The focus is on the differential experiences of those within the four clusters described in the previous section and the aim is to highlight the extent to which young people's objective routes are reflected in subjective experiences within the different countries. While patterns of unemployment may be largely determined by overall structures of opportunity in a society, it is not clear whether subjective responses are simply reflections of these underlying structures. The experience of unemployment may be conditioned by the perceived chances of finding work rapidly, but other factors, such as levels of financial security, supportive social networks and strength of work commitment within a culture are also likely to be significant.

To investigate these relationships, we first looked at overall satisfaction with life, which was strongly associated with labour market routes. Those who had followed routes dominated by unemployment were clearly more likely to express overall dissatisfaction with their lives than those who had followed other routes. Males who had followed mixed routes or routes dominated by unemployment tended to be more likely to express dissatisfaction than females following comparable routes. While these figures clearly highlight the negative impact of unemployment on life satisfaction, it is important to note that those who experience high levels of unemployment express general satisfaction with their lives (Table 3.6).

Table 3.6: General dissatisfaction with life, by labour market routes (%)

	Education-dominant	Employment-dominant	Mixed	Unemployment-dominant	X^2
Male	25	21	23	36	0.000
Female	20	21	24	28	0.004
Finland	17	16	14	26	0.000
Sweden	24	17	22	33	0.000
Scotland	33	42	52	54	0.000
Spain	21	17	23	31	0.001

On a country-specific level, we also tend to find that life dissatisfaction is more prevalent among those who have followed unemployment-dominant routes. However, despite high levels of unemployment in Finland, overall levels of life dissatisfaction among those who have followed routes dominated by unemployment are relatively low. Levels of life dissatisfaction are particularly high in Scotland, although this is not confined to those following the most disadvantaged routes. In Spain and Sweden, levels of life dissatisfaction are relatively low among those following routes dominated by unemployment. Here it is likely that in Sweden a generous welfare regime is likely to have an impact on patterns of life satisfaction, while in Spain other studies have shown that in terms of satisfaction, 'the impact of unemployment is less severe' (Whelan and McGinnity, 2000, p 306).

The experience of unemployment can lead to general dissatisfaction with life as a result of strong commitments to work as an area of achievement and a source of identity, and as a consequence of a deterioration in financial circumstances. Protracted unemployment, though, can lead to a deterioration in levels of work commitment, which in turn can reinforce patterns of disadvantage. Levels of work commitment were measured through a scale developed by Warr (1979) using six items that were scored from one (strongly disagree) to five (strongly agree)[1].

The distribution of scores (Table 3.7) shows, first, that differences in levels of work commitment between young people following different routes tend to be small and are only noticeably lower among those following routes that are dominated by unemployment. However, in Spain there is no relationship between unemployment-dominant routes and work commitment. Obviously, the cross-sectional design prevents us from distinguishing cause and effect.

Given the country-specific differences in levels of benefit, economic factors may help explain these variations in life satisfaction and work commitment. While there are sharp differences in the cost of living in the different countries, clearly some countries provide reasonably adequate levels of support while others barely provide for subsistence. The income received by unemployed members of the sample in the previous month varied from a low of €280 in

Table 3.7: Mean scores on the work commitment scale, by labour market routes

	Education-dominant	Employment-dominant	Mixed	Unemployment-dominant	Anova
Male	3.95	4.05	3.92	3.82	0.000
Female	4.13	4.15	4.04	3.95	0.000
Finland	4.00	3.99	4.02	3.77	0.000
Sweden	3.99	4.14	3.99	3.96	0.001
Scotland	3.97	4.04	3.97	3.80	0.000
Spain	4.14	4.15	4.14	4.11	0.051

Scotland to a high of €626 in Sweden. Average monthly salaries also varied significantly: in their last or most recent job, average income varied from €603 in Spain to 1,207 in Sweden.

In all countries except Scotland, young people who were unemployed received an income equivalent to half that of an employed person of the same age (51% in Finland, 58% in Spain and 69% in Sweden). In Scotland, unemployed people only received the equivalent of 37% of the income of a same-aged employed person. It should be noted here that income reported is not just that provided by the state, but includes that provided by family and friends (which in Spain forms a large part of young people's overall income).

To provide further elaboration of these apparent trends, young people were also asked about things which they had had to give up in the past 12 months due to a lack of money. While economic hardship was manifest in different ways and at different levels in each of the countries, the main trend that stood out was that the Spanish were consistently less likely than those from any other country to have had to give anything up due to financial hardship, whereas the Scots tended to have given more things up than those in other countries. This reflects low levels of state support in Scotland combined with low familial subsidies, while in Spain it provides further evidence of strong family support. Similar findings are reported by Gallie and colleagues where in a 10-country comparison, Spain was reported as having a lower level of disadvantaged of the unemployed (Gallie et al, 2000, p 52).

These trends are confirmed through an economic hardship scale produced through responses to the question on activities and goods given up due to a lack of money (Table 3.8). In each country, levels of economic hardship were higher among those following routes dominated by unemployment. Despite high overall levels of affluence in Sweden, young people there suffered relatively high levels of economic hardship, perhaps due to the relative affluence of the society as a whole.

While generous benefit systems can have an impact on the overall experience of unemployment, it is also important to recognise that social exclusion is

Table 3.8: Mean scores on the economic hardship scale, by labour market routes

	Education-dominant	Employment-dominant	Mixed	Unemployment-dominant	Anova
Male	2.2	2.1	2.0	3.0	0.000
Female	2.5	2.5	2.9	3.2	0.000
Finland	2.8	2.4	2.5	3.0	0.006
Sweden	2.8	2.4	2.7	3.5	0.000
Scotland	2.5	2.8	2.9	3.6	0.003
Spain	1.7	1.7	1.6	2.2	ns

Note: ns = not significant.

Table 3.9: Mean scores on the sociability index, by labour market routes

	Education-dominant	Employment-dominant	Mixed	Unemployment-dominant	Anova
Male	19.8	19.9	19.1	18.9	$p<0.001$
Female	20.7	20.0	19.5	19.3	$p<0.001$
Finland	18.3	18.5	18.0	18.4	ns
Sweden	19.4	20.0	19.2	19.4	ns
Scotland	19.3	19.2	18.5	18.4	ns
Spain	21.7	21.6	21.7	21.4	ns

Note: ns = not significant.

linked not only to economic factors, but also to social involvement (Levitas, 1998). Information was collected on peer and family support networks, but there was little variation either between country or between different status groups. However, a sociability scale was developed using information on the frequency of participation in a range of social activities (Table 3.9). Seven activities were included, for each of which young people were asked to say if in a normal week they undertook these activities never, less than once a week, once a week, several times a week or daily[2].

Compared with those who had followed educational or employment-dominated routes, young people who had followed unemployment-dominated routes tended to have slightly lower sociability scores. This difference was most marked in Scotland, with the Scottish position confirming the conclusions of Emler and McNamara (1996) on the strength of the relationship between unemployment and social exclusion. In contrast, a number of Scandinavian studies have argued that due to generous benefit levels, the link between unemployment and social isolation tends to be weak (Heikkinen, 2001).

Conclusion

In this paper we set out to analyse the links between labour market experiences and patterns of economic and social exclusion. Given the extremely high levels of youth unemployment in Finland and Spain compared with the other two countries, we had expected to find correspondingly high levels of marginalisation and exclusion. This was not the case: it was Scotland (where overall levels of youth unemployment were lowest) in which young people appeared to suffer most from the experience of unemployment. Indeed, while unemployment can lead to marginalisation or exclusion, its impact can be mediated by a number of different factors. First, it is not overall levels of unemployment that we should focus on, but long-term unemployment and particularly histories of dependence. In this context we noted that in Finland and Scotland, young people's labour market experiences were most heavily dominated by unemployment. We also noted that in Scotland routes out of unemployment are particularly constrained. Second, material factors provide an important mediating link and where benefit levels are high or where there is a tradition of strong financial support from the family, the subjective experience of unemployment tends not to be so negative. Here the strong family support provided in Spain helps to negate the difficulties experienced on a structural level. While generous benefit levels have sometimes been regarded by politicians as something that may lower the commitment to finding paid work, we suggest that inadequate benefits can be counterproductive in that they may reinforce social exclusion, as was the case in Scotland. Third, social activity can also provide some protection against social exclusion. While the ability to participate in a wide range of social activities is often affected by economic factors (especially benefit levels), this is not always the case.

In sum, the ability to maintain high levels of life satisfaction despite enduring prolonged unemployment would seem to be dependent on an equilibrium between the different dimensions of the unemployment experience. High levels of labour market exclusion may be tolerable subjectively if, for example, adequate recompense is provided (as in Sweden) or if levels of family support are strong (as in Spain). Conversely, high levels of labour market exclusion combined with inadequate income and low levels of social activity mean that the experience of unemployment is likely to lead to despondency and a sense of no future (as in Scotland) – factors that are central to the process of social exclusion.

Notes

[1] The work commitment scale was constructed from the following questions: 'It is very important for me to have a job'; 'If I won lots of money I would still want to work'; 'I hate being unemployed'; 'I feel restless if I do not have a job'; 'Work is one of the most important things in my life'; and 'I would prefer to work even if unemployment benefits were generous'.

[2] The sociability scale included the following activities: helping friends and relatives; doing voluntary work in the community; going to the pub, restaurant or dancing; going to the cinema, theatre or a concert; with the family; with friends; with a boyfriend or girlfriend.

References

Atkinson, T. (1998) *Exclusion, employment and opportunity*, London: Centre for Analysis of Social Exclusion, London School of Economics and Political Science.

du Bois Reymond, M. (1998) "'I don't want to commit myself yet": young people, citizenship and questions of social responsibility', *Journal of Youth Studies*, vol 1, no 1, pp 63-79.

Emler, N. and McNamara, S. (1996) 'The social contact patterns of young people', in H. Helve. and J. Bynner (eds) *Youth and life management*, Helsinki: Helsinki University Press.

European Commission (1997) *Youth in the European Union: From education to working life*, Luxembourg: Office for Official Publications of the European Communities.

Furlong, A., Cartmel, F., Biggart, A., Sweeting, H. and West, P. (2003) *Reconceptualising youth transitions: Patterns of vulnerability and processes of social exclusion*, Edinburgh: Scottish Executive.

Gallie, D. and Paugam, S. (eds) (2000) *Welfare regimes and the experience of unemployment in Europe*, Oxford: Oxford University Press.

Gallie, D., Jacobs, S. and Paugam, S. (2000) 'Poverty and financial hardship among the unemployed', in D. Gallie. and S. Paugam (eds) *Welfare regimes and the experience of unemployment in Europe*, Oxford: Oxford University Press.

Heikkinen, M. (2001) 'Social networks of the marginal young: a study of young people's social exclusion in Finland', *Journal of Youth Studies*, vol 4, no 1.

Jensen, P. (1987) 'Transitions between labour market states: an empirical analysis using Danish data', in P.J. Pedersen and R. Lund (eds) *Unemployment: Theory, policy and structure*, New York, NY: de Gruyter.

Levitas, R. (1998) *The inclusive society? Social exclusion and New Labour*, London: Macmillan.

O'Brien, G. (1986) *Psychology of work and unemployment*, Chichester: Wiley.

Silver, H. (1995) 'Social exclusion and social solidarity: three paradigms', *International Labour Review*, vol 133, no 5/6, pp 531-78.

Strobel, P. (1996) 'From poverty to exclusion', *International Social Science Journal*, no 148, pp 173-89.

Warr, P. (1979) *Work, unemployment and mental health*, Oxford: Clarendon.

Whelan, C. and McGinnity, F. (2000) 'Unemployment and satisfaction: a European analysis', in D. Gallie and S. Paugam (eds) *Welfare regimes and the experience of unemployment in Europe*, Oxford: Oxford University Press.

FOUR

Processes of marginalisation at work: integration of young people in the labour market through temporary employment

Ivan Harsløf

Introduction

Exclusion, marginalisation, and the contrasting concept, integration, are all metaphors subscribing to the underlying notion of a social space with a centre and a periphery. They denote the dynamic processes rendering movement of individuals and groups of individuals between these figurative poles. In relation to the labour market, however, these spatial metaphors are often anchored in temporal definitions. Thus, one is conventionally defined as being excluded from the labour market when one is of working age but out of the labour force for a certain longer period. Similarly, one is defined as being marginalised when one is in the labour force but occupying a position as long-term unemployed[1].

In discussing the social functioning of the labour market, a political concern has increasingly gone beyond the strictly temporal understanding of exclusion and marginalisation. There is growing awareness that even within the seemingly integrated position of employment, latent processes of marginalisation might be operating. Thus, the European Commission acknowledges that there is "a close linkage between job quality and social exclusion" (European Commission, 2001, p 66). "Those employed in jobs of poor quality are also at much higher risk of becoming unemployed or of dropping out of the labour force" (European Commission, 2001, p 66).

By the time of this survey, a little more than a third of the young people forming part of the present youth unemployment study had entered employment. During the six- to 12-month period that passed between the time the young people were sampled and the time the survey was conducted, this group had apparently succeeded in overcoming a position on the margin of the labour market. However, about a third of this group was employed on a temporary basis and another tenth reported doing occasional work (see Table 4.1).

Table 4.1: Young people 18- to 24-years-old (sampled on the basis of having been continuously unemployed for at least three months) by their main activity at the time of the survey, 6-12 months later (%)

| | Total | Employed (% of which) | | | Unemp-loyed[a] | Other status | Total | n |
		Stand-ard	Temp-orary	Occas-ional				
Denmark	44	80	19	1	34	22	100	1,171
Finland	21	39	44	17	53	26	100	1,735
France	52	47	38	15	31	17	100	2,001
Germany	27	35	64	1	42	32	101	1,419
Iceland	50	81	12	8	23	28	101	1,284
Italy	24	63	19	18	32	44	100	1,317
Norway	32	54	38	7	39	29	100	1,101
Scotland	41	63	37	1	46	13	100	817
Spain	43	37	53	10	36	21	100	1,440
Sweden	31	44	42	14	46	23	100	2,447
Unweighted average	37	54	37	9	38	26	100	14,732

Notes: The respondents were asked, 'What have been your *main* activities during the last week?'.
For some countries the total percentages exceed 100 due to rounding.
[a] In the group of unemployed is included the group that reported being in a training scheme for the unemployed.

The objective of this chapter is to evaluate on which terms the group in 'Temporary' and 'Occasional' employment can be regarded as being on an integrative track into the labour market in four strategically selected countries: Finland, Norway, Scotland and Spain.

From Table 4.1 it appears that the German respondents were those most likely to be employed on a temporary basis. However, less than 1% of the Germans reported doing occasional work, so their total share in 'non-standard' employment is not dramatically high compared with countries such as Finland, Sweden, Spain and France. The Danish and Icelandic respondents were those who, to the highest extent, had achieved standard employment.

Temporary work is normally understood as employment on a fixed-term contract (for instance, doing seasonal work or working as a substitute) or on a contract that terminates when the employee has fulfilled certain tasks specified in the contract (Rosdahl, 1984, p 126). In the questionnaire, the different types of work status were not defined more specifically. The Spanish version of the questionnaire deviated from the rest by including a sub-question dealing with the specific type of temporary contracts. It appeared that in Spain about 21% of the temporarily employed were doing seasonal work, 5% were working as substitutes, 38% were doing task-specific work, 19% were employed on apprenticeship[2] or internship contracts and 18% were doing other kinds of temporary work.

'Occasional' work might be even more difficult to comprehend in a comparative perspective. One interpretation would regard occasional work as a sub-category – as *very short-term temporary work* (for instance, day labour contracting). Another possible meaning, not necessarily excluding the former, would be work *without a formal contract*. One indicator supporting this latter interpretation, which the questionnaire elaborates further, is that those reporting to be occasionally employed would tend (in a question concerning types of income) also to report having income from informal employment. The results from a bivariate analysis of this relationship are presented in Table 4.2. For Italy and Spain, it appears that those respondents reporting having informal sources of work income are three to four times more numerous among those doing occasional work as their main activity, in the reference week, than among other employed youth. This finding indicates that for these two countries, doing occasional work in many cases implies working without a formal contract. This pattern is also found in Norway and to a lesser extent in Iceland, although, in general, income from informal activities does not appear to be as widespread here as it is in the two southern European countries. In the remaining countries, either no such relationship is found, or it is not possible to carry out the analysis due to the composition of the data (in Denmark, Scotland and Germany, almost no one reports having done occasional work in the reference week).

In this chapter 'temporary work' is regarded as a generic term that also encompasses occasional employment. However, in the separate analysis for Spain, as well as for the pooled analysis including all four countries, the group of occasionally employed will be treated as a separate category, because occasional employment in Spain probably not only means a very short-term arrangement, but, in addition, also implies an informal arrangement.

Table 4.2: The percentage of young people 18- to 24-years-old reporting to have income from informal employment by employment status (occasionally employed and otherwise employed) (%)

	Occasionally employed	Otherwise employed (temporary and standard)	Significance (Chi-square test)	n
Denmark	–	7	–	512
Finland	12	12	ns	421
France	–	–	–	–
Germany	–	2	–	540
Iceland	24	14	*	737
Italy	45	16	***	762
Norway	14	5	*	416
Scotland	–	4	–	335
Spain	51	14	***	1,402
Sweden	11	9	ns	947

Note: The respondents were asked, 'During the last 12 months, what have been your most important sources of income?'. The table shows the percentage of respondents checking the answer category 'Working in the black economy'.

– = No observations or less than 25 observations; *** = $p<0.001$; * = $p<0.05$; ns = not significant.

It is the purpose of this chapter to delve deeper into the quality of the temporary and occasional employment relationships by analysing subjective as well as objective aspects of these relationships. The background for this perspective is presented in the following section, which deals with the increase in the use of temporary contracts for young people. The chapter goes on to discuss the nature of the temporary contract. This is done by identifying a number of functions served by this type of contract. Throughout this discussion, three operational indicators of integration into the labour market are identified. Prior to the empirical analyses, a section is dedicated to a brief review of other studies of temporary employment. As the background for selecting four countries for the empirical analysis, the wider context of welfare, market and family are introduced. Finland, Norway, Scotland, and Spain are selected because they represent different youth labour markets in terms of employment probabilities and regulation of temporary employment. A comparative study containing such different cases offers the possibility of examining the effects of temporary employment on labour market integration in the context of high and low youth unemployment patterns.

The prevalence of temporary employment

In the past decade there has been an increase in the use of temporary contracts in Europe. Over the period 1994 to 1998, more than half of the net additional jobs created within the member states of the European Union (EU) were temporary ones. The relative growth in this type of employment took place in almost all member states. Denmark was the only member state experiencing a relative decline in the number of temporary contracts (European Commission, 1999, pp 37-42).

Especially for young people who are entering the labour market, being employed in temporary positions is increasingly common (Schömann et al, 1998, pp 101-5). Aside from those on training contracts (apprentices, trainees), about a third of all jobs held by new European school leavers aged 16-29 years were based on temporary contracts (author's calculation based on OECD, 1998, p 97)[3]. Utilising a traditional *life-cycle perspective*, one might argue that the proportion of young people on temporary contracts is so high because such contracts are used as extended probation periods during which employers are able to screen new, untested labour power. Schömann et al, however, emphasise the fact that in a number of European countries deregulation of the use of temporary contracts took place only within the recent decades. "Considering", they go on to say, "that mostly new labour market entrants will receive such wage contracts ... it is expected that mainly the young labour market entrants will have to carry most of the adjustment of the legal framework concerning more flexible employment contracts." (Schömann et al, 1998, p 139). What the authors hereby imply is that the use of temporary contracts could gradually be expected to extend to other age groups, young people today being only the first cohort to experience this phenomenon. In this *cohort perspective*, their over-representation as temporarily employed could be explained not only by the fact that as newcomers they comprise untested labour power that must undergo a certain screening process. In addition, they are newcomers in the sense that no previous generation in recent history has entered a labour market in which the use of temporary contracts was allowed to such an extent as is the case today.

Parallel with the demand-side strategies regarding deregulation, the increase in temporary employment for young people in Europe could be explained by the supply-side strategies in a number of countries implementing an active line in the unemployment protection systems. Such recommodifying strategies may force the young unemployed to accept types of temporary employment that they would otherwise have rejected (see Gallie and Paugam, 2000, p 10; Forde and Slater, 2001).

Approaching the integrative dimension of temporary contracts

One can identify a number of interrelated functions of the temporary contract explaining why employers are using this type of employment as a means to enhance efficiency and competitiveness. Understanding which functions the temporary contracts provide for the employer, one can approach the integrative impact of this type of contract on the young employee.

First, the use of temporary contracts clearly functions as a way of organising production according to a changing environment in terms of a demand for products, availability of input (such as raw materials) to the production and the availability of qualified labour. By using such contracts, employers strengthen their continuous control of the size of the workforce (numerical flexibility), acquiring the ability to organise production to match a product market characterised by fluctuations (Torp, 1998, p 111). "The use of fixed-term employment relationships allows enterprises to shift the responsibility from the employer to the employee in insecure circumstances by rendering a proportion of the personnel easily manoeuvrable and flexible. Thanks to this flexibility ... it becomes easier for enterprises to adapt to changing operating environments" (Sutela, 1999, p 137).

Second, as mentioned previously, temporary contracts can provide employers with the possibility of screening workers for longer-term positions. According to McGinnity and Mertens (2002, p 5), this function is especially important for employers hiring young people. The temporary contract serves as a suitable basis for extended probation, overcoming the *problem of asymmetric information* – in this case, the employer's limited knowledge about the relevant skills and work capacities of the jobseekers. Not only the single temporary workers, but also the position itself, can be screened in this process. Through temporary employment, employers can experiment with different combinations of employment positions related to productive outcomes.

Third, it could be argued that temporary contracts have a disciplinary effect on their incumbents. The temporary employee's knowledge that s/he must qualify in order to receive a renewed or permanent contract allows these contracts to function as a way of enhancing productivity.

If employers were free to hire and fire without regard for public legislation and collective agreements, the functions discussed above could be said to be irrelevant. However, this is not the case, in fact, the important feature of the temporary contract is its *legal-technical* function. By hiring on a temporary basis, employers avoid dismissal costs, which, depending on national regulations, are attached to standard employment contracts. It has often been argued that this function of temporary contracts explains their national variance. In flexible labour markets characterised by a low degree of state regulation, which allows employers to easily part with an employee without cost, temporary contracts would be expected to be less widespread. Labour markets characterised by rigid legislation, on the other hand, encourage employers to bypass such legal arrangements through the application of temporary contracts. This link between degree of regulation and prevalence of temporary contracts is questioned in a recent review. In a comparison of the OECD indicator for degrees of regulation of the labour market on the one hand and the distribution of temporary contracts in 12 EU member countries on the other, no clear-cut relationship was found (Institut der deutschen Wirtschaft Köln, 1999).

Temporary contracts may also be used in labour markets characterised by lax legal employment protection because the act of dismissing, even if easy and cost-free, is still controversial, from an industrial relations perspective. One must consider what Lindbeck and Snower have theorised as the *morale effects of labour turnover*. This theory states that the productivity of employees decreases if they are confronted with an overtly high labour turnover that implies poor internal career prospects for the entire staff (Lindbeck and Snower, 1984; see also Langager, 1993, p 12). This argument leads us to the third function of the temporary contract, which we shall refer to as the *social-symbolic* function of the temporary contract. The social-symbolic function relates to the human resource management strategies within the workplace. Sociologist and social anthropologist Erving Goffman has argued that a basic purpose of using the temporary contract is to make the employee *feel less integrated*, by making "it clear to the person that he must maintain his ego in readiness for the loss of his job, or, better still, that he ought not to think of himself as really having the job" (Goffman, 1952, p 460). When the employee is not feeling integrated, it follows that the employer can avoid potential conflicts if the need for the employee's labour ceases to exist and the employer wants to terminate the employment. Elaborating on Goffman's theory, it is likely that creating such a feeling may be important not only on an individual level (regarding the reactions of the individual on a temporary contract), but even more strongly on a social level (with regard to the colleagues' perception of the temporary employee's degree of integration). If those employed on a temporary basis are not regarded by their colleagues as 'really having the job', termination of such contracts will eventually correspond to natural wastage. The passive and tacit act of not reappointing may be more opportune – that is, a better peace-keeping strategy – for the employer than the overt act of dismissing[4].

It is assumed that the various functions of the temporary contract affect the integrative impact of being employed in this way. When temporary contracts are used in order to achieve numerical flexibility, succession in the present workplace through contract renewal is highly dependent upon external circumstances in the product and labour markets, as well as the financial market. The legal-technical function suggests that parting with a particular temporarily employed person is easy and cost-free – that the person is replaceable. The social-symbolic function predicts that the social-retention mechanisms, originating in pressure from other employees to retain their dismissed colleagues, will be weakened.

These functions of the temporary contract should imply that, in theory, a temporary employment position is indeed an *open* position, in the sense suggested by Sørensen (Sørensen, 1983; Gross and Vogel, 2001). Open positions are directly linked to the performance of the incumbent and the availability of more qualified candidates. According to Sørensen, the openness of an employment position has some further implications for the integrative impact of being employed in such a position. To be in an open position means that, to a high degree, one is exposed to market mechanisms. Partly for this reason, the bargaining power of the temporarily employed, compared with those in *closed* positions and sheltered by their standard contracts, is weak. Thus it is to be expected that the terms of temporary contracts are of a poorer quality than are the terms of a standard contract. Because of the functions of the temporary contract, it is expected that the group of young people who were employed on temporary contracts at the time of the survey would be less integrated than the group on standard contracts.

A combined subjective and objective perspective on labour market integration

In order to evaluate the integrative impact of temporary employment positions, which a large proportion of the young interviewees had taken by the time of the interview, three dimensions will be examined.

First, a subjective dimension related to the temporal integration of the employee will be considered. The employee's satisfaction with the terms of temporal integration will be operationalised by considering the gap, if any, between the number of weekly working hours provided by the work contract and the number of weekly working hours preferred by the employee. A negative gap will be regarded as indicating that the employee has not been capable of negotiating a satisfactory number of working hours according to his or her subjective preferences. A positive gap indicating that the person was 'overemployed' (working more hours than s/he preferred) will not be addressed in this study, although it could be argued that being overemployed constitutes a problem similar to being underemployed. For the purpose of the present study, which deals with the integration of unemployed youth into the labour market, the group of overemployed will be regarded, on this dimension, as being integrated.

A second subjective dimension of integration to be studied is the employee's expectations of returning to unemployment, which could, in fact, be regarded as the simplest indicator of integration. Even if employees are later shown to be wrong in their assessment of future unemployment – of being too pessimistic or too optimistic – their reports, while still in employment, say something important about their subjective beliefs regarding their integration into the labour market. As it will be argued below, these beliefs, especially when applied to young people, may have severe implications for their abilities to act and make plans in other spheres of their lives.

As a more objective indicator of integration, the issue of whether employees are receiving on-the-job training will be regarded as an important indicator of integration for two reasons. First, an employer's investment in its human capital can be taken as a sign of longer-term interests in the employee. Thus one might expect that receiving training increases the chances that the employer will not dismiss an employee on standard contract or will offer the employee a new temporary or standard contract when the present temporary contract expires. Second, even if the present employment relationship ends, the person who received on-the-job training should be more likely to re-enter employment. Empirically, these assumptions have been supported by several studies (see Lynch, 1989, pp 41-4; Hammer, 1997, pp 23-6).

Temporary contracts as either integrative or marginalising positions

Even if the functions of the temporary contract, discussed above, appear to open such positions, these contracts might also be regarded in an integrative perspective. If the issuing of temporary contracts was not possible, the young person in temporary employment may not have been offered any job (see Korpi and Levin, 2001, pp 127-8). Thus, whereas on one level the temporary contract appears to assign the individual worker a marginal or marginalising position, on another level this type of contract might integrate young school leavers on the labour market by creating new job openings. In the more abstract framework of Ulrich Beck (1999), temporary contracts can expose the individual worker to the risk of unemployment, but overall these risks are *democratised* – employment and unemployment are dispersed more equally among the working population.

According to Schömann et al, the creation of more jobs for the unemployed and new labour market entrants was in fact the political intention of deregulation, facilitating the use of temporary contracts and the operation of temporary employment agencies in a number of European countries during the 1980s and 1990s. Despite this clear intention of promoting integration, the authors conclude (based on studies of the temporarily employed in 12 European countries) that, overall, the increased application of temporary contracts has resulted in the perpetuation of structural deficiencies, such as labour market segmentation and segregation (Schömann et al, 1998, pp 164-5). Studying the impact of the deregulation of temporary employment in Spain, Polavieja finds that it has resulted in increased polarisation in the labour market. The increase in this type of insecure employment has been accompanied by increased job security (measured as higher survival probabilities) and increased earnings for permanent workers (Polavieja, 2001, p 314). By analysing longitudinal Labour Force Survey data for the UK, Forde and Slater find that "despite recent employment growth, for the majority, temporary work does not provide a route into more stable employment" (Forde and Slater, 2001, p 26). In another British study using 1992 data, Gallie et al found that the short-term temporarily employed were far more likely than were the permanently employed to report being exposed to the risk of dismissal on short notice if they failed to do a proper job. There was no significant difference in this respect when comparing the group of long-term temporary employees with their permanently employed counterparts. However, both the short-term and long-term temporary employees reported feeling in a considerably less secure job position than did those on a permanent contract. They were more likely to think that they would be forced out of their job within a year for reasons beyond their control. But even if the groups employed on a temporary basis felt less secure, the long-term temporarily employed were in fact more likely than were the permanently employed to report that their occupation had a recognised career ladder (Gallie et al, 1998, pp 172-85). One might say that this British group of long-term temporary employees is exposed to a certain degree of *suspense*, balancing on the knife-edge between unemployment risks (processes of marginalisation) and promotion chances (processes of integration).

Summing up, whether one regards temporary positions as integrative or marginalising depends to some extent on what one regards as being counterfactual to temporary employment: standard employment, unemployment, perhaps informal employment (without a contract). For this reason, in addition to the groups on standard and temporary contracts, the group still unemployed is taken as a basis for comparison where relevant. And for Spain, as well as in the pooled analysis, the group reporting occasional employment is treated separately.

The context of market, state and civil society

Even if the end of the contract brings new career opportunities, being temporarily employed means essentially that one's present employment relationship will end in the foreseeable future. Thus this type of contract involves a certain risk of finding oneself without a market income. The degree and qualitative impact of the risk one is exposed to, however, is contextual. The structural conditions set by the national/regional labour market, in terms of one's chances of regaining a market income by being re-employed, constitute an important contextual factor. Indeed, when the demand for the labour power one can provide is high, it may actually be to one's advantage to place one's labour power on the market on a temporary rather than a permanent basis. Similarly, the prevalence and quality of compensating social benefits and services in case of unemployment is of vital importance. In addition to these structural and institutional conditions relating to market and state, the way in which these systems relate to the civil society constitute a third dimension of the context mediating the risks to which one is exposed as a temporarily employed person. The existential consequences of losing one's market income by the expiry of the labour contract might differ depending on whether one resides with one's parents or is living independently (see Bison and Esping-Andersen, 2000).

A contextual perspective on the risks related to temporary employment is of particular importance when regarding young people. According to Coles, youth should be regarded as a time in which one experiences a series of at least three interrelated transitions. In addition to the school-to-work transition, he points to the family formation transition (from family of origin to family of destination), and to the transition involved in leaving home and establishing oneself independently (Coles, 1997, pp 70-2). In other words, the phase of life in which one is to undergo such transitional processes is a decisive period for the constitution of perhaps even long-term life chances.

The interrelatedness pointed out by Coles is important when examining the impact of the work contract. An instability caused by the nature of one's employment position might extend beyond one's working life, creating instability in other spheres, thus affecting a young person's success in undertaking other parallel transitions. For instance, the risk of losing one's market income in the future due to a fragile employment status might constitute an obstacle for a person trying to obtain a bank loan for a housing investment. Poor housing conditions may inhibit or delay the possibility of forming a family. Similarly, to not know what job, if any, to hold within a foreseeable future could affect the ability to make important biographical choices related to the other transitional courses.

Four countries – Finland, Norway, Scotland and Spain – constituting rather different youth labour markets, are selected for the empirical analysis. They differ substantially in terms of employment probabilities for young people according to the time the national surveys were conducted. The regulation of temporary employment and the prevalence of temporary contracts also differ among these countries.

Due to the economic recession in Finland, unemployment rose dramatically during 1990s, reaching its peak in the mid-1990s (Nyyssölä, 1998). Youth unemployment was as high as 30% in 1996 when the survey was conducted in Finland – twice as high as unemployment in general. At that time the probability of employment was relatively low – only 37.6% – for young new school leavers. Between 1989 and 1997 the proportion of temporary work increased steadily from 12% to 17%. The shift from typical to atypical forms of employment was most evident among the young workers. Whereas in 1989 57% of the young workers were working full-time and permanently, in 1997 this proportion fell to 32% (Julkunen and Nätti, 1999). Few Finns are voluntary employed in these atypical jobs. According to a 1997 survey, about 80% of the males and 90% of the females are employed in this way against their own will (Sutela, 1999, p 139).

Although unemployment for people of all ages has been relatively low in Norway in recent decades – around 5% in 1996 (Mjøset, 2001) – the Norwegian youth labour market provides employment probabilities that are only about average for the industrialised countries (57.8% in 1994). Coming into force on 1 February 1995, the use of temporary contracts was slightly restricted by an amendment to the law on protection in labour and the working environment. Variation in the demand for products no longer provided a sufficient reason for a firm to hire on a temporary basis. The law allowed such contracts to be issued only when the nature of production demanded it or when the temporarily employed person was hired as a substitute worker (Nergaard and Stokke, 1996, p 18).

The Scottish/British labour market provides relatively high probabilities of employment (67.6%) for young people (OECD, 1998)[5]. Forde and Slater argue that a more restrictive line in the unemployment benefit system as well as the introduction of active labour market measures in the UK contributed to the increase in temporary work between 1984 and 1997. The 1996 Jobseeker's Allowance, for example, has now included temporary employment in the types of jobs for which the unemployed are required to apply in order to be eligible for support. Allegedly, these strategies place increased pressure on the unemployed to register with private employment agencies and to accept precarious jobs (Forde and Slater, 2001).

Spain represents a typical segmented labour market that newcomers have difficulty entering (Polavieja, 2001). This is reflected in OECD figures. An employment probability of only about 40% for new school leavers in 1996 makes the Spanish labour market one of the most difficult in Europe to enter (OECD, 1998)[6]. By 2000, the time of the Spanish survey, youth unemployment was still high, affecting 25.5% of the young population. In Spain, specific government policies were implemented in order to encourage the use of temporary contracts. However, as the resulting growth in temporary jobs did not result in a corresponding overall net growth in employment (Esping-Andersen, 1996, p 19), several measures were adopted to counter the development. Thus it was made more attractive to convert temporary contracts for young people into permanent ones. Reducing by 40-60% the social security quota that the employer is supposed to pay when granting permanent contracts to young people was one such strategy. Another strategy was to offer a reduction of about 40% in the penalty for unfair dismissal as the condition for permanent contracts that have been converted from temporary contracts (Spanish background report). It should also be mentioned that reforms in 1999 made former temporarily employed individuals eligible for social security rights on the same terms as people previously on standard contracts (Guillén and Matsaganis, 2000, p 128).

Methodology

In the questionnaire, respondents were asked what had been their *main* activities during the previous week. They were offered up to 20 different categories of answers, including an open response category. Subsequently, several categories have been combined. Those who reported that they were in an activation measure during the reference week were categorised as being unemployed. Apprentices were regarded as being in education and therefore were not counted as being among the temporarily employed.

As the respondents were given the opportunity to check several answer categories, their answers have been recoded for the purpose of identifying the four main groups important for the present study: those on a standard contract, those on a temporary contract, those doing occasional work, and those who were unemployed. It was decided to exclude from the temporary employment category those respondents who declared themselves to be temporarily employed if they also declared themselves to be engaging in some type of education. Those who reported being unemployed *as well as* in being in temporary work were defined as unemployed. The purpose of these recoding procedures was to isolate the possible effects of being in temporary work from the potential 'noise' stemming from the effects of simultaneously taking other positions[7].

In these analyses, the effect of employment status is controlled for a number of other variables: respondents' gender and age, whether the respondent belongs to an ethnic minority (born in a country not a member of or affiliated with the EU or having parents, neither of whom were born in a country member of or affiliated with the EU), educational level (using a compressed Casmin scale), occupation (ISCO 88 occupational classification scheme on a one-digit level), and employment sector (public, private, self-employed[8]). In addition to the single-country analyses, the data were pooled in order to expand the number of observations available. In the pooled analyses, country was used as an additional control variable.

Tables 4.3, 4.4, and 4.5 summarise the results of the logistic regression analyses by presenting odds ratios related to the three different indicators that were singled out. The effects that can be related to employment status in the reference week will be discussed in the following sections (the variance explained by the control variables will not be discussed in this chapter). The employment status is a categorical variable. The odds ratio for the categorical variables demonstrates the extent to which the odds of belonging to the predicted group differ from those of the reference group. The reference group in the employment status variable is the group reporting to be in standard employment. The odds ratios presented for the group of temporarily employed, occasionally employed, and unemployed approximate how much more likely it is for the outcome being present among these groups, as compared with the reference group in standard employment (see Hosmer and Lemeshow, 1989, pp 41-2).

Table 4.3: Respondents underemployed by 10 hours or more (logistic regression analyses, odds ratios)

	Finland	Norway	Scotland		Spain	All
Standard employed (Ref)						
Temporary employed	4.72**	2.50*	3.14***		2.75***	2.57***
Occasional employed	†	†	†	3.49** 4.23***		
Female (male = Ref)	0.71	1.23	1.05		1.73***	1.21
Age (continuous)	0.91	0.98	0.95		0.95	0.95
Ethnic minority (majority = Ref)	0.07	1.69	0.56		‡	1.35
Elementary education (Ref)						
Full secondary	1.37	0.78	0.64		0.60	0.79
Higher or lower tertiary	0.01	1.45	0.67		1.37	1.02
Other or missing	0.84	0.79	0.30		2.22	0.78
Managers	‡	‡	0.00		‡	0.01
Professionals	0.01	0.00	0.83		1.64	0.97
Technicians/associated professions	3.58	4.87	2.36		1.37	1.78~
Clerks	3.09	0.10~	1.75		0.80	1.08
Service/shop sales workers	1.95	0.96	3.03*		1.65	1.93**
Skilled agricultural/fishery workers	1.28	0.00	0.00		1.28	0.61
Craft and related workers	0.40	0.00	0.66		0.92	0.64
Plant operators/assemblers	2.78	0.14~	0.52		1.34	1.17
Others or missing	8.06*	0.28~	3.66~		0.66	1.10
Elementary workers (Ref)						
Public sector (Ref)						
Private sector	2.46	2.89~	0.86		1.77*	1.52*
Self-employed	3.77	0.56	1.57		1.60	1.32
Finland (Ref)						
Norway	–	–	–		–	2.74**
Scotland	–	–	–		–	2.40**
Spain	–	–	–		–	1.40
Constant	0.00***	0.10~	0.04***		0.05***	0.05***
Chi-square	26.5~	38.5**	34.2*		33.5*	84.2***
2LL	144.669	171.663	236.990		458.627	1,070.615
n	250	204	286		565	1,305

*** p<0.001, ** p<0.01, * p<0.05, ~ p<0.10
† = the group is collapsed with the group in temporary employment; ‡ = no observations;
– = not included in this analysis.

Table 4.4: Respondents receiving/received no training on the job (logistic regression analyses, odds ratios)

	Finland	Norway	Scotland	Spain	All
Standard employed (Ref)					
Temporary employed	1.62	1.55~	0.75	1.32	1.24~
Occasional employed	†	†	†	2.03*	1.92**
Unemployed	1.85*	1.70*	1.56*	1.70**	1.65***
Female (male = Ref)	0.64*	0.80	0.93	1.08	0.91
Age (continuous)	0.86**	1.00	1.02	1.02	0.99
Ethnic minority (majority = Ref)	0.32	0.52	1.60	‡	0.75
Elementary education (Ref)					
Full secondary	1.01	0.90	0.80	0.71	0.83~
Higher or lower tertiary	2.81	0.93	1.27	0.79	1.00
Other or missing	1.34	1.27	0.72	0.85	1.05
Managers	‡	‡	1.06	0.37	1.19
Professionals	1.14	0.36	0.46	0.59	0.59~
Technicians/associated professions	0.77	1.56	0.63	0.36***	0.55**
Clerks	0.49~	0.98	0.42**	0.42***	0.49***
Service/shop sales workers	0.88	0.81	0.39***	0.61*	0.58***
Skilled agricultural/fishery workers	0.41	0.80	4.22	0.50	0.72
Craft and related workers	0.64	0.63	0.39**	0.51**	0.52***
Plant operators/assemblers	0.66	0.79	0.63	0.68	0.61**
Others or missing	0.53	0.61	0.37**	0.58~	0.48***
Elementary workers (Ref)					
Public sector (Ref)					
Private sector	0.61*	1.56*	1.32	1.25	1.17~
Self-employed	0.52~	1.59	1.17	1.50	1.19
Finland (Ref)					
Norway	–	–	–	–	0.44***
Scotland	–	–	–	–	0.18***
Spain	–	–	–	–	0.23***
Constant	18.7***	1.91	1.43	1.27	7.50***
Chi-square	36.8**	24.9	47.2***	42.7**	366***
2LL	713.714	789.874	758.245	1,244.344	3,571.446
n	948	672	582	945	3,147

*** $p<0.001$, ** $p<0.01$, * $p<0.05$, ~ $p<0.10$,
† = the group is collapsed with the group in temporary employment; ‡ = no observations;
– = not included in this analysis.

Table 4.5: Respondents expecting to be unemployed one year ahead (logistic regression analyses, odds ratios)

	Finland	Norway	Scotland	Spain	All
Standard employed (Ref)					
Temporary employed	5.49***	2,346	2.37	3.44*	6.34***
Occasional employed	†	†	†	7.19**	7.85***
Unemployed	7.24***	2,725	5.49*	7.40***	9.76***
Female (male = Ref)	0.60***	0.75	0.42~	1.28	0.72**
Age (continuous)	1.02	1.14~	0.88	1.05	1.03
Ethnic minority (majority = Ref)	0.51	0.80	0.00	‡	0.61
Elementary education (Ref)					
Full secondary	1.02	1.07	0.41	0.43~	0.94
Higher or lower tertiary	0.93	0.71	0.49	0.73	0.76
Other or missing	1.20	0.15~	0.88	0.41	0.94
Managers	‡	‡	0.00	0.00	0.02
Professionals	0.20	0.00	0.01	0.72	0.29~
Technicians/associated professions	0.86	0.00	0.00	0.94	0.76
Clerks	0.85	0.14~	1.12	0.55	0.64
Service/shop sales workers	0.95	0.53	1.32	0.55	0.77
Skilled agricultural/fishery workers	2.09	0.00	19.5**	1.06	1.65
Craft and related workers	1.09	0.99	0.92	0.44	0.98
Plant operators/assemblers	0.73	0.80	3.47~	1.61	0.92
Others or missing	0.92	0.69	1.73	1.47	1.05
Elementary workers (Ref)					
Public sector (Ref)					
Private sector	0.48***	0.45*	0.86	0.92	0.56***
Self-employed	0.55~	0.00	0.00	0.59	0.51*
Finland (Ref)					
Norway	–	–	–	–	0.42***
Scotland	–	–	–	–	0.26***
Spain	–	–	–	–	0.34***
Constant	0.08***	0.00	0.02***	0.02***	0.05***
Chi-square	94.2***	81.8***	63.7***	50.9***	390***
2LL	1,292.317	380.240	255.679	532.395	2,548.792
n	1,284	782	713	1,132	3,911

*** $p<0.001$, ** $p<0.01$, * $p<0.05$, ~ $p<0.10$,
† = the group is collapsed with the group in temporary employment; ‡ = no observations;
– = not included in this analysis.

Working hours according to subjective preferences

Temporary employment often goes hand in hand with part-time employment (Auer and Cazes, 2000, p 395). There can be several reasons why some people prefer to work on less than a full-time basis. Thus, in measuring integration in the labour market, the negative gap, if any, between actual and preferred number of working hours provides a better indicator than does the actual number of working hours. On the issue of whether one is capable of obtaining or negotiating a sufficient number of working hours according to one's subjective preferences, a logistic regression analysis was conducted. Those who were substantively 'underemployed' (here defined as those who were working at least 10 hours per week less than they would have liked to be working) were coded '1'. The remaining group – those underemployed fewer than 10 hours per week, those working exactly the number of hours they wanted to be working, or those who were overemployed (working more hours than they would like to) – were coded '0'.

For the temporarily/occasionally employed Finns, the odds of reporting themselves as underemployed increased with a factor of 4.7 over their counterparts in standard employment. This same factor is 2.5 in Norway and 3.1 in Scotland. In Spain, both groups of non-standard employed, which are treated separately, are similarly substantively underemployed to a higher degree than are their counterparts in standard employment. The pooled analysis recapitulates these unambiguous findings: for the youth labour markets analysed in this study, both temporarily employed and occasionally employed youth on this dimension are less well integrated into the labour market.

Formal training as part of the job

Respondents were asked whether they were receiving formal training as part of their job. In the modern 'knowledge-driven' economies, receiving such training can be expected to be crucial for the person's longer-term integration into the labour market. In order to track differences, if any, by employment status in the likelihood of receiving such training, logistic regression analyses were conducted. Not receiving training was coded '1'.

The differences, as a function of contract found on this dimension, are not dramatic. Concerning the temporarily employed, the tendencies indicating that temporary employees receive less training are barely significant. Being a temporary/occasional employee in Norway increases by 55% the odds of reporting that one did not receive training. In the Scottish sample, the tendency is actually the other way around, indicating that in the Scottish youth labour market the temporarily employed are more likely to receive training, however, this finding is not significant. For Spain, as could be expected, due to the shorter-term and probably informal nature of occasional jobs, those doing occasional work are more likely not to receive such training. In the pooled analysis, which benefits from a larger number of cases, there is also a tendency for the temporarily employed to be slightly less likely to receive training while employed. Those who are occasionally employed are also less likely to receive training. In all countries the group of unemployed, referring to their last job, are less likely than those presently in standard employment to report having received formal training[9]. The increase in the odds of not having received training ranges from 56% in Scotland to 85% in Finland, for those unemployed at the time of the survey. Even if the present study is not designed specifically for investigating the relationship between on-the-job training and longer-term integration, these findings indicate that, for young people, not receiving such training makes it more difficult, in relative terms, to get a foothold in the labour market. As previously stressed, this finding is in line with findings from other studies.

The perceived risk of becoming unemployed

Youth is a dynamic period of life, characterised by frequently changing statuses in employment, sometimes interrupted with periods of education, travelling abroad, maternity leave and so on. The respondents were asked what they saw themselves doing one year in the future. They could choose between a number of different possible statuses. The question then becomes: are the temporarily employed more likely than those in standard employment to report thinking of themselves as unemployed in the near future?

The results of the analyses show that in Finland and Spain, the two countries in the study characterised by particularly slim employment chances for young people, a divide is found between those who are in standard employment and those who are not, the latter group appearing, to a much greater degree, to feel exposed to the risk of unemployment. In Norway, one of the low-unemployment countries in the study, the non-significant results reflect that almost no one, not even those presently unemployed, thinks of themselves as likely to be unemployed one year in the future. The relatively good opportunities for employment in Norway might not be the only reason for such optimism, for at the time of the survey there were plentiful opportunities for (re)entering education or various other positions outside the labour market encouraged by the Norwegian welfare state. For Scotland, on the other hand, the odds of unemployed youth reporting that they expected to be unemployed in a year increases with a factor of around 5.5 compared to the group in standard employment. Even more pronounced in the pooled analysis is the tendency seen in Finland and Spain for young people in temporary or occasional employment to expect to become unemployed to a greater extent than their counterparts in standard employment. The relative pessimism among the temporarily and occasionally employed people regarding their future work prospects – a pessimism which almost compares to the still-unemployed group – indicates that temporary contract positions tend not to make their incumbents feel fully integrated in the labour market.

Conclusion

In the expanding literature on new forms of flexible employment, a main concern has been whether temporary employment constitutes an entrapment outside of, or a stepping stone into, stable positions in the labour market. However, in a European labour market where young people are increasingly being offered temporary contracts, one should be concerned about terms implied in such contracts, even if the jobs are, in fact, stepping stones in the long run. As is stressed in this chapter, labour market integration is but one of several critical transitions to be made by young people.

In several ways the empirical analyses supported the theoretical understanding of temporary jobs as being open employment positions. Those respondents on temporary contracts appeared to be in a weaker negotiating position regarding their preference for the number of hours worked each week. Those on temporary contracts were also somewhat less likely than permanent employees to receive formal on-the-job training. The type of contract appeared to have an effect on the subjective feeling of integration into the labour market. The temporarily employed were found to be more likely to report that they expected to be unemployed one year later. In Norway and Scotland, the two countries with relatively high employment opportunities for young people, this finding was not significant, however. In Spain, and especially in Finland, temporary employees, compared with those on standard contracts, seemed to bear (or rather, perceived themselves as bearing) most of the risks of being in a labour market characterised by high youth unemployment. If the tendency to employ more young people on temporary contracts continues, it is likely that subjective insecurity will also increase. As has been argued in this chapter, this situation may have important implications for young people's life chances in a broader perspective.

In comparing four different youth labour markets, some systematic differences were identified, but the patterns were not clear-cut. In the two countries with high youth unemployment (Finland and Spain), the contract effect was most pronounced, but also in the low youth unemployment countries (Norway and Scotland) the temporarily employed were found to be subjectively underemployed. Perhaps more important are the differences in the quality of support that young people can obtain from the state and the civil society when underemployed or when their contracts expire. Such important differences in welfare regimes and family structures will be the subject of several chapters in this volume.

Relying on the empirical analyses of the present study as well as the secondary literature discussed, we can conclude that being temporarily employed as a young person does not appear to imply that one is sufficiently integrated into the labour market. For a large proportion of the group in the youth unemployment study, who at the time of interview had succeeded in finding employment, processes of marginalisation are still at work.

Acknowledgements

The author wishes to thank Anders Rosdahl, Martin Munk and Søren Jensen from the Danish National Institute of Social Research, Torild Hammer, Ann-Helén Bay, Einar Øverbye and Axel West Pedersen from NOVA (Norwegian Social Research), and the members of the European Youth Unemployment and Social Exclusion research group for helpful comments to the draft of the present chapter.

Notes

[1] Of course, the exact period varies between definitions. The Danish Economic Council, for instance, has been operating with a definition of marginalisation that requires the person to have spent 80% of the past three years in a state of being gross unemployed (besides those being regular unemployed, this includes those participating in a labour market scheme, being on vocational rehabilitation, or on leave from employment) (Danish Economic Council, 2000, pp 136-8).

[2] As far as apprenticeship or internship contracts are concerned, it has to be stressed that these contracts can not be compared with the institution of apprenticeship as it functions in countries like Germany, Austria or Denmark because in Spain the formative content of such contract is not regulated.

[3] This share is the unweighted 1996 average for Denmark, Finland, France, Germany, Greece, Ireland, Italy, Luxembourg, the Netherlands, Portugal, Spain and the UK.

[4] This social function, dividing employees according to type of contract, can have implications for interest formation at the workplace level. In a qualitative study of a Danish workplace, Thaulow and Friche show how those in steady employment and those being temporarily employed tend to have opposing interests. They find that those employed on standard contracts have entered into a 'political alliance' with the management, which "determines that an employee on a short contract, by definition, is in a very marginal position within the enterprise" (Thaulow and Friche, 2000, pp 11-12).

[5] The OECD defines the group of employed as those in regular jobs, those in subsidised jobs, and those working full time while in education.

[6] *Employment probability* refers to the probability of being employed (either as regular employed, in an apprenticeship, in a labour market measure *with* a labour contract, or as full-time employed while in education) after having left initial education. The population for which these probabilities was calculated by the OECD was young people aged 16-29, who in t_1 were classified as being in initial education (either primary, secondary or tertiary) *and* who in t_2 – 9-10 months later (12 months later for Norway) – were classified

as having left education (or being full-time employed while in education) (see OECD, 1998, pp 114-15).

[7] For instance, the group both in education and being temporarily employed might have additional financial support through grants, and, on similar terms, the group both being unemployed and declaring to be temporarily employed might be receiving additional support through unemployment benefits.

[8] By definition, being self-employed means that one is not covered by a work contract as one cannot enter into contract with oneself. However, the tasks one is fulfilling for others as self-employed might be of a temporary nature.

[9] The group of unemployed who had never been employed, meaning that they had no job to refer to in the question, did not form part of this analysis.

References

Auer, P. and Cazes, S. (2000) 'The resilience of the long-term employment relationship: evidence from the industrialized countries', *International Labour Review*, vol 139, no 4, pp 379-408.

Beck, U. (1999) *Schöne neue Arbeitswelt: Vision: Weltbürgergesellschaft*, Frankfurt/ New York: Campus Verlag.

Bison, I. and Esping-Andersen, G. (2000) 'Unemployment, welfare regime, and income packaging', in D. Gallie and S. Paugam (eds) *Welfare regimes and the experience of unemployment in Europe*, Oxford/New York: Oxford University Press.

Coles, B. (1997) 'Vulnerable youth and processes of social exclusion: a theoretical framework, a review of recent research and suggestions for a future research agenda', in J. Bynner, L. Chisholm and A. Furlong (eds) *Youth, citizenship and social change in a European context*, Brookfield: Ashgate.

Danish Economic Council (2000) 'Marginalisering og udstødning' ('Marginalisation and exclusion'), in *Dansk Økonomi forår 2000* (*The Danish Economy spring 2000*), pp 133-217.

European Commission (1999) *Employment in Europe 1999: Employment and social affairs*, Brussels: Directorate-General for Employment Industrial Relations and Social Affairs, Directorate V/A.

European Commission (2001) *Employment in Europe 2001: Recent trends and prospects*, Brussels: Directorate-General for Employment and Social Affairs Unit EMPL/A.

Esping-Andersen, G. (1996) 'After the golden age? Welfare state dilemmas in a global economy', in United Nations Research Institute for Social Development, *Welfare states in transition: National adaptations in global economies*, London: Sage Publications, pp 1-31.

Forde, C. and Slater, G. (2001) 'A temporary solution to unemployment?', Paper prepared for the ESF conference 'Labour market change, unemployment and citizenship in Europe', Helsinki.

Gallie, D. and Paugam, S. (2000) 'The experience of unemployment in Europe: the debate', in D. Gallie and S. Paugam (eds) *Welfare regimes and the experience of unemployment in Europe*, Oxford/New York: Oxford University Press.

Gallie, D., White, M., Cheng, Y. and Tomlinson, M. (1998) *Restructuring the employment relationship*, Oxford: Clarendon Press.

Goffman, E. (1952) 'On cooling the mark out: some aspects of adaptation to failure', *Psychiatry*, vol 15, pp 451-63.

Gross, M. and Vogel, C. (2001) 'Flexible employment and income inequality in Great Britain and West Germany', Paper prepared for conference 'Winners and losers in the new economy', Nottingham.

Guillén, A.M. and Matsaganis, M. (2000) 'Testing the "social dumping" hypothesis', *Journal of Social Policy*, vol 10, no 2, pp 128-43.

Hammer, T. (1997) 'History dependence in youth unemployment', *European Sociological Review*, vol 13, no 1, pp 17-33.

Hosmer, D. and Lemeshow, S. (1989) *Applied logistic regression*, New York, NY: John Wiley and Sons.

Institut der deutschen Wirtschaff Köln (1999) 'Befristete Arbeitsverträge: Sprungbrett für Einsteiger', *Informationsdienst des Institut der deutschen Wirtchaft Köln*, 39/1999.

Julkunen, R. and Nätti, J. (1999) *The modernization of working times: Flexibility and work sharing in Finland*, Jynäskylä: SoPhi.

Korpi, T. and Levin, H. (2001) 'Precarious footing: temporary employment as a stepping stone out of unemployment in Sweden', *Work, Employment and Society*, vol 15, no 1, pp 127-48.

Langager, K. (1993) *Rekruttering, afskedigelse og marginalisering (Recruitment, dismissal and marginalisation)*, Copenhagen: The Danish National Institute of Social Research.

Lindbeck, A. and Snower, D. J. (1984) *Labour turnover, insider morale, and involuntary unemployment*, Seminar Paper No 310, Stockholm: Institute for International Economic Studies, University of Stockholm.

Lynch, L.M. (1989) 'The youth labor market in the eighties: determinants of re-employment probabilities for young men and women', *Review of Economics and Statistics*, vol 71, pp 37-45

McGinnity, F. and Mertens, A. (2002) 'Fixed-termed contracts in East and West Germany: low wages, poor prospects?', Paper prepared for the 5th International GSOEP conference.

Mjøset, L. (2001) 'Types of welfare states, unemployment, and European integration', in P. Petit and L. Soete (eds) *Technology and the future of European employment*, Cheltenham: Edward Elgar.

Neergaard, K. and Stokke, T.Å. (1996) *Midlertidige ansettelser i norsk arbeidsliv: Hvor mange, hvem, hvor og hvorfor? (Temporary employment on the Norwegian labour market: How many, who, where and why?)*, Fafo Report 198, Oslo: Fafo Institute for Applied Social Science.

Nyyssölä, K. (1998) 'From school to where? Labour market transitions of young Finnish people in 1980-1993' (www.minedu.fi).

OECD (Organisation for Economic Co-operation and Development) (1998) *Employment outlook*, Paris: OECD.

Polavieja, J.G. (2001) *Insiders and outsiders: Structure and consciousness effects of labour market deregulation in Spain (1984-1997)*, Madrid: Centro de Estudios Avanzados en Ciencias Sociales.

Rosdahl, A. (1984) *Ledighedens sammensætning (The composition of the unemployed)*, Copenhagen: The Danish National Institute of Social Research.

Schömann, K., Rogowski, R. and Kruppe, T. (1998) *Labour market efficiency in the European Union: Employment protection and fixed-term contracts*, London: Routledge.

Sutela, H. (1999) "Fixed-term employment relationships and gender equality", in A.-M. Lehto and H. Sutela (eds) *Gender equality in working life*, Helsinki: Statistics Finland.

Sørensen, Å.B. (1983) 'Processes of allocation to open and closed positions in social structure', *Zeitschrift für Soziologie,* vol 12, no 3, pp 203-24.

Thaulow, I. and Friche, C. (2000) *Changing work and new mechanisms of marginalisation in the work place*, Working Paper, Copenhagen: The Danish National Institute of Social Research.

Torp, H. (1998) 'Midlertidig ansatte: hvor arbeider de?' ('Temporary employees: where are they employed?'), *Søkelys på arbeidsmarkedet*, no 15, pp 111-18.

FIVE

Recurrence of youth unemployment: a longitudinal comparative approach

Isabelle Recotillet and Patrick Werquin

Introduction

The transition from school to work is of primary interest to researchers in labour economics. Because of the high rate of youth unemployment in Europe, researchers now tend to evaluate the effects of unemployment on early labour market experience. Young people tend to be unemployed for shorter periods than adults but the frequency of their unemployment is higher. Because young people encounter successive spells of short unemployment during their first years in the labour market, it is of interest to measure the impact of this recurrence longitudinally. Specifically, one might ask if unemployment causes unemployment or if selection effects cause this pattern of recurrence (Roed et al, 1999). Are young people unemployed because they have difficulty escaping the unemployment spiral, because of specific individual characteristics, or because of the macroeconomic environment?

Beyond this lies the question of how young people accumulate human capital and how they manage their returns on investment in education and training (Bratberg and Nilsen, 2000). Level of education may also affect the impact of recurring unemployment on patterns of labour market mobility. An individual with a higher level of education is likely to have better job prospects and be less affected by jobless periods. However, specificities of national labour markets, educational systems and the economic context may have an impact on the role of unemployment during the transition from school to work (Raffe, 2001). Thus, youth unemployment policies may differ according to the origin of the persistence of unemployment (Fougère et al, 2000).

This chapter is devoted to the analysis of recurring unemployment among young people who have experienced at least one period of unemployment. The empirical findings are generated from several national surveys that were conducted using identical questionnaires, and the analysis was based on comparisons of France, Germany and Sweden. A Poisson model has been used for count data in order to model the process of unemployment recurrence. Two sets of factors were included in the model: micro-level data such as age, gender and education, and macro-level data such as youth unemployment rate, adult unemployment rate and the proportion of long-term unemployed in the country. In addition, unobserved heterogeneity in the count model is controlled. Because young people can be selected into recurring unemployment by unobserved characteristics, state dependence is controlled for when analysing this process (Van den Berg and Van Ours, 1996).

Recurring unemployment can be interpreted as either a positive phenomenon in the trajectories of newcomers to the labour market or as a depreciation of human capital. As Hammer and Stavik (2000) note, the recurrence of unemployment is structurally different depending on whether it follows a job, a return to an educational programme, or a youth scheme. Government policy has a major influence on the transition from school to work, because it organises the way young people enter and re-enter unemployment (Werquin, 1997). In industrialised countries, turnover can be described as alternating between jobs and short spells of unemployment. Following this pattern, Ryan (2001) assumes that high flows in and out of unemployment involve labour market matching and a labour market efficiency problem. To summarise, the turnover between jobs and unemployment is necessary to reach an optimal match according to the job-matching theory (Jovanovic, 1984). A certain period is needed in order to reveal individual abilities, interests and tastes before young people find a job in which they wish to remain. However, this type of theoretical argument ignores employer behaviour. Signalling theories could complement matching arguments. For example, education is a signal for newcomers: employers associate a value to each type of education, allowing them to sort young people who are searching for a job. Vishwanath (1989) has developed a theoretical model in which employers sort jobseekers on the basis of individual characteristics and the number of previous employers. The greater the number of previous employers, the lower the probability of obtaining a job. Unemployment recurrence follows the same pattern. Major research reveals that the probability of re-entering unemployment increases with the number of previous spells of unemployment (Van den Berg and Van Ours, 1994). According to Hammer (1997), repeated participation in different training schemes raises the probability of returning to unemployment. Unemployment might not be problematic if it is considered inherent in the transition from school to work. Unemployment recurrence – in the case of short spells – could even lead to a more efficient labour market. However, signalling theory suggests that young people who have a strong history of unemployment find themselves at the back of the line in their jobsearch. Furthermore, many studies of unemployment duration show that the probability of exiting the unemployment cycle decreases with time. Several hypotheses, such as human capital depreciation and personal discouragement, might be utilised to explain this exit. Higher levels of education involve lower unemployment rates and fast exit from spells of unemployment. Young people with lower levels of education are more vulnerable to recurring unemployment. Because unemployment – even as early labour market experience – is considered to be a social and economic problem that probably does not lead to labour market efficiency, the principal aim of this chapter is to highlight the phenomenon of recurring unemployment in a comparative perspective. The types of young people most often unemployed will be described, as well as the ways in which the probability of their re-entrance into the labour market varies as the number of spells of unemployment increase.

The comparison in this chapter is limited to France, Germany and Sweden. The choice of these three countries is based on the observed differences in their educational systems. According to Verdier (2001), the French and German education systems can be distinguished by their organisation and their links to the labour market. The French education system is referred to as meritocratic in that it is based on school outcomes and founded on an equity principle. The German education system is more professional than the French, notably concerning professional tracks: competence is acquired prior to entering the labour market, producing a signal to be used in job competition, as in the Thurow (1975) model. Furthermore, the social partners are highly involved in the certification process. This way of operating leads to a social and economic legitimacy, allowing the use of the theoretical framework developed by Thurow (Möbus and Verdier, 2000). As French and German education systems are based on very different structures, they create specific links between school and work and, consequently, different early labour market paths.

The choice of Sweden is related to the particular nature of youth unemployment in that country. As shown by Ryan (2001), young people who have great difficulties finding jobs are more likely drop out the labour force and become inactive. In Sweden in 1997, 10% of the youth cohort was inactive, compared with 3% in France. A link could be made between youth inactivity and macroeconomic deterioration and introducing macroeconomic factors in the model should lead to a better explanation of the comparison among national unemployment patterns.

Describing youth unemployment among the different countries

The overall European unemployment rate in 2000 was approximately 8.4% (OECD, 2001), its lowest level since 1990. In France and Germany, the unemployment rate rose gradually until the end of the 1990s, to a rate of approximately 10%, which is in contrast with the low level in Sweden (6% in 2000 and less than 2% at the beginning of the 1990s) and the generally lower rates of the Nordic countries. In Germany, the level of unemployment is closer to that of France than of Sweden.

The youth unemployment rate is the first index we examine when analysing youth unemployment problems (Figure 5.1). In France, the youth unemployment rate (20.7% in 2000) is twice that of adults, but it is relatively low in Germany (7.7%) and Sweden (11.9%). However, these figures should be interpreted with caution because of the low participation rates in the under-25 age category.

Figure 5.1: Youth unemployment rates

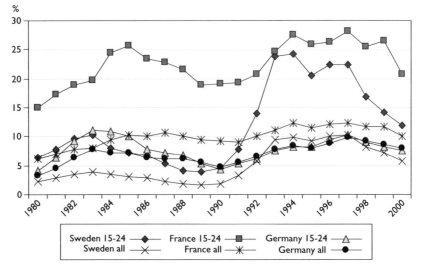

Source: OECD (2001)

Modelling the recurrence of youth unemployment: a count model with unobserved heterogeneity

Due to the structure of the sample, all the young people surveyed have at least one spell of unemployment. The mean number of these spells is around 3 for the Nordic countries, Spain and Scotland and less than 2 for the other countries (Table 5.1). Except in Italy and France, half the sample has been unemployed more than twice in the period (75% in Finland).

Table 5.1: How many times unemployed

	25% quartile	50% median	75% quartile	Mean	*n*
Denmark	1	2	3	2.4	1,125
Finland	2	2	3	2.7	1,590
France	1	1	2	1.6	2,001
Germany	1	2	2	1.8	1,917
Iceland	1	2	3	2.6	1,215
Italy	0	1	1	1.0	1,410
Norway	1	2	3	2.6	1,014
Scotland	1	2	4	2.6	734
Spain	1	2	4	2.8	1,846
Sweden	1	2	4	2.7	2,252

The Poisson model is typically recommended for analyses of this type of data: it allows for the probability that a person experiences a new event – in this case, another spell of unemployment – other things being equal and conditional on a vector of explanatory variables (Lancaster, 1990). As the number of events is relatively low, the dependent variable is discrete: linear methods do not apply in this case, and so we turn to count models[1]. First, we present the basic formulation of the Poisson model. Assuming a discrete random variable, Y, and observed frequencies, $y_i=1...n$, the time-dependent Poisson process at rate l is given by:

$$\text{prob}(Y=y_i) = \frac{e^{-\lambda_i}\lambda_i^{y_i}}{y_i!} \qquad [1]$$

Writing this formula in the form of a regression:

$$\ln y_i = \beta' x_i \qquad [2]$$

Using maximum likelihood estimation, the log likelihood function is:

$$L = \sum_i -\lambda_i + \beta' x_i y_i - \ln y_i! \qquad [3]$$

A more robust specification of this model allows for individual heterogeneity, so that the distribution of y conditional on ε follows a Poisson distribution with mean:

$$\lambda|\varepsilon = \exp(\beta' x_i + \varepsilon) \quad \text{where} \quad \varepsilon \sim N(0,\sigma^2) \qquad [4]$$

If there is no individual heterogeneity, $\sigma^2=0$, and we obtain the basic Poisson formulation. Formally, the Vuong test is used to perform the test $\sigma^2=0$ against $\sigma^2>0$.

Using a heterogeneity term allows for the control of the selection bias that arises, in particular, when estimating a model with multiple spells of unemployment. This situation occurs because the unemployment recurrence can be attributed to individual characteristics (whether or not they are observed) or to the fact that individuals have already experienced unemployment (state dependence). Even if several effects due to individual characteristics such as gender, age and level of education are controlled for, there always exists a set of individual characteristics that are beyond control, namely the unobserved characteristics. Because they are unobserved, we hypothesise that they are normally distributed. Other statistical distributions are possible, but the normal distribution has better properties when modelling unobserved heterogeneity. However, using a term that controls for the unobserved variables does not prevent one from searching for the best possible specification for the estimated model, given the individual characteristics provided by the survey data collected for this particular case. As a consequence, a number of explanatory variables are used at both the microeconomic and macroeconomic level.

Microeconomic factors included in the x vector are gender, education (Casmin scale), age, age when first unemployed, and the presence of children. To this set of variables is added information on early labour market experience, namely participation in a training scheme during the period and the average duration of a spell of unemployment. Using a dummy variable for training scheme participation allows us to approximate the link between schemes and the recurrence of unemployment. As schemes have been elaborated by government institutions to reduce the likelihood of unemployment among youth, especially the less qualified, it is expected that entering a training scheme would lead to a lower probability of re-entering unemployment. The measurement of the impact of the duration of unemployment on the recurrence mechanism is more delicate, however. Currently, there are no data that would allow researchers to test the presence of a positive relationship between unemployment duration and the probability of becoming unemployed again. Nonetheless, using an estimator controlling for unobserved heterogeneity, it can be assumed that the parameter for 'mean duration of spells of unemployment' is partly purged of selectivity bias. A positive parameter should indicate that, as the mean duration rises, the number of spells of unemployment also increases, so that there is a state-dependent selection mechanism in this case. Conversely, a negative parameter might be more difficult to interpret because of an observation period that is too narrow. For example, the last French cohort – the cohort with the strongest frequencies – enters the labour market one year before the interview. Research conducted in France shows that the transition from school to work should be studied for at least three years after the individual has entered the labour market (Recotillet, 2000).

Introducing the macro-level in the comparison: some methodological remarks

Two types of models are proposed: first, models including dummy variables representing the three countries and, second, models excluding these dummies[2], but including youth and adult unemployment rates as well as long-term unemployment indexes for each country (OECD, 2001) at the time of sampling in 1998. In this way, an explanatory rather than a descriptive approach has been adopted (Russell and O'Connell, 2001).

By utilising a cross-country comparison, two main lines of complementary investigation can be pursued. Estimated parameters (size and sign) can be compared for each country separately; thus one model is estimated for each of the three countries. This is the first approach followed. However, this approach does not allow for the measurement of a 'country effect' for the phenomenon under study, namely the recurrence of unemployment for individuals. As a consequence, it is also proposed here to follow an alternative (and complementary) approach, which consists of using additional variables that are supposed to characterise the national labour market in which young people are job hunting. This is an interesting alternative to the usual method that consists of adding dummy variables for each country: the utilisation of macroeconomic variables seems like a more appropriate way of measuring the country effects that are likely to appear in modelling recurrence in unemployment, in countries with different economic backgrounds at the time of the survey.

Main findings

A first comparative approach to estimating the recurrence of unemployment for young people

The first estimation of the probability of experiencing an additional spell of unemployment shows two highly significant effects for each of the three countries. The order of magnitude of these effects does, however, differ according to the country (Table 5.2). The first most significant effect for young people is their age at the time of the first spell of unemployment. It seems clear, from this set of estimates, that the older a young person is when experiencing

Table 5.2: A first approach: Poisson regression models for count data

	France $n = 1,827$		Germany $n = 1,805$		Sweden $n = 2,252$	
	Coefficient	SE	Coefficient	SE	Coefficient	SE
Constant	0.84	3.38	−2.05	2.10	−0.05	2.27
Male (Ref: female)	−0.04	0.04	0.04	0.03	0.13***	0.03
Casmin 2c	0.01	0.05	0.06	0.07	−0.01	0.05
Casmin1, 2a	−0.30	0.05	0.08	0.05	−0.02	0.05
Casmin other (Ref: Casmin 3a, 3b)	−0.03	0.01	−0.22	0.22	0.02	0.05
Age	0.07	0.31	0.34*	0.18	0.27	0.22
Age squared	−0.00	0.01	−0.00	0.05	−0.00	0.05
Age when first time unemployed	−0.07***	0.02	−0.15***	0.01	−0.18***	0.08
Children (Ref: no children)	0.04	0.07	−0.04	0.05	−0.002	0.04
Training scheme in the past	−0.02	0.06	0.14***	0.04	0.15***	0.03
Training scheme now and/or in the past (Ref: no training scheme)	−0.09	0.06	0.02	0.05	0.15***	0.04
Mean duration of each unemployment spell	−0.04***	0.00	−0.02***	0.00	−0.05***	0.03
Log likelihood	−2,564.67		−2,480.10		−3,719.60	

Note: SE = standard error
*** $p<0.01$; ** $p<0.05$; * $p<0.10$.

unemployment for the first time, the lower the likelihood of that person experiencing unemployment in the future. In other words, when unemployment hits young people early in their careers, they tend to be more vulnerable and to be unemployed more often in the future. This effect is clearly linked with the educational level of the individual: first of all, to experience early unemployment, young people must abandon education and training at a young age and enter the labour market. When estimating the same model without the variable 'age at the first spell of unemployment', all the dummy variables representing educational attainment become statistically significant again. The age of the individual when s/he first experienced unemployment appears to be a good proxy for the educational attainment. This finding is not a new one: a high level of education, if it does not always provide a good job, often prevents a young person from becoming unemployed.

The order of magnitude of this effect varies according to the country under consideration. The effect is more pronounced in Sweden than in Germany and less so in France. Stated differently, young people who experience their first spell of unemployment at a relatively late age are less likely to experience further unemployment. However, in France the likelihood of further spells of unemployment is higher than in Germany and Sweden. Overall, it is clear that in Germany and Sweden level of education is among the key factors influencing multiple spells of unemployment.

Another effect, which is highly significant in the three countries under study, can be identified from this first estimated model: the impact of the average duration of a spell of unemployment. It shows that the average duration of unemployment and the probability of being unemployed in the future are inversely correlated. In other words, long-term unemployed young people are less likely to experience recurrent unemployment than are unemployed young people who do not have long periods of unemployment. Although this finding may not make intuitive sense, there are at least two possible explanations for the effect. First, the long-term unemployed are actually less likely to be unemployed again, possibly because of the support they receive from youth training programmes and active labour market policies targeted at long-term unemployment. Second, there is a statistical bias due to the fact that the window of observation (the time between the beginning and the end of the follow-up) is too short. That is to say that long-term unemployed young people may well be unemployed again just as often, or even more often, than their non-long-term counterparts, but that the survey does not allow for a correct observation of those recurrences. At this stage, it is difficult to disentangle these two possibilities, and both may be operating to some extent. Long-term unemployment is relatively scarce among young people, whose careers are better characterised by alternating unemployment and employment. It is possible that these data do not cover a sufficient time span to provide clear answers.

Confronted with a high level of youth unemployment, many European countries have instituted programmes and schemes designed to ease the transition from school to working life (OECD, 2000). France, where more than 10 major programmes were in place during the 1990s, is one of the best examples

(Recotillet and Werquin, 2000). Although the statistical model does not account for the specificities of the different youth programmes, the findings do show a positive correlation in both Sweden and Germany between the number of programmes in which individuals engaged and the number of spells of employment they experienced. Hammer (1997) has found similar patterns among Norwegian young people. In France, this parameter is not statistically significant, probably because there are different programmes working simultaneously in that country: some have a training component, others do not; some are targeted at the private sector, others are confined to the public sector, and so on.

Young people in Sweden and Germany who experienced recurrent spells of unemployment were found to have participated in youth schemes more often than other unemployed youth. However, this finding by no means represents an evaluation of the youth schemes in these countries. Although there is a positive correlation between youth programmes and number of spells of unemployment, one cannot conclude that youth programmes lead to greater unemployment, as we have no way of knowing what these young people would have done in the absence of those youth programmes. In order to be able to assess youth programmes, it would be necessary to assimilate the fact that some of the characteristics that predict programme participation may also lead to recurrent spells of unemployment. An evaluation of youth programmes would require an estimation of an instrumental equation for the variable that measures the use of the youth programmes. The only evidence available from this model in Sweden and Germany is, therefore, that the young people who experience more recurring unemployment are also those who attained the greatest benefit from youth programme(s).

A more comprehensive approach to recurrent unemployment among young people

We now propose to use a more original approach to compare the explanatory factors in recurring unemployment for young people. Parameters for individual characteristics, as previously seen, are estimated in a single equation model, and some of the national discrepancies are controlled through variables measuring the tightness of the labour market: youth (15-24 years of age) unemployment rate; adult unemployment rate (as there is some degree of competition between generations); and/or the proportion of long-term unemployed.

The main results on unemployment recurrence concern national effects and experience of unemployment (Tables 5.3 and 5.4). Comparative analysis is largely confronted in the structural effects of national economies: differences in educational systems, production systems and patterns of labour market mobility, for example. Generally, methodological problems appear when econometricians are required to control for micro- and macroeconomic information (Van den Berg and Van der Klaauw, 1999). Whatever the model used, educational attainment using the Casmin scale is always insignificant in favour of national dummy variables or national unemployment rates. Parameters associated to educational level become statistically significant when we exclude any element on national difference. Level 1a–2 becomes significant in Model 2, indicating that less qualified unemployed youth have a higher probability of being unemployed again.

Table 5.3: Count model using macroeconomic factors (*n*=5,884)

	Poisson model without individual heterogeneity				Poisson model with individual heterogeneity			
	Model 1		Model 2		Model 1		Model 2	
	Coefficient	SE	Coefficient	SE	Coefficient	SE	Coefficient	SE
Constant	1.30	1.04	2.35**	1.04	1.64	1.15	2.35**	1.14
Male (Ref: female)	0.07***	0.02	0.09***	0.02	0.07***	0.02	0.09***	0.02
Casmin 2c	0.04	0.03	0.04	0.03	0.04	0.04	0.04	0.04
Casmin1, 2a	0.03	0.03	0.06**	0.03	0.05	0.03	0.06*	0.03
Casmin other (Ref: Casmin 3a, 3b)	0.05	0.04	0.05	0.04	0.03	0.04	0.05	0.04
Age	0.19**	0.09	–0.14	0.09	–0.04	0.11	–0.14	0.10
Age squared	–0.01	0.002	0.01**	0.03	0.003	0.002	0.01**	0.002
Age when first time unemployed	–0.16***	0.01	–	–	–	–	–	–
Children (Ref: no children)	–0.10	0.03	0.06**	0.03	0.04	0.03	0.06*	0.03
Training scheme in the past	0.13***	0.02	0.26***	0.02	0.22***	0.04	0.03***	0.02
Training scheme now and/or in the past (Ref: no training scheme)	0.06**	0.03	0.13***	0.03	0.11***	0.03	0.13***	0.03
Mean duration of each unemployment spell	–0.04***	0.00	–0.04***	0.002	–0.04***	0.002	–0.04***	0.002
Unemployment rate 15-24	0.03***	0.002	–	–	0.03***	0.003	–	–
Unemployment rate 25-54	–0.02***	0.01	–	–	–0.02***	0.01	–	–
Long-term unemployment	–	–	–0.02***	0.001	–	–	–0.02***	0.002
Sigma	–	–	–	–	0.03	0.12	0.03	0.12
Log likelihood	–8,849.90				–9,289.20		–9,308.80	
Vuong Test					0.75		0.82	

*** *p*<0.01; ** *p*<0.05; * *p*<0.10.

Table 5.4: Count model using national dummies (*n*=5,884, Model 1)

	Poisson without individual heterogeneity		Poisson with individual heterogeneity	
	Coefficient	SE	Coefficient	SE
Constant	0.74	1.04	0.74	1.15
Male (Ref: female)	0.07***	0.02	0.07***	0.02
Casmin 2c	0.04	0.03	0.04	0.04
Casmin 1, 2a	0.05*	0.03	0.05	0.03
Casmin other (Ref: Casmin 3a, 3b)	0.03	0.04	0.03	0.04
Age	−0.04	0.09	−0.04	0.11
Age squared	0.003	0.002	0.003	0.002
Children (Ref: no children)	0.04	0.03	0.04	0.03
Training scheme in the past	0.23***	0.02	0.23***	0.02
Training scheme now and/or in the past (Ref: no training scheme)	0.12***	0.03	0.12***	0.03
Mean duration of each spell of unemployment	−0.04***	0.002	−0.04***	0.002
France	−0.34***	0.03	−0.34***	0.03
Germany (Ref: Sweden)	−0.35***	0.03	−0.35***	0.03
Sigma	–	–	0.03	0.12
Log likelihood	−9,290.21		−9,287.82	
Vuong Test	–		0.75	

*** $p<0.01$; ** $p<0.05$; * $p<0.10$.

Unemployment entry rates increase with the national youth unemployment rate, indicating that there is competition for jobs in the early years on the labour market. In a context of high youth unemployment (Table 5.5), turnover in the labour market is more intensive. This is especially so in France, where the youth unemployment rate is high and where young people on short-term contracts have a higher probability of turnover between jobs and unemployment (Recotillet, 2000). The effect of the adult unemployment rate on the other hand is less clear. With a negative parameter (but close to zero) for this unemployment rate, it could be assumed that, in a context of high unemployment among adults, either young people stay jobless longer (the probability of a new spell of unemployment does not increase but the mean duration of each spell does), or it becomes so difficult to find a job that they drop out of the labour market. It would be useful to investigate these possibilities. However, data on

Table 5.5: Unemployment rates in France, Germany and Sweden (1998) (%)

	France	Germany	Sweden
Unemployment rate 15-24	25.4	9.0	16.8
Unemployment rate 25-54	10.8	8.4	7.6
Overall unemployment rate	11.8	9.2	8.3

Source: OECD (2001)

unemployment duration would be necessary, as our data set does not include the duration of each spell of unemployment; only an average duration – the ratio between the cumulated duration of unemployment and the number of spells – is available.

Controlling for unobserved components leads to smaller standard errors, implying a more robust estimation. While the Vuong test unobserved heterogeneity test is insignificant, the estimation of the count model with unobserved heterogeneity shows declining *t*-values, primarily for training scheme and unemployment mean duration effects. The count model with unobserved heterogeneity captures components containing selection terms, especially for these two explanatory variables (training scheme and unemployment mean duration) for which selection bias is very likely to occur.

Whatever the model, whether it employs national dummies or macroeconomic factors, the parameter associated with mean unemployment duration is negative. As previously stated, a negative sign is harder to interpret. Strictly speaking, it should be concluded that as the mean duration of spells of unemployment increases, the probability of another spell of unemployment falls slightly. This result should be put into perspective with the length of the observed period, which induces a mechanical relation between the unemployment duration and the number of spells. The primary conclusion is that data should be collected over a longer time frame.

Correlation between overall duration of unemployment and number of spells of unemployment

Many empirical studies aimed at testing the jobsearch theory demonstrate that the odds of finding a job decrease as the duration of unemployment increases (Van den Berg and Van Ours, 1994). From the estimated model displayed above, it seems that when the duration of unemployment increases, the odds of being unemployed decreases. Because this finding contradicts the usual one – and even if it might partly be a statistical artefact due to the short period of observation for the survey data – an additional indicator has been adopted to further assess this correlation. This indicator is derived from the total duration of unemployment and the number of spells of unemployment. The average duration of unemployment is conditional on having been unemployed once, twice, three

Figure 5.2: Cumulated unemployment duration and number of spells of unemployment

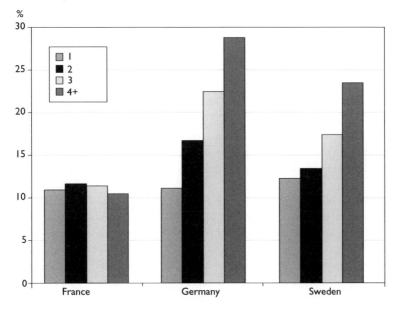

times, four times or more. Overall, recurring unemployment seems to follow different patterns in the three countries under study (Figure 5.2). With the exception of France, the greater the number of spells of unemployment, the longer the total duration of unemployment. In France, the distribution of the cumulated duration of unemployment is relatively flat and lies below the two other countries: thus recurring unemployment is characterised by short spells of unemployment. In Germany, on the other hand, individuals with multiple spells of unemployment display a much longer cumulated duration of unemployment than do their counterparts in Sweden and France. For people unemployed only once, the three countries are similar, with France displaying the shortest average duration, followed by Sweden and Germany.

Conclusion

For the past two or three decades, most European countries have witnessed a rate of youth unemployment twice as high as the adult rate. They are also more concerned by recurrent unemployment, whereas adults are more affected by long-term unemployment. The aim of this study has been to identify the main factors that exert an impact on the recurrent unemployment across three countries. The three countries – France, Germany and Sweden – have been chosen according to various criteria, but primarily because they display relatively radical unemployment patterns. For these three countries, there are common factors that explain the recurrence of unemployment:

- age of first unemployment: the younger an individual, the higher the likelihood of being unemployed again;
- the average duration of unemployment: the shorter the average duration, the higher the risk of being unemployed again;
- participating in a youth programme: in Germany and Sweden only, participating in a youth scheme increases the probability of being unemployed again;
- the labour market situation in the country as measured by the youth unemployment rate in the country: the number of spells of unemployment increases with the youth unemployment rate.

Beyond these common findings, national differences remain: the order of magnitude of the effects described is different, as are the patterns of recurring unemployment.

Most of the literature over the past couple of decades has focused on the determinants of the duration of one spell of unemployment (or the hazard function) according to, among other relevant variables, the unemployment history of the individuals. Available evidence from the literature suggests a positive relationship between duration of unemployment and number of spells of unemployment; that is, the probability of leaving unemployment (hazard function) decreases with the number of spells of unemployment. A different method has been used for this study: estimating a model in which the number of times the individuals have been unemployed is the dependent variable and using, among other variables, the duration of each of the previous spells of unemployment as an explanatory variable. This new approach leads to somewhat different findings: there is a negative relation between the probability of being unemployed again (unemployment recurrence) and the duration of the different spells. This new approach is complementary to most of the models used in the literature, because it focuses on re-entry into unemployment as opposed to a duration model that addresses the issue of leaving unemployment.

In addition, strong national discrepancies appear when using the cumulated duration of unemployment and the number of spells of unemployment. In Germany, to experience several spells of unemployment is to face a longer cumulated duration of unemployment, as opposed to experiencing only one spell, for instance. The Swedish case is similar to the German case, but cumulated duration of unemployment is shorter. In France, to experience many spells of unemployment does not necessarily mean a longer cumulated duration of unemployment.

Acknowledgement

This paper is the responsibility of the authors and does not necessarily reflect the views of the OECD or the governments of its member countries. The authors would like to thank Torild Hammer for her constant support as well as Bridget Gee and Steve Bazen for their comments on previous versions.

Notes

[1] This kind of modelling is used to count number of accidents or rare events (Greene, 1993).

[2] National dummies are excluded when we introduce macroeconomic factors because of colinearity.

References

Bratberg, E. and Nilsen, O.A. (2000) 'Transitions from school to work and the early labour market experience', *Oxford Bulletin of Economics and Statistics*, no 62, pp 909-29.

Fougère, D., Kramarz, F. and Magnac, T. (2000) 'Youth employment policies in France', *European Economic Review*, no 44, pp 928-42.

Greene, W.H. (1993) *Econometric analysis* (2nd edn), London: Macmillan.

Hammer, T. (1997) 'History dependence in youth unemployment', *European Sociological Review*, vol 13, no 1, pp 17-33.

Hammer, T. and Stavik, T. (2000) *Unemployment in a segmented labour market? A study of youth unemployment in Norway*, NOVA Report, 4/00.

Jovanovic, B. (1984) 'Matching, turnover and unemployment', *Journal of Political Economy*, vol 92, no 1, pp 108-22.

Lancaster, T. (1990) *The econometric analysis of transition data*, Econometric Society Monographs.

Möbus, M. and Verdier, É. (2000) 'Diplômes professionnels et coordination de la formation et de l'emploi: l'élaboration d'un signal en France et d'une règle en Allemagne', *Économie publique*, vol 1, no 5, pp 271-301.

OECD (Organisation for Economic Co-operation and Development) (2000) *From initial education to working life: Making transitions work*, Paris: OECD.

OECD (2001) *Labour force statistics, 1980-2000*, Paris: OECD.

Raffe, D. (2001) 'Insertion professionnelle: quels enseignements tirer des comparaisons internationales', *Formation-emploi*, no 76, pp 51-6.

Recotillet, I. (2000) 'Modélisation empirique des mobilités professionnelles des jeunes', PhD thesis, EHESS, Paris.

Recotillet, I. and Werquin, P. (2000) *Youth unemployment in France*, French Background Report for the YUSE Project.

Recotillet, I. and Werquin, P. (2001) 'Sortir du chômage: quelques résultats sur données françaises', Paper prepared for the Annual Workshop of the Transition-in-Youth (TIY) Network, Lisbon, 5-7 September.

Roed, K., Raaum, O. and Goldstein, H. (1999) 'Does unemployment cause unemployment? Micro evidence from Norway', *Applied Economics*, no 31, pp 1207-18.

Russell, H. and O'Connell, P. (2001) 'Getting a job in Europe: the transition from unemployment to work among young people in nine European countries', *Work, Employment & Society*, vol 15, no 1, pp 1-24.

Ryan, P. (2001) 'The school-to-work transition: a cross national perspective', *Journal of Economic Literature*, vol 39, pp 34-92.

Thurow, L.C. (1975) *Generating inequality: Mechanics of distribution in the US economy*, New York, NY: Basic Books.

Verdier, É. (2001) 'La France a-t-elle changé de régime d'éducation et de formation?', *Formation-emploi*, no 76, pp 11-34.

Van den Berg, G.J. and Van der Klaauw, B. (1999) *Combining micro and macro data in microeconometrics models*, Working Paper, Amsterdam: University of Amsterdam.

Van den Berg, G.J. and Van Ours, J. (1994) 'Unemployment dynamics and duration dependence in France, the Netherlands and the United Kingdom', *The Economic Journal*, no 104, pp 432-43.

Van den Berg G.J. and Van Ours, J. (1996) 'Unemployment dynamics and duration dependence', *Journal of Labour Economics*, vol 14, no 1, pp 100-27.

Vishwanath, T. (1989) 'Jobsearch, stigma effect and escape rate from unemployment', *Journal of Labour Economics*, vol 7, no 4, pp 487-502.

Werquin, P. (1997) 'Dix ans d'intervention sur le marché du travail des jeunes en France, 1986-1996', *Économie et statistique*, vol 4/5, no 304, pp 121-306.

SIX

Scheme participation and employment outcome of young unemployed people: empirical findings from nine European countries

Hans Dietrich

Introduction: youth unemployment in European countries

Youth unemployment is an important issue in policy debates across European countries, and both the level of youth unemployment and the range of fluctuation in youth unemployment figures stimulate public discussion. The range of youth unemployment rates differs remarkably among countries and over time. According to Eurostat, for example, the unemployment rate for those aged under 25 in 2000 ranged from 7.3% in Denmark to 30.7% in Italy.

Taking a longitudinal perspective, significant variations in youth unemployment can be observed within the same country during the 1990s. For example, Finland began the decade with a relatively low youth unemployment rate of 9.3% and by 1994 had already reached a peak of 34%. Spain also reached its 1990s peak in 1994 at 45%, after which youth unemployment decreased to 26.2% by 2000. In Germany however, the national unemployment rate remained relatively stable over the 1990s, exhibiting a moderate range of fluctuation – between 8% and 10.8%. Also, the youth unemployment rate in Germany varies remarkably among regions: for example from 5% to 30% in 2000.

As can be seen in Figure 6.1, the youth unemployment rate varies dramatically across countries, across regions, within countries and over time. As discussed below, there is variation beyond these macro-indicators – variation related to individual characteristics such as gender, ethnic background, age and employment qualifications.

The labour market participation rate of the under-25s varies across countries and over time, and strongly influences the level and impact of youth unemployment. In Italy, for example, only 26.1% of 15- to 24-year-olds are

Figure 6.1:Youth unemployment rate in European states (1990-2000)

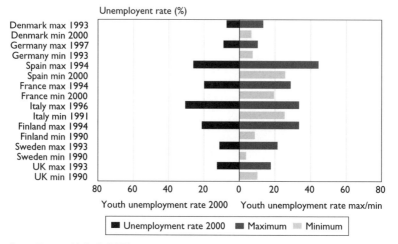

Source: Eurostat Jahrbuch (2002)

integrated into the labour market; the comparable participation rate for Denmark is 67.1%. From a longitudinal perspective, national participation rates differed across countries during the last decade: in Germany and Italy there was a decrease in the youth labour market participation rate, whereas Spain, France and the UK show a U-shaped curve. However, there is no clear association between the development of labour market participation rate and the level of labour market participation rate in 1990 across the European countries (see Figure 6.2).

Figure 6.2:Youth labour market participation rate in European states (1990-2000)

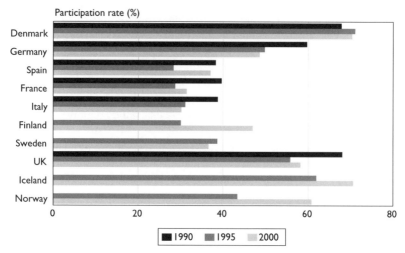

Source: Eurostat Jahrbuch (2002)

The varying levels of young people's labour market participation in European countries indicate that unemployment rates of young people are hardly comparable over countries. Using the age cohort of 15- to 24-year-olds instead of the workforce aged 15-24 as reference group for young unemployed people, the unemployment rates are remarkably lower in the observed European states. The extent of youth unemployment then varies from 4% in Germany to 10% in Italy (Dietrich, 1998). Beyond this descriptive perspective the risk of becoming unemployed and the average duration of spells of unemployment depend on individual characteristics such as gender, age, general qualifications and obtaining a vocational degree. From this point of view, country-specific patterns of school-to-work transition are embedded in an institutional, situation-specific and cultural framework, which includes different national concepts of youth policies supporting the school-to-work transition (Blanchflower and Freeman, 2000; O'Higgins, 2001; Ryan, 2001).

Theoretical background: institutions, time-specific factors and culture

From a life-span or school-to-work-transition perspective the individual path from a general school-based education (such as that in Germany) or a compulsory one (such as in the UK) to sustainable integration into the active labour force consists of a succession of events, including temporary jobs, formal education, vocational qualifications, military service, participation in labour schemes and unemployment (Dietrich, 2001). However, there are two core elements of the school-to-work transition pattern: first, access to vocational qualifications (school-based, firm-based or university-based) after finishing general or compulsory education and, second, entering stable employment after the qualification process.

From an empirical perspective, the individual school-to-work transition process could include temporary or occasional jobs, jobsearch activities, periods of unemployment, military or civil service, periods of sickness, drug withdrawal and even leisure time. Therefore an individual's school-to-work transition is conceptualised as a sequence of status positions. Relying on a school-to-work transition perspective, it will be assumed that status positions are normally temporary, and even the end of this process – a stable integration into the labour market – can be defined only approximately. In some countries this employment period could be identified as a fully protected, permanent and full-time job after successfully completing a first vocational qualification period. In other countries a stabilised job career after a period of on-the-job-training can be assumed as an end of the school-to-work transition (Ryan, 2001). Although numbers and types of status sequences within the school-to-work transition may vary among individuals, empirical findings document country-specific patterns of transition processes (Heinz, 1991; Furlong and Cartmel, 1997; OECD, 2000; Raffe, 2003).

From this life-span perspective, unemployment is seen not merely as a transition period but as a risk that arises at the end of each of the possible transitions. From an individual perspective within the school-to-work transition, periods of unemployment appear to have different functions, depending on the individual's stage in their life-span. This situation presents both empirical and theoretical questions.

From a neo-classical perspective, unemployment could be interpreted as search time. From an institutional perspective unemployment is discussed as process produced waiting time (such as waiting for the beginning of training courses, military service and so on); from a developmental perspective unemployment could be the result of a voluntarily selected period of orientation. The consequence of this assumption is that unemployment periods can be interpreted as the intended or unintended result of individual action in more or less market-organised matching processes embedded in specific institutional settings.

From an empirical perspective, individual characteristics such as gender, ethnicity, educational and vocational qualifications, competence, skills and social background, influence access to and outcomes of qualifications and employment to a high extent. From this perspective, the transition process is closely related to individual and familial characteristics.

Nevertheless, school-to-work transition (and the emergence of unemployment) depends on organisations and institutions, as determined by the general and vocational qualification system or the employment system. How far access to these institutions is market organised depends on the type of organisation and on the country. But not only is access to market organised, it is also influenced by demand-side and supply-side factors such as demographics (cohort-specific birth rates, migration and life expectancy), business cycles, cohort-specific qualifications and job choice (O'Higgins, 2001; Ryan, 2001).

A European comparative perspective clarifies the country-specific design of institutions and organisations of education, qualifications and employment, and related pathways (Shavit and Müller, 1998). There are remarkable differences in the qualification systems, but even the more harmonised employment systems are organised by countries independently. Even within the clusters of welfare system identified by Esping-Andersen (1990) and Gallie and Paugam (2000), there are remarkable differences in the details of the instruments of and concepts behind the welfare state.

Motivated by increasing youth unemployment figures in recent years, and implemented by active labour market policies for young people (European employment guidelines, 1997), training and employment schemes have become significant policy instruments across Europe. However, the design of active labour market policies for young people and the related instruments (in the following also called youth schemes; OECD, 2002) vary remarkably within and among countries (OECD, 2002; Serrano Pascual, 2001). Specific policies depend on each country's educational and vocational systems, the constitution of the employment system, the country-specific labour market situation and the welfare system, which are the core elements of the country-specific transition regimes.

On the one hand, national provision of youth schemes is motivated by the strengths and weaknesses of the labour market; on the other hand, youth schemes are motivated by the individual needs not only from disadvantaged people. In this sense youth schemes are both demand- and supply-oriented. During the past few years countries have developed a wide variety of schemes such as counselling and guidance, vocational training, work experience, wage subsidies and job creation. Whether a scheme focuses on job creation in less developed regions or compensation for insufficient qualifications obtained by disadvantaged young people, for example, indicates that even the policy objectives may vary from activation and motivation, integration of qualifications, training, or employment to the compensation of insufficient competencies, improving the financial situation of young people, or mental health provision. These differing schemes are closely related to the institutions of the national school-to-work and welfare systems. Active labour market policy can be programme based (as in the UK) or established primarily by legislation (as with Germany's social labour law), where it is supplemented with programme components. In accordance with national welfare principles, participation in labour market activities can be voluntary or compulsory (Lødemel and Trickey, 2000).

Independent of the country-specific design of the active labour market policy for young people, the quantitative dimension of employment or training scheme participation is impressive. In the UK, around 730,0000 young people have participated in publicly-funded schemes since 1998 (within New Deal 18+). In France, about 460,000 young people have joined the Nouveaux Services, Emplois Jeunes or Trace since 1997. In Germany, about 500,000 young people have spent some time participating in employment or training schemes, financed since 1999 by the German Immediate Action Programme for Young People (OECD, 2002). Remarkable numbers of young people have been integrated into additional German programmes and schemes financed by the federal government, the Länder, or local communities. On average, about 500,000 young people under the age of 25 participate in youth schemes annually. Thus, up to 10% of the 15-24 age group have joined at least one youth scheme (Dietrich, 2001), which suggests that such scheme participation can be identified as an empirically relevant aspect of the school-to-work transitions of young people. Active labour market policy and the role it plays in the lives of young people become relevant quantitative factors in school-to-work transitions. It is common for labour market schemes to be primarily financed independent of the regular educational process, vocational qualifications or employment systems. In most cases they are only weakly connected with the rules governing these systems. However, there is a close interrelation between scheme activities and the corresponding activities in the regular systems. Taking these theoretical and empirical assumptions into account, this chapter mainly focuses on the question of how far scheme participation supports young people under the age of 25, who have been unemployed for a period of more than three months (here considered longer unemployed) on their way into employment or re-employment.

After discussing the dataset and the included variables, an analysis is conducted on the extent to which longer unemployed young people, independent of their status at the time of the survey, have participated in youth schemes. These data supply information about the impact of youth schemes offered by the active labour market policies of the countries examined in this study. The following questions are asked: Who are the young people who had already participated in youth schemes in their country prior to completing the survey? Are there country-specific patterns? What are the causal effects for different scheme participation in the observed countries? A new set of questions is then generated: What is the consequence of individual scheme participation? To what extent does scheme participation support the transition from unemployment into the labour market? Who are the young unemployed who attained re-employment, as opposed to other possible outcome positions? And to what extent do scheme experience and type of unemployment experience influence the re-employment perspectives of young persons? The final question is: Does unemployment and scheme participation affect the income situation of longer-unemployed young people in the case of (re-)employment, and to which extent?

Data and variables: who are the longer unemployed young people?

A total of 12,731 longer unemployed 18- to 24-year-olds from nine European countries (Finland, Iceland, Norway, Sweden, Denmark, Scotland, Italy, Spain and Germany) are included in this analysis. With the exception of Scotland and Italy, the representative sample of longer unemployed youth was drawn from the national unemployment registers between 1995 and 1999. The samples comprised unemployed people under 25 years of age who were registered in continuous unemployment for a period of more than three months (with the exception of Iceland, where it was two months) within a given observation period that ranged, depending on the country, from six to 12 months. However, the definition of unemployment varies slightly across countries.

Surveys were completed between six and 12 months after the end of the observation period of registered unemployment. A coordinated survey was completed in the language of the country as a paper-pencil questionnaire, a personal face-to-face interview or as a CATI interview. Response rates varied from 50% in Spain to 76% in Denmark. The national data from the participating countries are combined in a unified dataset.

Given the design of this study, it is not possible to identify selectivity for this group of longer unemployed young people compared to the age cohort as a whole. It is obvious, however, that the risk for young people of becoming unemployed depends on their cohort, the year in which the young person is seeking work, the country, the region of that country and the young person's individual characteristics (Dietrich, 1998). Different transition regimes, the country-specific design of active labour market policy for young people, business cycles and demographic factors all influence the individual risk of becoming unemployed for unemployed youth in general, and for longer unemployed youth in particular. According to this assumption, there are country- and group-specific differences in the observed group of longer unemployed young people (see Table 6.1).

As shown in Table 6.1, there are no significant gender differences among the long-term unemployed over the full sample. However, three different gender patterns do occur within the observed countries: in Finland, Norway, Scotland, and Germany young men are over-represented among the long-term unemployed; in Spain women are over-represented; and in Iceland, Sweden, Denmark and Italy there is a gender balance in longer unemployment among young people.

Only the young unemployed aged between 18 and 24 were included in this analysis. Although the age limit for participation in youth employment schemes differs from country to country, 25 years of age does appear to be the critical borderline and respondents who were over 24 on the day they completed the survey were therefore excluded from further analysis. The overall mean age of our sample was 21.5 years, with the Scottish sample being significantly younger (20.7 years) and the Danish, German and Spanish young people being significantly older than average (at 22.2, 22.1 and 22.2 respectively).

Parenthood differentially influences the labour market access of men and women. Whereas the employment orientation of young fathers tends to increase their access to employment, young mothers are often temporarily excluded from the labour market (Dietrich, 2001). The proportion of young longer unemployed parents varies across the countries, with the highest proportion in Iceland, Norway and Denmark, the lowest in the Mediterranean countries, and Sweden, Germany and Finland falling between these two extremes.

Health problems or disabilities preventing the young unemployed people from obtaining work vary remarkably from country to country. This difference may exist as a function of country-specific definitions of health problems and disabilities and country-specific labour-market restrictions. At least three country groups can be distinguished: the Nordic countries with a relatively large proportion of the young unemployed mentioning health problems, the Mediterranean countries with a small proportion, and Germany in an intermediate position.

Immigration background is a recognised variable in discussions of unemployment, independent of national definitions of immigration and minority groups. Additionally, enrolment into the unemployment register depends, in many countries, on a recognised status of immigration. Thus, if the respondent or both of his or her parents were born abroad the respondent was assumed to have an immigrant background. According to this definition, immigrant background of registered unemployed young people varies among countries, with a larger proportion of immigrants in Germany and Sweden.

Table 6.1: Longer unemployed young people, by country (descriptive statistics)

Variable	Label	Finland	Iceland	Norway	Sweden	Denmark	Scotland	Italy	Spain	Germany	Total
F1 gender	0 male	56.9	50.8	57.3	51.2	47.6	64.5	50.6	40.1	57.0	52.3
	1 female	43.1	49.2	42.7	48.8	52.4	35.5	49.4	59.9	43.0	47.7
F2n age	18	7.2	14.0	3.6	2.2	–	19.9	4.5	–	0.6	5.0
	19	18.8	12.8	9.2	10.9	–	14.4	14.4	2.7	3.7	9.9
	20	19.5	15.6	17.5	20.2	12.0	14.3	17.2	14.1	12.5	16.5
	21	14.3	16.4	17.7	17.5	19.8	14.4	14.2	16.1	17.9	16.5
	22	14.8	13.6	16.9	16.9	22.2	13.6	16.2	19.2	22.6	17.5
	23	13.7	15.7	16.6	16.8	24.0	13.2	16.2	20.6	22.1	17.6
	24	11.6	11.5	17.9	25.4	21.9	10.0	17.3	27.2	20.7	17.0
	Age mean (years)	21.0	21.0	21.6	21.5	22.2	20.7	21.4	22.2	22.1	21.5
F49	Ill-health/disability (1 = yes)	19.7	22.2	23.4	16.6	18.8	12.7	3.7	5.9	13.3	15.9
F3a2kor	Immigrant background (1 = yes)	4.4	2.8	8.5	13.4	3.4	4.8	1.1	–	12.9	5.0
Barn1kor	Children (1= yes)	10.1	38.2	28.1	15.2	20.4	10.0	2.2	5.3	10.1	15.0
F44Schol	School experience	1.9	1.8	1.7	1.7	1.7	1.9	1.9	1.6	1.7	1.8
SCASMINR qualification respondent	1 1a+1b	23.2	64.0	15.8	8.4	17.8	49.1	39.0	36.0	26.8	28.5
	2 1c+2a	26.6	1.3	25.6	28.8	9.9	–	7.4	28.4	43.9	21.3
	4 2c gen+2c voc	37.4	25.5	41.0	38.3	55.3	13.7	51.7	16.3	28.5	23.9
	5 3a+3b	1.8	6.0	9.7	6.4	16.0	30.1	1.9	16.9	0.5	8.5
	6 other education	0.7	1.6	6.6	9.6	–	–	–	1.9	–	4.1
	99 missing	0.9	1.6	1.4	8.4	0.9	7.1	0	0.6	0.4	2.7

continued..../

Table 6.1: contd.../

Variable label	Label	Finland	Iceland	Norway	Sweden	Denmark	Scotland	Italy	Spain	Germany	Total
SCASPARqualification	1 1A+1B	39.3	30.3	26.3	26.5	24.9	33.8	49.9	77.4	12.3	35.5
parents	2 1c+2a	19.4	2.4	15.2	11.7	1.1	–	10.2	8.3	54.6	14.6
	4 2c gen+2c voc	25.6	49.1	36.7	22.8	33.2	6.4	27.7	6.7	12.5	24.5
	5 3a+3b	9.9	14.8	10.4	21.6	24.1	27.3	10.6	5.3.	13.8	15.1
	99 missing	5.8	3.4	11.4	17.4	16.7	32.3	1.6	2.2	6.7	10.2
F33fruh former scheme participation	Yes	43.6	31.2	46.3	59.7	29.8	43.0	10.7	35.8	48.4	40.6
F36BNEU unemployment periods	Mean (spells)	2.8	2.6	2.6	2.7	2.4	2.7	1.6	2.8	1.8	2.5
F36CD unemployment duration cumulative	Mean (month)	20.9	10.7	18.7	14.9	13.8	20.7	26.1	26.3	12.6	17.8
COMIT work commitment	Mean	3.88	4.29	4.14	4.04	3.61	3.93	3.82	4.12	4.09	4.00
F9 place of living	3 Community (b 2,000)	28.8	19.6	29.4	20.0	25.3	27.0	2.5	15.7	9.2	19.4
	4 Small town (b 10,000)	15.9	16.7	22.6	14.9	17.0	17.5	13.1	23.2	19.9	17.5
	5 Medium town (b 150,000)	38.3	55.0	30.6	41.4	33.3	27.9	46.1	32.9	46.4	39.9
	6 Big town (150,000am)	17.0	8.7	17.4	23.6	24.4	27.5	38.3	28.2	24.5	23.2
Outcom11	1 unemployed	40.4	18.5	27.2	29.4	28.1	41.0	27.6	26.0	22.8	28.8
Current	2 employed	15.9	45.2	29.2	25.6	25.4	40.3	19.4	37.8	24.4	29.7
employment	4 scheme	15.2	5.2	12.8	18.8	19.2	7.3	7.8	11.5	23.0	13.2
status	5 education	17.4	17.9	17.3	15.4	15.5	3.3	37.6	12.9	13.7	17.1
	9 other	11.1	13.2	13.5	10.8	11.8	8.1	7.6	11.8	16.1	11.2
F24SDT_1	Mean	6.98	6.12	9.44	8.39	12.2	6.01	4.72	4.81	7.80	7.61
employment income	(dev)	(4.49)	(3.69)	(3.41)	(3.52)	(4.12)	(3.26)	(3.17)	(4.06)	(4.21)	(4.47)
n	*n* (=100%)	1.735	1.276	1.101	2.279	1.171	817	1.317	1440	1.414	12.555340

– = data not available.

Source: TSER ProjectYUSE

National information on respondents' educational qualifications is translated into the Casmin scale (Müller, nd), which identifies the highest level of general and vocational qualifications that respondents have reached. According to different qualification systems and country-specific risks for different qualification groups of becoming longer unemployed, the distribution of the qualification levels of respondents do vary significantly among the countries. While in most of the Nordic countries and in Italy the young unemployed finished their education at the upper secondary level, the majority of young unemployed in Iceland (60%) and in Scotland (49.1%) left school at a low Casmin level (Casmin 1a and 1b). In Germany, lower- and medium-level general secondary qualifications, supplemented with qualifications in the dual system (1c+2a) is the dominating qualification level, but about 50% of all the longer unemployed have not finished their vocational qualifications and are not well prepared to join the labour market. This situation indicates a country-specific transition pattern and related functions of unemployment periods within the school-to-work transition process.

As Müller et al (2002) have shown, parents' educational qualifications are important predictors of children's qualifications and employment success, and also determine the school-to-work process. Because of different qualification systems in the observed European countries and a country-specific history of development of these systems, this variable provides only weak information about the relative class position across countries – merely within countries

In addition to the variables mentioned above, a five-item school experience scale (Cronbach's alpha 0.55) was entered into the analysis. Based on factor analysis, items 1 and 5 from the original scale were excluded, leaving a scale in which increasing scores indicated a bad experience with school.

The longer unemployed youth in this study had already experienced an average of more than two periods of unemployment. This repeated unemployment experience indicates that the entry into unemployment is not accidental, rather, it is an ongoing integration problem in the school-to-work transition (Hammer, 1997; Stavik and Hammer, 2000). With the exception of Italy and Germany, where periods of unemployment are shorter than average, variation among countries is low. However, remarkable variation occurs across countries in the accumulated duration of unemployment. Respondents have experienced an average of 17.8 months of unemployment in their ongoing school-to-work transition. Again, strong country-specific differences occur, with extremely long-term unemployment experiences in Italy (26.3 months), Spain (26.1 months) and Finland (20.9 months), compared to Iceland (10.7 months) and Germany (12.6 months).

Active labour market policy for young people was enormously extended in the 1990s and became an important part of the so-called 'employment guidelines' of the European Community in 1997, strongly influencing the national labour market action plans. As a result of this process the number of participants at youth schemes increased considerably. From an empirical perspective, however, participants are only able to identify scheme participation at a very simplistic level, and it is difficult to compare youth schemes across countries. Thus, in order to avoid over-interpretation of respondents' answers with respect to scheme participation, participation is identified in this analysis at the most general level (compare Julkunen, 1998). A generated variable identifies the former scheme participation of respondents dichotomously (participation = yes/no). On average, 40.6% of the respondents had already participated in active labour market schemes, independent of their current labour market status at the time of completing the survey. On this variable scheme participation does vary significantly among countries. While in Italy only 10.7% reported scheme participation, 59.7% of Swedish respondents had already acquired scheme experience. These findings strongly reflect the different concepts involved in school-to-work transition in different countries and the different strategies of active labour market policy for young people. While Sweden, Germany and Norway had developed a highly quantitative, elaborate system of schemes targeting the different positions within the school-to-work transition, Italy offered only weak support for longer unemployed young people.

Work orientation differs significantly among countries (Inglehard, 1989) and among social groups within countries (Gallie and Vogler, 1994). According to Gallie and Vogler (1994, p 124), job-seeking unemployed people exhibit more positive attitudes toward work than do those who are employed or inactive in the labour market. These findings are valid for the population as a whole, but do not necessarily apply to young people in the school-to-work process. Data used in this unemployment study include the six-statement Warr's Work Commitment Scale (Warr et al, 1979). There is a significant difference in work commitment across countries, which is weakened but still significant when one controls for current labour market position. Whereas in Germany work commitment is significantly higher among unemployed young people than in any other labour market status group, the opposite is the case in the other European countries in this study. These findings correspond to results from other current youth studies, which show a high work orientation among unemployed youth in Germany (Deutsche Shell, 2002).

Young unemployed people differ according to their job-search strategies (Julkunen, 2002, pp 161ff) and exploratory factor analysis identifies at least two distinct strategies. First, a formal strategy, in which official labour office information is utilised, advertisements are placed or replied to, and local employers are contacted. Second, an informal strategy that focuses on information from members of social networks like relatives or friends. Figure 6.3 visually presents the components of these two factors.

Information about the regional background of respondents controls for regional variation of the qualification system and the labour market situation. Unfortunately, only weak regional information is included in the common dataset. Included is a measure of population density that shows that unemployed youth in the Nordic countries are more likely to live in small communities (less than 2,000 inhabitants); that unemployed youth in the southern countries, including Germany, are more likely to live in medium-sized towns (10,000 to

Figure 6.3: Jobsearch strategies

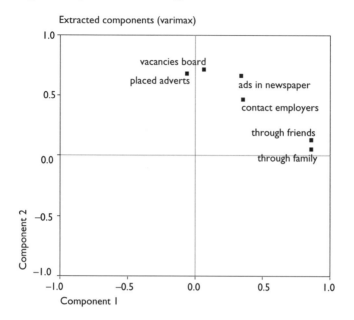

150,000 inhabitants) or big cities (more than 150,000 inhabitants). Again, the regional effect is not comparable across countries.

The outcome variable identifies the labour market status at the time the survey was conducted. It differs among the following status groups: unemployment, employment, scheme participation, education and 'other'. Overall, 29% of the longer unemployed were still unemployed or re-unemployed at the time they completed the survey; 30% were regularly; 13% had joined a employment or training scheme; 17% had returned to an educational programme; and 11% were engaged in other activities such as homemaking or military service (Table 6.1). Again, the outcome varies strongly over countries. The risk of re-unemployment is particularly high in Finland and Scotland, while the re-employment risk is high in Scotland, Iceland and Spain. Training scheme participation is highest in Germany and Sweden, while a return to education is higher in the Nordic countries. Compulsory military or civil service participation supports the category 'other labour market status', especially in Germany where it appears to be used as an instrument for reintegrating young unemployed people.

Who had already participated in youth schemes?

In most of the observed countries a remarkable proportion of longer unemployed young people had already participated in youth schemes within their school-to-work transition. In this section, we address the questions: Which of these young people have already participated in youth schemes in the different countries? Are there factors that indicate scheme participation, and do these factors vary between countries? A logistic regression model was estimated for the entire sample and country-specific models were calculated with respect to country-specific school-to-work transition patterns and related differences in the educational and employment systems.

As shown in Table 6.2, the probability of former scheme participation varies between countries. In the binomial logit model the country variable shows a strong effect. Scheme participation is highest in Sweden, followed by Norway and Germany, all of which offer extensive labour market schemes to support the school-to-work transition of longer unemployed young people. The probability of scheme participation is significantly lower for long-term unemployed youth in the other countries.

Overall, women show a higher probability of joining a scheme than do men, which indicates a gender-specific pattern of labour market integration. Women are a recognised target group in labour market policy, which corresponds with the findings for the general (pooled) model and the country-specific models. Individual characteristics such as parenthood or immigration background reduce scheme participation in most of the countries, while young people with health problems or disabilities have a higher probability of accessing youth schemes.

In the pooled model the probability of former scheme participation increased with the age groups. In contrast to this pooled model effect, the county-specific models show a different result. According to the country-specific transition pattern and the related risk of becoming unemployed, even the probability of former scheme participation increased, which corresponds with country-specific qualification effects. Although the pooled model shows only weak significant qualification effect according to former scheme participation, country-specific models do show specific effects. In Scotland, Denmark and Germany, better qualified youth were less likely than those in the lowest qualification group (Casmin 1a+1b; no general qualification, no vocational qualification) to have attained scheme participation, whereas in Sweden both low qualified and high qualified show a better access to youth schemes than average.

Independent of the level of education and vocational qualifications that respondents had reached at the time they completed the survey, Table 6.2 shows a positive effect of bad school experience on increasing scheme participation.

Work commitment is weakly related to scheme participation, which is also the case with formal jobsearch strategies. Informal jobsearch strategies, however, are positively correlated with scheme participation and indicate a weaker labour market performance among respondents across most of the countries.

Common to all countries is the fact that the number of periods of unemployment and the accumulated duration of unemployment increased the risk of former scheme participation considerably. Long-term unemployment was defined here as unemployment for more than one year. In recent years this definition was changed, in the case of youth unemployment, to more than six

Table 6.2: Former scheme participation (logistic regression: 1 = former scheme participation), exp (B)

Variable	Label	Pooled	Finland	Iceland	Norway	Sweden	Denmark	Scotland	Italy	Spain	Germany
FI	Gender (1= female)	1.178***	1.559***	0.778*	1.252	1.287**	1.329*	0.859	1.479**	1.147	1.142
Age18	Age 18-19	0.644***	0.555***	1.527***	0.723	0.388***	–	0.667*	0.422**	0.812	0.619
Age20	Age 20-22	R	R	R	R	R	R	R	R	R	R
Age23	Age 23-24	1.154***	0.837	1.408**	1.053	0.879	1.221	0.566***	1.093	1.287*	1.498***
CasminR(1)	1a Inad compl elementary education	1.454***	0.619	0.899	1.764	13.136**	0.594	1.050	–	0.209	2.255**
CasminR(2)	1b compl (comp) element education	R	R	R	R	R	R	R	R	R	R
CasminR(3)	1c compl element edu. and voc qual	1.062	–	–	–	–	–	–	–	0.929	0.832
CasminR(4)	2a sec intermed voc qualification	0.942	0.984	0.978	0.919	1.653**	0.610*	–	0.556	1.421	0.652**
CasminR(5)	2b sec intermded gen qualification	0.678***	–	–	–	–	–	–	–	0.662*	0.606**
CasminR(6)	2c gen full general maturity	0.950	0.936	1.206	1.005	1.885***	0.578**	0.283***	1.303	–	0.455***
CasminR(7)	2c voc full voc maturity	0.944	1.324*	1.373	0.844	1.407*	0.633**	–	–	–	0.478**
CasminR(8)	3a Low tertiary education	1.252*	–	–	–	–	–	0.809	–	1.178	0.005
CasminR(9)	3b Higher tertiary education	0.940	1.832	1.195	0.778	1.696*	0.883	0.232***	1.634	0.807	1.627
CasminR(10)	Other qualification	0.765**	0.864	1.334	0.823	1.067	0.710	–	–	1.060	–
CasminR(11)	Missing	0.990	0.951	0.969	0.652	1.367	–	1.050	–	1.982	1.055
Comit	Work commitment	0.965	1.086	0.804**	0.990	0.909	0.921	0.834	1.297	1.177	1.131*
F36CD	Total unemployed duration (months)	1.003***	1.031***	1.040***	1.025***	1.027***	1.051***	1.008	0.998	1.002	1.006
F49	Ill-health/job disability (1 = yes)	1.156**	1.048	1.124	1.173	0.928	1.345*	1.205	1.311	1.200	1.037
Schol	School experience	1.208***	1.174	1.277	1.374*	1.074	0.993	1.099	1.166	1.206	0.746**
Fac1_1	Factor 1 formal job search	1.022	0.927	0.983	1.025	1.207***	0.988	1.206	0.947	1.005	0.953
Fac2_1	Factor 2 informal job search	1.189***	1.080	1.477***	1.216**	1.334***	0.876*	1.247	1.269**	1.238**	1.061
Barn1	Children (1= yes)	0.789***	0.781	0.805	0.7306***	0.606***	0.845	0.708	1.564	0.649	0.804
F3Alt	Immigration background (1 = yes)	0.825**	0.692	1.125	0.742	0.782*	1.447	0.890	0.395	–	0.844

/continued

Table 6.2: Former scheme participation (logistic regression: I = former scheme participation), exp (B)

Variable	Label	Pooled	Finland	Iceland	Norway	Sweden	Denmark	Scotland	Italy	Spain	Germany
Scasp1	Casin parents: 1a+1b	R	R	R	R	R	R	R	R	R	R
Scasp2	1c+2a	1.054	0.882	0.770	1.113	0.992	0.519	–	1.315	1.098	1.218
Scasp4	2c gen+2c voc	1.022	1.132	1.100	1.144	0.933	0.768	1.262	0.838	1.472	0.835
Scasp5	3a+3b	0.975	0.999	0.980	1.211	1.090	0.642**	1.126	1.116	1.389	0.844
Scasp7	Missing	1.064	0.881	0.794	0.966	1.118	0.585***	1.010	2.951*	0.626	1.900**
F9Com	<2,000 inhabitants	0.923	0.976	0.586**	0.908	1.015	0.986	1.193	0.905	0.746	1.157
F9Smal	<10,000 inhabitants	1.104*	1.078	0.923	1.105	1.359*	0.945	1.449	1.285	1.134	1.111
F9Med	<150,000 inhabitants	R	R	R	R	R	R	R	R	R	R
F9Big	>150,000	0.812***	0.861	1.035	0.656**	0.704**	0.791	1.364	0.958	0.943	0.921
Land(1)	Finland	0.851*									
Land(2)	Iceland	0.507***									
Land(3)	Norway	0.946									
Land(4)	Sweden	1.612***									
Land(5)	Denmark	0.472***									
Land(6)	Scotland	0.775**									
Land(7)	Italy	0.136***									
Land(8)	Spain	0.655***									
Land (10)	Germany	R									
		12,555	1,735	1,276	1,101	2,279	1,171	817	1,317	1,440	1,419
Pseudo R² (Nagelkerke)		0.145	0.098	0.157	0.089	0.128	0.139	0.139	0.066	0.062	0.086

* p< 0.1; ** p<0.05; *** p<0.01.
R = reference category; – = no data.

months. Long-term unemployment in this sense and repeated unemployment is targeted by active youth labour market policies in almost all European countries, according to European employment guidelines.

Parents' qualifications and regional effects vary among countries and were introduced into the model primarily as controls. Place of living as a regional indicator shows weak a significant model effect, but indicates better conditions in small and medium-sized towns compared to villages (small communities) or big cities (with more than 150,000 inhabitants). To summarise, the included countries differ not only according to quantitative aspects of scheme participation, but also with respect to the individual characteristics of the scheme participants. These differences are caused by the country-specific transition systems. Furthermore, such time-dependent factors as business cycle and related youth unemployment problems may have an influence. Consequently, these findings favour country-specific models over pooled models across all the countries included in this analysis.

From unemployment to employment

This section asks: How do long periods of unemployment or former scheme participation affect the current labour market perspective of young people? A bivariate logit model was calculated to estimate the probability of becoming employed. Again, pooled and country-specific models were estimated.

According to most of the current definitions of unemployment, employment is to be regarded as the recognised outcome of periods of unemployment. In contrast to this labour-law-focussed concept, from an empirical point of view this is not necessarily the case for unemployed people under 25 years of age. For this age group alternative recognised outcomes are a transition to general or vocational qualifications, a transition into training or employment schemes, and a transition to military or civil service. It is also clear that not all unemployed young persons are enrolled in the unemployment registers of their countries (MacDonald, 1997; Bentley and Gurumurthy, 1999; Dietrich, 2001). Enrolment in the unemployment register, especially for this group, depends on push-and-pull factors such as the design of the school-to-work transition system and its institutions, but also on benefits derived from the welfare system. The access to social assistance or housing benefits depends to a country-specific degree on registered unemployment status (Lødemel and Trickey, 2000).

The transition from unemployment to employment can be regarded as just one possible pathway for longer unemployed youth. As seen in Table 6.1, only 29.7% of the longer unemployed was employed in an unsubsidised or scheme-based employment contract at the time of the survey. But the proportion of employed respondents differs substantially, from 45.7% in Iceland to 15.9% in Finland. An alternative outcome from unemployment is to return to school to complete one's general or vocational qualifications, either through the general educational system or through a training scheme. This path varies and depends on the country-specific pattern of entering the labour market. In Germany youth unemployment is primarily concentrated on young people without a vocational degree – a necessary prerequisite for obtaining stable employment position in that country. In the UK job experience appears to be a more relevant factor for improving individual labour market prospects and in the Nordic countries an appropriate level of general education appears to be required.

According to country-specific re-employment patterns, the effects of qualifications, school experience, jobsearch strategies and work commitment vary between countries (see Table 6.3). Education and vocational qualifications have country-specific effects on the employment prospects of the young unemployed. Work commitment and negative school experience increase employment prospects in most of the countries, while informal jobsearch strategies reduce them.

Re-employment prospects are both age dependent and gender specific. According to the pooled model, there is a positive relationship between age and labour market access. Furthermore, women have a weaker access to the labour market than do men. However, gender is closely related to parenthood, for females with young children tend to be excluded from the labour market, whereas males with children are more labour-market oriented. Yet, significant gender effects and most of the effects related to children disappear when we control for the gender x child interaction. However, health problems, job-related disabilities and immigration background reduce the re-employment prospects of unemployed young people in most countries.

People from small communities and small towns have better access to the labour market and countries show distinct variation in their re-employment prospects, even in the multivariate model. According to this cross-sectional data design, it is not possible to control for time-dependent labour-market conditions, effects of the business cycle (O'Higgins, 2001, p 11), or demographic effects (Mayer, 1990). As a consequence, these effects are included in the country effect, which should not be over-interpreted. The transition into non-subsidised employment depends on both the country-specific school-to-work transition system and individual characteristics.

Under the control of country-specific and individual characteristics, both scheme participation and total duration of unemployment reduces the risk of re-employment in a non-subsidised contract. Scheme participation reduces labour market perspectives in the pooled model. This country-specific effect is significant only in Sweden, however. Only in the two Mediterranean countries of Italy and Spain former scheme participation show weak, non-significant positive employment prospects, suggesting country-specific differences in labour market schemes, but even a greater variation among schemes within countries (Schröder, 2000 for Sweden; Dietrich, 2001 for Germany).

The increasing cumulative duration of periods of unemployment significantly reduces the re-employment perspective in the pooled model and in all country-specific models. Each month of unemployment reduces the probability of employment by approximately 3%.

Table 6.3: Longer unemployed young people currently employed (logistic regression: 1 = employed), exp (B)

Variable	Label	Pooled	Finland	Iceland	Norway	Sweden	Denmark	Scotland	Italy	Spain	Germany
FI	Gender (1 = female)	0.877***	0.749***	0.880	0.755*	0.713**	0.622***	1.098	1.402**	1.023	1.172
Age18	Age 18-19	0.823***	0.744	0.938	1.150	0.723*	–	0.808	0.457***	0.975	1.324
Age20	Age 20-22	R	R	R	R	R	R	R	R	R	R
Age23	Age 23-24	1.481***	1.744***	1.167	1.683***	1.093	1.589***	1.483*	1.769***	1.983***	1.454**
CasminR1	1a Inad compl element education	0.697***	1.551	1.223	0.846	1.983	0.944	0.608*	–	0.287	1.160
CasminR2	1b compl (comp) element education	R	R	R	R	R	R	R	R	R	R
CasminR3	1c compl element edu. and voc qual	1.182	–	–	–	–	–	–	–	0.796	1.892**
CasminR4	2a sec intermed voc qualification	1.011	0.998	0.780	0.952	0.792	1.063	–	0.627*	1.046	1.902**
CasminR5	2b sec intermded gen qualification	0.544***	–	–	–	–	–	–	–	0.390***	0.765
CasminR6	2c gen full general maturity	0.789***	0.913	1.099	0.684*	0.870	1.088	1.352	0.352***	–	0.364**
CasminR7	2c voc full voc maturity	0.906	0.894	0.884	0.762	1.058	1.030	–	–	–	0.743
CasminR8	3a Low tertiary education	0.788*	–	–	–	–	–	0.872	–	0.586**	1.056
CasminR9	3b Higher tertiary education	0.924	1.367	0.916	0.951	0.650	1.225	0.818	1.050	0.484*	5.377
CasminR10	Other qualification	0.689	0.896	0.633	0.894	0.819	1.476	–	–	0.818	–
CasminR99	Missing	0.664**	0.004	0.624	1.505	0.850	–	0.502*	–	0.461	3.047
Comit	Work commitment	1.349***	1.576***	1.374***	1.472**	1.214**	1.484***	1.190	1.506**	1.199	1.023
F33Fruh	Former scheme experience	0.863***	0.796	0.959	1.041	0.789**	0.865	0.862	1.292	1.063	0.903
F36CD	Total unemployment duration (months)	0.974***	0.960***	0.973***	0.978***	0.957***	0.980**	0.961***	0.991**	0.966***	0.983**
F49	Ill-health/job disability (1 = yes)	0.735***	0.868	0.648**	1.053	0.655**	0.628**	0.692	1.108	0.283***	0.753
Schol	School experience	1.097*	1.337	1.020	1.058	0.715**	1.139	1.095	1.797**	1.489**	1.270
Fac1_1	Factor 1 formal job search	1.040	1.019	1.008	0.826**	1.015	0.940	0.911	1.168*	0.977	1.166**
Fac2_1	Factor 2 informal job search	0.943***	1.074	1.020	0.901	0.891*	0.893*	0.730*	0.953	0.847*	0.942
Barn1	Children (1 = yes)	1.180*	0.552***	0.916	0.702*	0.740*	0.651*	0.511**	0.528	0.276**	0.449***

/continued

Table 6.3: contd.../

Variable	Label	Pooled	Finland	Iceland	Norway	Sweden	Denmark	Scotland	Italy	Spain	Germany
F1*Barn1	Interaction: gender x child	0.371***	0.132***	0.302***	0.333***	0.428**	0.346**	0.226**	0.694	0.0163*	0.167***
F3Alt	Immigration background (1 = yes)	0.762**	1.218	1.117	0.816	0.782	0.557	0.377**	0.575	–	1.196
Scasp1	Casmin parents: 1a+1b	R	R	R	R	R	R	R	R	R	R
Scasp2	1c+2a	0.677***	1.173	0.513	1.098	1.024	1.070	–	0.667	0.706	0.942
Scasp4	2c gen+2c voc	1.002	1.250	0.928	1.095	1.059	1.292	0.985	0.644**	0.817	1.032
Scasp5	3a+3b	1.034	1.374	0.938	1.489	1.202	1.134	1.081	0.296***	0.368**	0.943
Scasp7	Missing	0.958	0.739	0.699	1.088	1.056	1.438*	0.713*	0.434	1.117	0.903
F9Com	<2,000 inhabitants	1.227***	1.171	1.349*	1.189	0.968	1.513**	1.156	2.351**	1.016	0.619*
F9Smal	<10,000 inhabitants	1.286***	1.096	1.644***	1.273	1.039	1.130	1.120	1.288	1.284	1.127
F9Med	<150,000 inhabitants	R	R	R	R	R	R	R	R	R	R
F9Big	>150,000	0.914	0.754	0.981	0.962	0.981	0.878	1.204	0.804	0.944	1.138
Land(1)	Finland	0.746***									
Land(2)	Iceland	2.574***									
Land(3)	Norway	1.533***									
Land(4)	Sweden	1.185*									
Land(5)	Denmark	2.462***									
Land(6)	Scotland	2.846***									
Land(7)	Italy	0.767**									
Land(8)	Spain	2.463***									
Land (10)	Germany	R									
n		12,246	1,687	1,276	1,088	2,248	1,167	817	1,212	1,417	1,334
Pseudo R² (Nagelkerke)		0.094	0.121	0.086	0.098	0.116	0.134	0.203	0.140	0.216	0.106

* $p<0.1$; ** $p<0.05$; *** $p<0.01$.
R = reference category, – = no data.

Table 6.4: Income of (re-)employed longer unemployed young people (OLS regression: Ln income), Beta

Variable	Label	Pooled	Finland	Iceland	Norway	Sweden	Denmark	Scotland	Italy	Spain	Germany
FI Gender	Gender (1 = female)	-0.099***	-0.197**	-0.191**	-0.212**	-0.159***	-0.041	-0.048	-0.29***	-0.199***	-0.165***
Age18	Age 18-19	-0.042***	-0.147*	-0.062	-0.043	-0.045	—	-0.065	-0.089	-0.009	-0.029
Age20	Age 20-22	R	R	R	R	R	R	R	R	R	R
Age23	Age 23-24	0.082***	0.322***	0.067	0.036	0.15**	0.116**	0.092	0.058	0.156**	0.081***
Scasp1	1a+1b	R	R	R	R	R	R	R	R	R	R
Scasp2	1c (other)+2a+2b	0.025*	-0.066	-0.042	-0.04	-0.034	-0.01	—	0.089	-0.064	0.198***
Scasp4	2c gen 2c voc	0.037**	0.11	-0.022	-0.012	0.002	-0.04	0.004	0.193**	0.038	0.201***
Scasp5	3a+3b	0.035**	-0.002	-0.043	0.035	0.04	-0.015	0.08	0.022	0.127**	-0.175***
Scasp6	Other	-0.012	0.054	-0.067	-0.207***	-0.032	—	—	—	0.038	—
Scasp7	Missing	0.006	—	-0.109*	0.004	-0.092	-0.014	0.074	—	0.052	-0.018
F21ISC1	Manager	0.028**	—	0.078	—	—	0.053	0.061	—	—	0.058
F21ISC2	Professionals	0.116***	0.112	-0.001	0.111	0.175**	0.212***	0.339***	0.127	0.244***	—
F21ISC3	Technicians/associate professionals	0.108***	0.182*	0.165**	0.271***	0.194***	0.192***	0.134**	0.066	0.091*	0.163***
F21ISC4	Clerks	0.061***	0.019	0.065	0.166*	0.002	0.109**	0.12*	0.066	0.171**	0.082
F21ISC5	Service/sales workers	R	R	R	R	R	R	R	R	R	R
F21ISC6	Skilled agricult/fishery workers	0.048***	-0.08	0.216***	0.041	0.046	0.09**	0.066	0.009	0.125**	0.081
F21ISC7	Craft and related trade workers	0.108***	0.051	-0.059	0.01	0.202**	0.268***	0.288**	-0.119	0.24***	0.164**
F21ISC8	Plant/machine operators and assemblers	0.084***	0.118	0.055	0.156*	0.087	0.085	0.157**	0.097	0.217**	0.102*
F21ISC9	Elementary occupations	0.039**	-0.004	-0.178**	0.196***	-0.003	0.059	0.191**	0.006	0.181**	0.061
F21ISC99	Missing including armed forces	0.063***	0.115	0.016	0.318***	-0.023	0.105**	0.119*	-0.034	0.113**	-0.04
F23Pub	Public sector	-0.012	-0.132	-0.16**	0.024	-0.131**	0.009	-0.037	0.186	0.047	0.02
F23Priv	Private sector	R	R	R	R	R	R	R	R	R	R
F23Self	Self-employed	-0.018*	0.013	-0.004	-0.097	-0.044	0.004	0.092	-0.014	-0.045	-0.218***
F23Rest	Others/missing	-0.024**	0.021	-0.06	—	0.042	-0.115**	-0.123**	—	-0.045	-0.031

/continued

Table 6.4: contd.../

Variable	Label	Pooled	Finland	Iceland	Norway	Sweden	Denmark	Scotland	Italy	Spain	Germany
Comit	Work commitment	0.026*	-0.049	0.062	0.179***	0.051	0.008	0.002	0.105	0.031	-0.031
F27Partt	Part-time (1 = yes)	0.002	-0.031	0.127**	-0.085	0.079	-0.02	0.01	0.204**	0.112**	-0.193***
F33Fruh	Former scheme e-perience	-0.034**	0.071	0.019	0.061	-0.034	-0.072	-0.041	0.007	0.001	-0.074
F36Bneu	Total unemployment spells	0.007	-0.162*	-0.058	0.024	-0.034	0.015	0.098	-0.128	0.035	0.114**
F36CD	Total unemployment duration (months)	-0.054***	-0.128	-0.089	-0.047	-0.042	-0.073	-0.088	-0.159**	0.07	-0.108*
F49	Ill-health/job disability (1 = yes)	-0.006	-0.01	-0.089	0.008	-0.007	-0.012	-0.047	0.141*	0.018	-0.051
Schol	School e-perience	-0.004	0.126	0.031	-0.044	0.023	0.038	-0.091	0.107	-0.043	0.066
Fac1_1	Factor 1 formal job search	-0.015	-0.041	-0.072	0.02	0.012	0.015	-0.138**	-0.08	-0.047	0.075
Fac2_1	Factor 2 informal job search	-0.004	0.06	0	-0.041	-0.007	0.039	-0.122*	0.132	-0.042	-0.02
Barnl	Children (1 = yes)	-0.007	-0.16*	-0.04	0.011	0.066	0.004	-0.105*	0.071	-0.039	0.001
F3Alt	Immigrant background (1 = yes)	-0.012	-0.105	-0.017	-0.141*	-0.099	0.027	0.048	0.008	–	0.008
F9Com	<2,000 inhabitants	-0.025*	0.048	-0.045	-0.065	0.098*	-0.226***	-0.01	0.026	-0.072	-0.108*
F9Smal	<10,000 inhabitants	-0.006	-0.047	-0.031	-0.121	-0.001	-0.098*	-0.048	-0.044	0.009	0.101*
F9Med	<150,000 inhabitants	R	R	R	R	R	R	R	R	R	R
F9Big	>150,000	-0.011	0.086	0.006	-0.046	-0.028	-0.062	-0.115	-0.249	0.015	0.036
FI	Finland	-0.044**									
IS	Iceland	-0.165***									
NO	Norway	0.125***									
SV	Sweden	0.07***									
DA	Denmark	0.349***									
SC	Scotland	-0.135***									
IT	Italy	-0.267***									
SP	Spain	-0.445***									
Germany	Germany	R									
Adjusted R²		0.608	0.146	0.024	0.113	0.119	0.144	0.216	0.301	0.193	0.29
n		2,899	194	335	240	416	467	282	163	495	307

* $p< 0.1$; ** $p<0.05$; *** $p<0.01$.

103

To summarise, the unemployment-to-work transition is highly dependent on country-specific conditions and on individual characteristics. Even under the control of these dimensions, the re-employment perspective decreases remarkably with the duration of unemployment. Furthermore, labour market schemes generally show a weak and statistically non-significant negative effect in the Nordic countries and Germany, while in the Mediterranean countries this effect tends to be positive. However, variations on the schemes are legion, and most of them are time-dependent and highly target-oriented. These scheme-specific conditions cannot be controlled within these empirical data.

Income effects of unemployment and scheme participation

In this final section, the effect of the duration of unemployment and scheme-participation on gross hourly income is discussed. As shown above, the transition to employment is only one of several possible outcome options for the unemployed. According to the sample design of the dataset utilised, employment duration and the possible job tenure after leaving unemployment must be short with a country-specific job tenure averaging from six to 12 months, depending on the country's sample design. According to the life-span position, it will be assumed that in most cases the jobs reported are entry positions into the labour market; already realised job careers are assumed to be the exception. From this point of view, a reduced human capital perspective is chosen, supplemented by the individual characteristics of job starters. From this perspective, information on unemployment experience and scheme participation is included in the model as relevant labour market-related dimensions. Both a pooled model and country-specific OLS regression models are estimated to identify the effect of unemployment experience and scheme participation on the income of re-employed young people under the control of further individual and country-specific characteristics. As dependent variables, the logarithm of hourly gross income information was used.

A highly significant pooled income model shows a strong country effect. Furthermore, the pooled model, but also most of the country-specific models, identifies a significant negative income effect for women and a positive age effect. Consistent with the human capital theory, there is also a qualification-level effect and an occupation effect. Managers (ISCO 1) and professionals (ISCO 2) earn more money than the reference category of service and sales worker (ISCO 7), but crafters and related workers score highest on the income ladder. Only in Norway do elementary occupations (ISCO 7) attain the highest scores. This finding seems to be typical for job starters, who can earn above-average incomes, even in the low qualification segment. For some groups of less qualified young people this appears to be both an opportunity and a trap – a trap that prevents them from completing higher general or vocational qualifications and related career perspectives.

From a sector perspective, when other variables are controlled, income does not differ significantly as a function of public and private industry. It is remarkable, however, that self-employment reduces income in most of the countries studied. In contrast to European employment strategies for young people, self-employment appears not to improve the income prospects of young unemployed people. Although the income effect of part-time versus full-time employment exerts only a marginal effect in the pooled model, there are some effects of working time on income in the country-specific models. Part-time occupations have a positive effect on income in the Mediterranean countries and Iceland, whereas it reduces hourly income in most of the other Nordic countries and has a significant negative effect in Germany.

Under the control of this country-specific dimension, scheme participation has a weak but significant effect in the pooled model that is not repeated in the country-specific models. According to these findings, there is no indicator for a scheme participation-related penalty if former participants become re-employed. The opposite is the case according to the duration of unemployment (see also Ackum, 1991). Duration of unemployment reduces income remarkably month by month, whereas the number of spells of unemployment does not have a significant effect in the pooled model. Even the country-specific models, with the exception of Germany, show small differences. In Germany, the cumulated duration of unemployment has a negative effect on income, whereas the number of periods of unemployment has a positive effect. Germany's complex transition process and the reward in that country for active jobsearch may explain this result.

To summarise, former scheme participation of longer unemployed young people does not significantly reduce income compared to non-participation, but neither does it substantially improve income. In contrast to this finding, an increasing duration of unemployment tends to reduce income in almost all countries. But at least human capital-oriented variables, such as qualifications, occupation and age, are identified as the dominant income determinants, even among job starters who are facing problems starting a career.

Discussion

Longer unemployed young people (under 25 years of age), who were registered as unemployed for at least three months, form a distinct group of unemployed youth within individual countries. However, this group differs significantly between countries. This is mainly due to the country-specific school-to-work transition process, framed by country-specific institutions and organisations, and time-specific restrictions and opportunities in individual countries. Beyond these differences, European employment guidelines and their recommendations for youth-specific labour market policies urge countries to develop and adjust their national labour market policies for young people. Empirical findings about the scheme participation of longer unemployed young people generally fit this political development well. Scheme participation in all countries is remarkably high, at approximately 40%. There is, however, variation between countries, with comparable low scheme participation in the Mediterranean countries and comparable high scheme participation in Sweden, Germany and Norway. Independent of this distribution, 13% of all longer unemployed young people reported that they were participating in a scheme at the time they completed the survey. These findings should be interpreted carefully, of course, because of methodological problems, particularly identifying individuals' scheme participation and distinguishing it from regular education, qualifications or employment activities. These findings also present some arguments for considering country-specific targeting processes in the observed countries (OECD, 2002). In accordance with these assumptions, findings from a multivariate logit model confirm country-specific determinants of scheme participation. It is common to all of these models that qualifications, school experience and respondents' labour market behaviours, such as jobsearch strategies, have a strong influence on the outcome of periods of unemployment.

At least for young people, it is obvious that employment is one of several possible outcomes of unemployment. Access to employment that is not scheme based depends on the country-specific transition system and on the individual's characteristics. Qualifications, school experience and work commitment support the integration of unemployed young people into the labour market. Health problems, disabilities and immigrant background render young people's integration more difficult. Having children supports the labour market integration of men, but impedes that of women. Beyond these characteristics, duration of unemployment and former scheme participation do reduce the probability of entering non-subsidised employment in most countries. Again, because these findings are sensitive to methodological changes (Holm, 2002), they should be interpreted with care.

The findings suggest that different mechanisms operate between the obtaining of a job and job outcome (measured as the gross hourly income of employed respondents). If the threshold of successful re-employment is conquered, income is much more dependent on such 'classical' human capital-based indicators, such as qualifications and type of occupation. There is no clear evidence for scheme punishment. In fact, the opposite appears to be the case. If duration of unemployment is used as a measure of reward, an increasing duration of unemployment reduces income considerably. From this point of view, scheme-based labour market policy shows some effect and supports integration to a certain degree. But for a noteworthy increase in youth unemployment caused by business cycle or demographic processes, a scheme-based labour market policy may be limited. However, even in that case, equalising labour market opportunities and smoothing the effect of individual characteristics remains a substantial policy-oriented objective in democratic societies.

References

Ackum, S. (1991) 'Youth unemployment, labour market programmes and subsequent earnings', *Scandinavian Journal of Economics*, vol 93, no 3, pp 531-43.

Bentley, T. and Gurumurthy, R. (1999) *Destination unknown: Engaging with the problems of marginalised youth*, London: Demos.

Blanchflower, D.G. and Freeman, R.B. (2000) *Youth employment and joblessness in advanced countries*, Chicago, IL: University of Chicago Press.

Deutsche Shell (ed) (2002) *Jugend 2002*, Shell Jugendstudie 14, Frankfurt am Main: Fischer.

Dietrich, H. (1998) *Arbeitslose Jugendliche in Europa – Methodische Überlegungen und empirische Befunde aus dem LFS 1984-1996*, Gutachten für Eurostat, Nürnberg: IAB.

Dietrich, H. (2001) 'Wege aus der Jugendarbeitslosigkeit – Von der Arbeitslosigkeit in die Maßnahme?', *Mitteilungen aus der Arbeitsmarkt- und Berufsforschung*, vol 34, pp 419-39.

Esping-Andersen, G. (1990) *The three worlds of welfare capitalism*, Cambridge: Polity Press.

European employment guidelines (1997) http://europa.eu.int/comm/employment_social/empl&esf/docs/guideen.htm/

Furlong, A. and Cartmel, F. (1997) *Young people and social change: Individualization and risk in late modernity*, Buckingham: Open University Press.

Gallie, D. and Paugam, S. (eds) (2000) *Welfare regimes and the experience of unemployment in Europe*, Oxford: Oxford University Press.

Gallie, D. and Vogler, C. (1994) 'Unemployment and attitudes to work', in D. Gallie, C. Marsh and C. Vogler (eds) *Social change and the experience of unemployment*, Oxford: Oxford University Press, pp 115-53.

Hammer, T. (1997) 'History dependence in youth unemployment', *European Sociological Review*, vol 13, pp 1-17.

Heinz, W.R. (ed) (1991) *Theoretical advances in life course research*, Weinheim: Deutscher Studien Verlag.

Holm, A. (2002) 'The effect of training on search durations: a random effects approach', *Labour Economics*, vol 9, pp 433-50.

Inglehard, R. (1989) *Cultural change*, Princeton, NJ: Princeton University Press.

Julkunen, I. (1998) 'Active labour market policy and integration', in I. Julkunen and J. Carle (eds) *Young and unemployed in Scandinavia: A Nordic cooperative study*, Copenhagen: Nordic Council of Ministers, pp 65-77.

Julkunen, I. (2002) *Being young and unemployed: Reactions and actions in northern Europe*, Helsinki: University of Helsinki Press.

Lødemel, I. and Trickey, H. (2000) *'An offer you can't refuse': Workfare in international perspective*, Bristol: The Policy Press.

MacDonald, R. (ed) (1997) *Youth, the 'underclass' and social exclusion*, London: Routledge.

Mayer, K.U. (1990) 'Lebensverläufe und sozialer Wandel. Anmerkungen zu einem Forschungsprogramm', in K.U. Mayer (ed) *Lebensverläufe und sozialer Wandel*, Sonderband 21 der KZfSS, Opladen: Westdeutscher Verlag, pp 7-21.

Müller, W. (nd) 'Casmin educational classification' (at www.nuff.ox.ac.uk/Users/Yaish/NPSM/Casmin%20Educ.pdf).

Müller, W., Brauns, H. and Steinmann, S. (2002) 'Expansion und Erträge tertiärer Bildung in Deutschland, Frankreich und Vereinigten Königreich', *Berliner Journal für Soziologie*, vol 12, no 1, pp 37-62.

OECD (Organisation for Economic Co-operation and Development) (2000) *From initial education to working life: Making transitions work*, Paris: OECD.

OECD (2002) *Employment outlook*, Paris: OECD.

O'Higgins, N. (2001) *Youth unemployment and employment policy: A global perspective*, Geneva: ILO.

Raffe, D. (2003) 'Pathways linking education and work: a review of concepts, research, and policy debates', *Journal of Youth Studies*, vol 6, no 1, pp 3-19.

Ryan, P. (2001) 'The school-to-work-transition: a cross-national perspective', *Journal of Economic Literature*, vol 39, March, pp 34-92.

Schröder, L. (2000) *The role of youth programmes in the transition from school to work*, Sofi Working Paper, Stockholm: Sofi.

Serrano Pascual, A. (2001) *Enhancing youth employability through social and civil partnership*, Brussels: ETUI.

Shavit, Y. and Müller, W. (1998) *From school to work: A comparative study of educational qualifications and occupational destinations*, Oxford: Clarendon Press.

Stavik, T. and Hammer, T. (2000) *Unemployment in a segmented labour market? A study of youth unemployment in Norway*, Oslo: NOVA.

Warr, P., Cook, J. and Wall, T. (1979) 'Scales for the measurement of some work attitudes and aspects of psychological well-being', *Journal of Occupational Psychology*, vol 44, pp 47-68.

SEVEN

Youth participation in the labour market in Germany, Spain and Sweden

Floro Ernesto Caroleo and Francesco Pastore

Introduction

The European Social Agenda defined in the Council of Nice declared: "social cohesion, the rejection of any form of exclusion or discrimination and gender equality are all essential values of the European social model". Moreover, "employment is the best protection against social exclusion", but "quality" in work, both in job characteristics and in the work and wider labour market context, is essential to strengthen the social model. Within the European Employment Strategy (EES), young unemployed people are one of the main target groups of employment policy, and education and training are the main instruments used to raise young people's employability.

Across Europe, various proactive schemes have been implemented in the past two decades. According to international conventions, they include job-broking activities with the aim of improving matching between vacancies and unemployed people, labour market training and job creation (subsided employment). However, training schemes, such as work and training contracts, apprenticeships and scholarships, are the most suitable measures for young people, as they activate the accumulation of human capital necessary to find gainful employment. This chapter studies how educational attainment and past participation in training affect labour market participation of young long-term unemployed people (aged 18-24) within the EU. Participation in the labour market for young people includes not only unemployment and employment but also investment in human capital through education and training.

The nature of youth unemployment

The youth activity rate is generally lower than that of adults in almost every country. Low labour force participation crucially depends on educational, vocational and training systems on the one hand, and on labour market structure and institutions on the other. Cross-country differences in the degree of efficiency of the educational systems explain a large part of the differences in the participation rate of young people. In almost every country, teenagers (aged 15-19) tend to have lower participation rates due to school attendance, whereas for young adults (aged 20-24), participation is generally dependent on the effectiveness of training systems in favouring a smooth transition from school to work. Germany is the exception, where young adults have slightly higher unemployment rates than teenagers.

An efficient education system also reduces the share of young adults flowing into the unofficial economy and/or into social exclusion or marginalisation (see Chapter Eight of this book). In fact, a poor education and training system dramatically contributes to raise the number of unskilled young workers entering the labour market with little, if any, probability of finding a good job. Cultural problems may also contribute to this, such as individuals' family background and type of welfare system. The hypothesis that weak labour market conditions could generate social exclusion is based both on demand- and supply-side considerations. On the demand side, entrepreneurs tend to consider repeated unemployment spells early in a person's life as a sign of scant motivation to work. On the supply side, unemployment may lead to depression, family break-up and social isolation. Reducing the number of those experiencing unemployment spells early in their lives is an essential step for reducing the bulk of long-term persistent unemployment.

Common across all Organisation for Economic Co-operation and Development (OECD) countries is the large and perhaps growing number of unemployed workers among the youth population. The International Labour Organization (ILO, 1999, p 1) claims that, on average and almost everywhere, young people who enter the labour market are twice as likely to be unemployed as adults. For reasons that will be discussed later in this chapter, Germany and other countries such as Austria, Switzerland and Denmark are the exception. In these nations, the unemployment rate of young people has been almost the same as that of adults for many years.

When considering the causes of youth unemployment, one should bear in mind that a high unemployment rate mirrors the low employment rate among young people, which, in turn, depends on two groups of factors. First are the levels of aggregate demand and income growth. Nonetheless, holding constant the rate of income growth across countries, differences still exist in youth unemployment rates, suggesting that the structure and features of the youth workforce, as well as the institutions prevailing in the market, also matter (Jimeno and Rodriguez-Palenzuela, 2002).

Much evidence exists of the fact that flows in and out of employment are very high among the youngest workers (Clark and Summers, 1990). These flows are due to various factors, such as the tendency to return to education or to go into training or retraining schemes. Especially when on-the-job training is absent, young workers often prefer (or are forced) to stay out of the labour market to participate in formal off-the-job training. This means that when school-to-work transitions are not smooth, there is opportunity for frequent unemployment spells and fragmented labour market experiences, which could in some cases be conducive to long-term unemployment.

Also, the flows between employment and unemployment are very frequent for some sub-groups of particularly low-skilled young workers. Their unemployment and employment spells are generally shorter than those of highly skilled young and adult workers, due to their tendency to enter a chain of low-pay, temporary and/or part-time work. The low outflows from unemployment into a stable occupation[1] of some groups of young workers depend also on the tendency on the part of employers to prefer adults. This is because of the lower skill and experience levels of young workers, which an inefficient education and training system is unable to improve. The cost of providing on-the-job training for young workers significantly increases the cost of hiring them.

Furthermore, except for southern European countries such as Italy and Spain, young men are worse off in terms of lower job finding and higher job loss rates than their female counterparts (for a cross-country comparison, see Bowers et al, 1999; Ryan, 2001; O'Higgins, 2001).

Previous analysis strongly supports the view that two very different paths are offered to young workers in almost every country. Some young workers enter a positive virtuous circle that leads from education to (and) training to work, while some groups of young people get stuck in unemployment. Having entered unemployment early in life, a young worker has a higher probability of permanently entering long-term unemployment later on in life as well.

As noted, O'Higgins (2001), among others, suggests that youth unemployment and employment policies should be especially targeted at those young people who have a weak position in the labour market. The main focus of an employment policy targeted at young workers should be an efficient education system, as a high rate of school attendance reduces youth labour market participation, but increases the frequency and quality of participation of adults. Once the number of school dropouts among young workers is reduced, policy makers should then focus on increasing their probability of finding a job. To this end, labour market policy should not be confined to passive income support, but to actively affect their employability. Similarly, as also noted in Calmfors et al (2002), the direct employment of young workers in social or public services with little, if any, work experience or on-the-job training is not dissimilar to passive income support.

The choice of countries

The degree of flexibility in education and training systems plays a determinant role in providing the framework within which the school-to-work transitions of young people take place. They also determine the degree of effectiveness of active labour market policies (ALMPs) at a micro level.

Two different education systems can be found in Europe: *sequential* and *dual* systems. The first and more common sequential system is based on the assumption that young people should enter training after they have completed formal education. The sequential system is implemented with different degrees of flexibility in different EU countries. It is more flexible in Northern countries (including, in the Youth Unemployment and Social Exclusion [YUSE] survey sample, Finland, Norway, Scotland and Sweden) and more rigid in southern countries (including, in the YUSE survey sample, France, Italy and Spain).

Various factors determine the rigidity of the southern European education system. Its organisation is very complex and its main feature is a difficult path with various barriers to discourage transitions across different tracks. To complicate the matter, teenagers are already faced with the difficult choice of which educational track to take after compulsory schooling. Furthermore, particularly in Italy, until the recent reform of tertiary education, it takes seven years on average to obtain a university degree.

Another related issue is the tendency of southern European education systems to be centred on those students who are successful in their curricula. However, given the complexity of the system, the number of dropouts is quite high at every stage of the educational career. Until recently, no alternative in terms of training was offered to these young people. In fact, ALMP expenditure is traditionally very low. Market-based systems of training, such as temporary contracts, have been introduced only recently on a large scale in Spain and moderately in Italy. Consequently, especially in high unemployment areas, school dropouts create a stagnant unemployment pool.

Northern European countries have a more flexible sequential education system and, hence, more efficient school-to-work transitions. Northern education systems are commonly characterised by three tracks: a general education track that leads to work through higher education, a vocational track and a work training and/or apprenticeship track. Young people do have to make choices early in their lives concerning which 'pathway' they want to pursue, but they have the opportunity to move from the vocational to the academic pathway and vice versa. The Nordic system has a low dropout rate and higher expenditure in training for school dropouts. As noted in Calmfors et al (2002), over the 1990s, a period of emerging unemployment, ALMP was given the role of closing the circle of sequential education systems in Sweden, providing the last resort of human capital formation on a large scale.

The northern European system also has drawbacks. The main problem is the cost and the unavailability of young people and businesses to participate in the pathways foreseen by policy makers. Moreover, the 'stigma' surrounding some training schemes in northern countries has discouraged young people from participating (for England for example, see O'Higgins, 2001, p 119).

A different approach to gaining flexibility in the education system is pursued in Germany and other German-speaking countries. The dual education and apprenticeship system envisages the young person to experience a period of apprenticeship or traineeship while being involved in formal education. The dual system can be school-based as well as workplace-based. A large number of apprenticeship and vocational education schemes are combined with government-led programmes in the dual system. The apprentice is employed on a three- to four-year contract with an employer. Each year s/he is supposed to spend a certain number of weeks in vocational school. The wage during the apprenticeship is set through collective agreement and is subsidised by the state. In this way, when seeking employment at the end of formal education, the young person will have not only education but also some work experience. The dual system thereby aims to prevent potential market failure in the market for firm-specific human capital. The main drawback of the dual system is that it requires a strong commitment by all parties involved. In various countries, for instance, it is difficult to create a sufficient number of apprenticeships.

Moreover, the education and training systems are part of the more general welfare system and follow the same philosophy. In fact, our classification of countries by education system largely overlaps that by welfare system, laid down in Esping-Andersen (1990). In Spain, the family bears the highest cost of the welfare system and their assistance to young people is the main instrument of fighting the difficulties of a market economy. Germany and Sweden belong to the northern European type of state-based welfare system.

There are differences in the effectiveness of the two systems. A beneficial consequence of the dual system in Germany is the low youth unemployment rate, which was 9% for young adults (aged 18-24) compared to an EU average of 19.1% in the second half of the 1990s. The gap with the prime-age (those aged 25-54) unemployment rate has almost been closed. Nonetheless, young adults (aged 20-24) tend to have slightly higher unemployment rates than do teenagers (aged 15-19), which is a peculiarity of Germany (O'Higgins, 2001, Figure 2.1). This could be due to the fact that some teenagers easily find a job during their apprenticeship, only to lose it later. Therefore, the German system may simply postpone rather than eliminate the risk of unemployment. Unified Germany has represented an important testing ground for the dual system. The increasing unemployment rate of the 1990s suggests that the dual system works well when the average unemployment rate is low.

Although higher than in countries adopting a dual system, the unemployment rate of young people in northern European countries is traditionally lower than in southern European countries: for example, for those aged 18-24, in 1997, it was 17.8% in Sweden compared with 34.2% in Spain. The rigid sequential system is often associated with high and persistent youth unemployment. Confirming a finding of the literature relative to the previous decades, the youth unemployment rate also noticeably decreased in the second half of the 1990s, together with the average unemployment rate.

This chapter focuses on Sweden as an example of the more flexible northern European education system, Spain as an example of the more rigid southern European education system and Germany as the best example of the dual system.

Cross-country evidence on ALMP

This section attempts to assess the importance of ALMP in various EU and non-EU countries. Figures 7.1 and 7.2 show the evolution of expenditure for active and passive policies in 1985 and in 2000. The tick lines represent average

Figure 7.1: Ratio of expenditure for active to passive measures (1985)

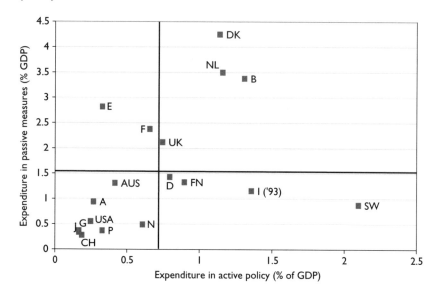

Figure 7.2: Ratio of expenditure for active to passive measures (2000)

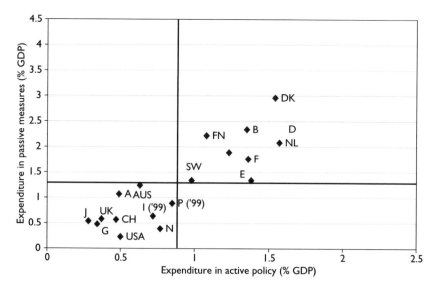

Note: A (Austria), AUS (Australia), B (Belgium), CH (Switzerland), D (Germany), DK (Denmark), E (Spain), F (France), FN (Finland), G (Greece), I (Italy), J (Japan), NL (The Netherlands), P (Portugal), UK (United Kingdom), USA (United States of America), SW (Sweden).

Source: OECD (2001)

values in the sample considered. In 1985, Sweden had higher than average expenditure in active income support but not in passive income support. The opposite holds true for Spain. Germany had a low share of expenditure both in active and passive schemes.

The overall expenditure in employment policy for the unemployed has decreased from 1985 to 2000 due, not only to the reduction in unemployment in many countries, but also to the growing emphasis on proactive measures. In fact, the reduction of expenditure in passive measures has been higher than in active ones (OECD, 2001, 2002).

Noticeable differences between countries can be detected. The relative size of active measures has remarkably increased in one group of countries, including Spain and Germany. Not surprisingly, these are either traditionally high or newly high unemployment countries. Italy is the exception. In Sweden expenditure on ALMP has been reduced since 1994, when it peaked to over 3% of GDP, although it remains one of the highest of the OECD members.

Column (a) in Table 7.1 denotes the expenditure in favour of young people as a share of total expenditure in ALMP at the end of the 1990s, about the time that the YUSE survey was conducted. Column (b) denotes the share of participants on proactive measures over the total labour force. Spain has higher

Table 7.1: Expenditure and participation on ALMP of young people by country (1999) (%)

Country	(a)	(b)
Australia	11.11	0.93
Austria	8.16	0.11
Belgium	0.82	0.24
Denmark	6.49	1.82
Finland	17.59	2.07
France	24.26	2.82
Germany	6.50	1.00
Greece	32.35	0.00
Italy	34.72	1.10
Japan	0.00	0.00
Norway	1.30	0.26
Portugal	36.47	2.64
Spain	6.12	2.10
Sweden	1.45	0.63
Switzerland	2.13	0.00
The Netherlands	2.55	0.56
UK	40.54	1.01
US	6.00	0.56

Source: OECD (2001)

than average share of participation and a lower than average share of expenditure, which suggests that the programmes implemented have a low cost per participant. Sweden and Germany are among the countries with the highest share of expenditure on ALMP over total GDP, but have a low share of expenditure in favour of young people and a low share of young participants.

Modelling labour market participation

An important part of the EES is stressing the need for continuous monitoring and evaluation of the results of the policy. However, while monitoring is now established in many EU countries, so far evaluation has mainly been carried out according to the conventional programme-oriented approach to policy evaluation. Not to mention the serious econometric shortcomings of such an approach, such as the sample selection bias, it is now widely believed to be too specific (for surveys of the literature see Schmid et al, 1996; Meager and Evans, 1998; Pierre, 1999). Our starting point is that a programme-oriented approach is insufficient to evaluate the overall effectiveness of ALMP, especially in the case of young people. In fact, the measures implemented include reforms of education, training and employment systems, arrangements that favour temporary employment and direct incentives to employ young workers. All these programmes affect not only the employability of young people but all the transitions between education, training, employment (regular, irregular, part time, full time) and inactivity (education, staying at home with children and social exclusion) in various ways. Focusing on individual programmes and on the so-called 'treatment effect' (that is, the ability of a training policy to increase the employability of young people) means neglecting the interaction of different policy interventions and their cumulative impact on the behaviour of the target group.

This chapter therefore follows a target-oriented approach, focusing on a specific target group, namely the youth registered as unemployed in a selection of EU countries. An overall evaluation of the impact of various policy instruments on the probability of this specific group to belonging to a given labour market status, controlling for individual and environmental characteristics, is conducted estimating a multinomial logit model for five labour market statuses.

Multinomial logit estimates of the probability of belonging to one of the five different labour market statuses – unemployment, employment, training, education and inactivity – provide a vivid picture of the features of youth unemployment in the three different labour markets studies here. The effects on labour market participation of various sets of individual characteristics are studied:

- demographics (age and gender);
- human capital endowment (education, training and work experience);
- reservation wage (proxied by the mother's university education attainment, degree of parental support and having children);

- length of previous unemployment spells and the intensity of jobsearch;
- social capital endowment (proxied by involvement in political and social activities and in voluntary work).

As noted in Calmfors (1994), despite the fact that ALMP is often regarded as the *deus ex machina* that will provide the solution to the unemployment problem, there is growing scepticism regarding the effects of such a policy on the ability to reduce unemployment. This conclusion is the result of so many studies that it cannot be due to only inadequate data and the econometric methodology adopted. In the case of Sweden, Calmfors et al (2002, p 85) claim that ALMP for young people has reduced open unemployment at the cost of lowering regular employment. The findings of this chapter appear to confirm such scepticism, focusing the analysis on a limited issue: assessing comparatively the role of different education and training systems in Europe on the labour market participation of young unemployed people.

The outcome variable

The analysis is based on the YUSE database, which comes from an ad hoc survey of about 17,000 young people (aged 18-24) interviewed in the mid- to late 1990s and sampled among those registered at the local unemployment office for at least three months in the year preceding the interview. Question f13 of the questionnaire is used to detect the labour market status of each individual at the time of the interview, asking: 'What has been your main activity during the last week?'. Based on the answer given, the respondents have been grouped into one of five homogeneous statuses forming our outcome variable, Y_i, with the individual $i = 0, 1, ..., n$:

- *Unemployment*, including those who are jobless, but actively seeking a job $(Y = 0)$.
- *Employment*, including those with a permanent or temporary contract or in occasional, casual or irregular work activity $(Y = 1)$.
- *Training*, including those on various types of on- or off-the-job training schemes $(Y = 2)$.
- *Education*, including those in compulsory school, vocational school, apprenticeship, academic or university education $(Y = 3)$.
- *Inactivity*, including those in domestic work, on maternity leave, in military service or involved in other activities $(Y = 4)$.

Some observations and caveats are required. First, unemployment has been labelled as $Y = 0$ to indicate that it is considered in the estimates the base alternative to which all the other alternatives are normalised to solve the so-called indeterminacy problem typical of multinomial logit models (Maddala, 1983; Greene, 2000). Second, grouping together formal and informal employment could be considered not completely satisfactory; however, the share of occasional work was low and brought together regular and irregular work in northern countries. Third, an outcome variable of 2 could be taken as a way of assessing how fine-targeted ALMP is to the needs of unemployed youth. In fact, the independent variables can be used to test whether young workers involved in training are those indicated as the most in need of training in the EES and in the National Action Plans of the countries considered, such as low-skilled, long-term unemployed people. Fourth, the inclusion of apprenticeship in educational status is mainly based on the German view of apprenticeship as part of the educational track.

Some caveats also apply to the modelling strategy adopted. The outcomes considered in the multinomial logit model should have neither particular ordering nor sequence. In the former case, one should use, for instance, the ordered PROBIT model. In the latter case, one could use the sequential response model if, for instance, the labour market choices of individuals occupying subsequent stages of the educational track are significantly different (Maddala, 1983). As for the ordering of the statuses included in the above outcome variable, it is apparent that the data do not naturally suggest any inherent ranking of the options considered, as, for instance, involvement in education or training cannot be considered any worse than employment, particularly for young people. Moreover, the so-called property of Independence of Irrelevant Alternatives (IIA) should apply in the case of a multinomial logit model. The IIA property implies that the probability of one status to be chosen over another status is independent of the availability or attributes of alternatives other than the two under scrutiny. In other words, the probability of choosing any status of the outcome variable should be independent of the probability of choosing any other status (McFadden, 1984). However, as noted in the seminal paper by Clark and Summers (1990), it is typical of young people, especially when unemployed, to be involved in various activities at the same time. In our sample, this also holds true. The answers to question f13 of the questionnaire were not mutually exclusive, as the interviewees could declare they were occupying two or more statuses at the same time. For instance, they could be registered as unemployed in the national employment office, but be in education and have occasional jobs. Also, workers involved in ALMP could be in need of finding paid formal or informal employment.

How was this problem tackled in the analysis? Following the general guidelines of the project group, it was assumed that declaring unemployment overrules any other labour market status. Then, sequentially, follows participation in training schemes, in education and employment. The remainder of the sample was considered to be outside the workforce.

In addition, McFadden claims that the IIA property:

> is theoretically implausible in many applications. Nevertheless, empirical experience is that the multinomial Logit model is relatively robust, as measured by goodness of fit or prediction accuracy, in many cases where the IIA property is theoretically implausible. (1984, p 1414)

Table 7.2 gives an overview of labour market participation in our sample of registered unemployed people at the time of the interview by gender. The first apparent feature of the data is the relatively low unemployment rate. With small differences across countries, only one third of the sample appears to remain unemployed one year after registration in the unemployment offices.

Similarly remarkable is the high share of employment. The higher than average share of employment in Spain depends essentially on a much higher than average share of temporary (30.7% compared with an average of 17.3%) and occasional (13.7% compared with 8.6%) work, but also the lower than average share of permanent employment in Sweden and Germany (14.7% and 10.0% respectively compared with 20.1%). This is evidence of the recent excellent performance of the Spanish labour market in providing gainful employment and labour market integration to young people, albeit at the cost of increasing the precariousness of job conditions.

The independent variables

In addition to the typical variables used to predict labour market participation, some variables have been included to test hypotheses relative to the role of social capital endowment. Individual characteristics include age and gender; the human capital endowment of young workers is measured, above all, by educational attainment, detected using the Casmin scale[2]. After some experimentation, four groups have been selected: tertiary education (3 in the Casmin scale), high secondary education (2c), low secondary education (2a and 2b) and compulsory education (1a, 1b, 1c). This last group is used as baseline.

Extensive literature points to the role of work experience as an important component of employability, especially for young people. In addition, education and work experience tend to be inversely correlated, particularly among young workers, as the higher the level of education, the lower the level of general and job-specific skills, which increase together with work experience. Of course, these differences tend to abate as time passes. Work experience has been measured in months and upper-truncated at a maximum of 108 months.

Table 7.2: Frequencies of the outcome variable

Outcome	Sweden			Germany			Spain			All		
	M	W	All	M	W	All	M	W	All	M	W	All
Unemployment	33.6	28.8	31.1	26.7	22.8	25.0	23.3	30.7	27.9	30.9	27.4	29.2
Employment	32.2	29.2	30.8	26.3	30.6	28.2	53.4	44.8	48.1	38.1	36.4	37.2
Training	15.8	14.4	15.1	17.7	20.2	18.8	5.7	6.7	6.3	9.0	10.2	9.6
Education	13.5	18.4	16.1	11.7	12.3	11.9	12.0	10.7	11.2	15.6	16.7	16.2
Inactivity	4.9	9.0	6.9	17.6	14.1	16.1	5.5	7.2	6.5	6.4	9.3	7.8

M = men; W = women

Source: authors' interpretation of YUSE data

Only those young people unemployed at the time of the survey declared the reservation wage. Moreover, the doubt exists that the younger the individual and the less their work experience, the lower their ability to evaluate their own possible contribution to economic activities. As a consequence, three different variables have been used as a proxy of the reservation wage.

The first variable refers to those whose mother has attained university education[3]. A favourable family background is expected to increase the reservation wage, thus increasing the probability of being in education, rather than in unemployment. These expectations are based on sound theoretical and empirical evidence. For example, Bohrman and Rosenzweig (1999) confirm that the significant positive correlation between women's educational attainment and that of their children, although possibly affected by 'ability bias' and various mating problems, is a result that is robust to conventional controls. Furthermore, young people from richer families tend to find gainful employment earlier.

The second variable is a dummy for individuals with children, which generally increases the reservation wage. However, having dependants also represents an important practical obstacle to work, which could increase the risk of inactivity and unemployment. When the latter prevails over the former, it suggests that the welfare system does not provide sufficient childcare facilities.

Furthermore, we test whether receiving parental support prevents young people from finding a job. This is potentially a very important issue, especially in southern European countries where the family plays an important role in the welfare system, but less so in the northern countries, where the pervasive role of the state stigmatises young people relying on family support.

As abundant literature has shown (see, for instance, Nickell, 1997; Barbieri and Scherer, 2001; Caroleo and Pastore, 2001), youth labour market participation in Italy – a country with a typical family-based welfare system – has a puzzling characteristic: labour market participation of young people and women is very low, despite the absence of unemployment benefits. One possibility that the advocates of labour market flexibility consider is that parental financial support works as a powerful substitute for unemployment benefits by substantially increasing the reservation wage of young people and women. Expectations based on this approach would be to find a negative coefficient of parental support on the probability of finding a job and, conversely, a positive coefficient on the probability of remaining unemployed or out of the workforce. On a more positive note, however, high parental support is seen as a necessary condition for many young people to go into tertiary education. The alternative approach stresses the fact that family support is essential to access better education early in a person's life and to better jobs later (for a study relative to the UK, see Gregg and Machin, 1999). Therefore, receiving parental support could increase the probability of being employed and reduce that of being unemployed.

We also tested for the presence of duration dependence in unemployment, that is, the possibility that, ceteris paribus, the longer the spell of unemployment experienced by the worker, the higher the probability of remaining unemployed. The questionnaire includes a question on the overall time spent unemployed[4].

Another way to represent the effect of duration dependence is by assuming that the longer spell of unemployment the less intensive jobsearch. This is measured by the average number of actions implemented, weighted by the number of search methods considered in each country's questionnaire[5]. The variable could capture two different effects according to the labour market status: first, in the case of employed workers, it captures the presence of jobsearch while involved in other activities; second, in the case of the unemployed, it captures the effects of past jobsearch on current labour market status. This suggests the results be viewed with caution.

The policy variable has been used to verify whether past participation on a proactive scheme affects the present probability of finding a job. In principle, the YUSE questionnaire includes questions that would allow the disentangling of different types of proactive measures[6]. However, the number of workers involved in proactive schemes is so low and the differences across countries so sizeable that we end up with only one policy variable.

Some experiments have been carried out to test whether some forms of social capital endowment affect the labour market participation of young people. Of course, social capital is a multidimensional asset, which is difficult to measure (Knack and Kiefer, 1997); however, the information available covers some important aspects of what is meant by social capital and is based on convincing theoretical rationales. Two variables have been used to designate social capital endowment. The first variable, participation in social and political activity, is based on question f57: 'Have you ever participated in any of the following activities or would you be prepared to do so?'. Various answers are considered, such as signing a petition, participating in boycott strikes, demonstrating, occupying factories, attending political, union or other organisational meetings and wearing a badge[7]. The independent variable is obtained as an average weighted by the number of questions included in each country's questionnaire. It is expected that social capital increase the participation in both employment and university education.

Another variable used is participation in voluntary work activity. Following Musella (2002), we assume that voluntary work increases individuals' generic human capital endowment by fostering their employability or, at least, their participation in university education.

Results

We find little evidence in favour of a positive role of training programmes in increasing the employability of young participants. Only in Sweden is the probability of being employed significantly dependent on participation in training programmes. The effect of ALMP on employment is weak in Spain and non-existent in Germany.

This result could also be due to the policy's poor targeting of the weakest groups, especially in Spain and, to a lesser extent, in Germany. Similar to Italy (Caroleo and Pastore, 2001), the variables included in the model are unable to predict participation in training schemes in these countries. The only exception is Sweden with a share of correct predictions equal to 32%, which confirms the importance and the practical effectiveness of ALMP in this country. The share of correct predictions of inactivity equals 27% for Germany and 17% for Sweden.

Our findings confirm existing doubts in the literature on whether ALMP is a good instrument for fighting youth unemployment. We argue that human capital formation is the most important objective for young people at the school-to-work phase of their lives. The best way of improving young people's labour market performance would be to make the general education system more 'effective', that is, able to integrate the largest possible number of young people and to have closer links to the labour market, in order to produce relevant qualifications. This conclusion aligns with that of important in-depth studies on youth unemployment (Booth and Snower, 1995).

Overall performance of the model

Table 7.3 reports the results of the multinomial logit model discussed above for Sweden, Germany, Spain and the entire sample. We chose to report directly the marginal and impact effects of the variables on the relative probabilities, rather than the estimated coefficients. The marginal (impact) effects measure the slope (the shift) of the cumulative distribution function for every unit increase of the independent variable in the case of continuous (discrete) independent variables. The marginal and impact effects in the table are computed at the mean of the covariates. This implies that the effect of each covariate on the dependent variable refers to an individual of average characteristics. The marginal and impact effects are obtained after opportunely manipulating the estimated coefficients and can be used to measure elasticity values. The marginal and impact effects are preferred to the coefficients, as the former should be more useful to find the elasticity values at the mean of the covariates[8] (Maddala, 1983; Greene, 2000).

The overall performance of the model is satisfactory. The variables have the expected sign and the overall significance level is high for a multinomial model. Two tests[9] for the overall significance level are provided in Table 7.4: the McFadden pseudo-R^2 and the Count-R^2. In the estimates reported, both tests are high for a multinomial logit model. The value of the latter test suggests that, for the model discussed here, over 40% of predicted outcomes are correct for each country and for the entire sample.

The values of the Count-R^2 are reported for every single outcome. This is useful information, as it shows that the performance of the model has to be attributed essentially to the ability of the independent variables to predict labour market participation, with shares of correct predictions that range between 64% for Sweden and 84% for Spain in the case of employment, and between 42% for Germany and 55% for Spain in the case of unemployment. The model also performs satisfactorily in the case of participation in education, with a Count-R^2 that varies between 18% for Sweden and 49% for Germany. However, the variables included in the model are unable to predict other types of inactivity. The only exception is Sweden for participation in training schemes (32%). This suggests that expenditure in ALMP in this country is well targeted. Moreover, the share of correct predictions of inactivity equals 27% for Germany and 17% for Sweden.

Table 7.3: Marginal and impact effects based on a multinomial logit model of the probability of belonging to various labour market statuses

Dependent variable	Unemployment ($Y = 0$)			
Independent variables	Spain	Germany	Sweden	All
Constant	−0.58 (0.33)	0.55 (0.79)	0.37***(0.00)	0.21***(0.00)
Age	−0.001 (0.12)	−0.03 (0.73)	0.002***(0.00)	0.0004 (0.32)
Women	0.84***(0.00)	−0.56***(0.02)	−0.51***(0.02)	−0.39***(0.00)
University education	−0.22***(0.00)	−0.27 (0.21)	0.13 (0.78)	−0.51***(0.00)
High secondary education	−0.15***(0.00)	−0.89***(0.02)	−0.19 (0.46)	−0.24***(0.01)
Low secondary education	−0.96***(0.00)	−0.76***(0.00)	0.09 (0.74)	−0.36***(0.00)
Months of work experience	0.03***(0.00)	−0.02***(0.01)	−0.004 (0.35)	−0.01***(0.00)
Mother with university degree	−0.15 (0.82)	0.02 (0.97)	−0.19 (0.51)	0.15 (0.30)
Having children	0.18***(0.00)	0.12***(0.00)	0.74***(0.02)	0.92***(0.00)
Having parental support	0.16***(0.00)	0.06 (0.80)	0.36 (0.21)	0.44***(0.00)
Duration of unemployment (in months)	−0.02***(0.00)	0.06***(0.00)	0.09***(0.00)	0.06***(0.00)
Past participation in training	−0.19 (0.36)	0.94***(0.00)	0.85***(0.00)	0.96***(0.00)
Active jobsearch	0.39 (0.18)	0.71 (0.24)	−0.19***(0.00)	−0.11***(0.00)
Active political participation	−0.03 (0.26)	−0.10***(0.00)	−0.15***(0.00)	−0.06***(0.00)
Doing voluntary work	0.42 (0.25)	−0.72 (0.12)	−0.32 (0.21)	−0.52***(0.00)
Number of observations for Y_i and country	687	480	784	4,772
Number of observations for Y_i	2,466	1,917	2,517	16,368
Count-R^2 [a]	0.55	0.42	0.45	0.46
Count-R^2 for every Y_i	0.43	0.52	0.52	0.45
Log likelihood	−3,220.589	−3,000.621	−3,750.453	−23,674.81
Chi-squared	779.33	668.64	836.05	4,173.16
McFadden pseudo–R^2	0.121	0.111	0.111	0.087

[a] The Count–R^2 is obtained as the ratio or percentage of correct predictions over the total number of observations.

/continued

Table 7.3: contd.../

Dependent variable	Employment (Y= 1)			
Independent variables	Spain	Germany	Sweden	All
Constant	0.48***(0.00)	0.16 (0.46)	0.13* (0.09)	0.19***(0.00)
Age	0.0001 (0.88)	0.12 (0.16)	−0.001 0.35	0.0002 (0.61)
Women	−0.88***(0.00)	0.62***(0.01)	−0.30 0.16	0.02 (0.79)
University education	0.18***(0.00)	0.16 (0.25)	−0.79* (0.09)	0.75***(0.00)
High secondary education	0.61* (0.8)	−0.50 (0.21)	0.07 0.79	−0.57***(0.00)
Low secondary education	0.15 (0.59)	−0.19 (0.45)	−0.29 (0.28	−0.45***(0.00)
Months of work experience	0.05***(0.00)	0.06***(0.00)	0.03 (0.00)	0.04***(0.00)
Mother with university degree	−0.13* (0.07)	−0.21 (0.73)	0.05 0.86	−0.49***(0.00)
Having children	−0.17***(0.00)	−0.13***(0.00)	−0.74** (0.02)	−0.13***(0.00)
Having parental support	−0.25***(0.00)	−0.03 (0.90)	−0.18 0.52	−0.12***(0.00)
Duration of unemployment (in months)	−0.02***(0.00)	−0.03***(0.00)	−0.10***(0.00)	−0.04***(0.00)
Past participation in training	0.48** (0.04)	−0.13 (0.66)	0.77***(0.00)	0.22***(0.01)
Active jobsearch	−0.71***(0.02)	−0.26***(0.00)	0.43 (0.33)	0.45***(0.00)
Active political participation	−0.02 (0.51)	−0.05 (0.13)	0.001 (0.97)	−0.05***(0.00)
Doing voluntary work	−0.93** (0.03)	0.51 (0.23)	0.12 (0.61)	0.07 (0.56)
Number of observations for Y_i and country	1,186	540	774	6,094
Count–R^2 for every Y_i	0.84	0.65	0.64	0.74
Dependent variable	**Training (Y = 2)**			
Constant	−0.12***(0.00)	−0.29* (0.10)	0.13 0.78	−0.09 (0.48)
Age	−0.0002 (0.45)	0.12* (0.09)	−0.001***(0.00)	−0.001***(0.00)
Women	0.07 (0.53)	0.46***(0.02)	0.05 (0.69)	0.16***(0.00)
University education	−0.19 (0.38)	0.64 (0.60)	0.44 (0.11)	0.07 (0.38)
High secondary education	0.36***(0.01)	0.04 (0.90)	0.23 (0.17)	0.13** (0.03)
Low secondary education	0.18 (0.16)	0.04 (0.84)	0.23 (0.19)	0.43***(0.00)
Months of work experience	−0.005* (0.09)	0.01 (0.28)	−0.01** (0.01)	−0.01***(0.00)
Mother with university degree	0.48** (0.03)	0.28 (0.56)	0.01 (0.93)	0.07 (0.43)
Having children	−0.16 (0.58)	−0.99***(0.00)	0.06 (0.77)	−0.09 (0.24)
Having parental support	0.31***(0.00)	−0.15 (0.46)	−0.21 (0.25)	−0.10** (0.05)
Duration of unemployment (in months)	−0.001 (0.64)	0.001 (0.83)	0.04***(0.00)	0.007***(0.00)
Past participation in training	−0.19* (0.08)	−0.10 (0.69)	−0.23***(0.00)	−0.94***(0.00)
Active jobsearch	−0.07 (0.63)	−0.20 (0.71)	−0.49* (0.08)	−0.46***(0.00)
Active political participation	0.02* (0.08)	0.04 (0.15)	0.02 (0.20)	0.006 (0.25)
Doing voluntary work	0.35** (0.02)	0.64* (0.07)	0.10 (0.50)	0.16***(0.02)
Number of observations for Y_i and country	156	360	380	1,574
Count-R^2 for every Y_i	0	0.03	0.32	0.003

/continued

Table 7.3: contd.../

Dependent variable	Education (Y = 3)			
Independent variables	Spain	Germany	Sweden	All
Constant	−0.23***(0.00)	0.78　(0.28)	−0.35***(0.00)	−0.27***(0.00)
Age	0.001**(0.06)	−0.06***(0.02)	−0.001　(0.11)	0.0001 (0.69)
Women	−0.13　(0.17)	0.14　(0.24)	−0.60***(0.00)	0.17***(0.00)
University education	0.49***(0.01)	0.88　(0.17)	0.06　(0.85)	−0.26***(0.01)
High secondary education	0.87***(0.00)	0.16***(0.00)	0.02　(0.90)	0.78***(0.00)
Low secondary education	0.11***(0.00)	0.34** (0.03)	0.02　(0.92)	0.22***(0.00)
Months of work experience	−0.01***(0.00)	−0.02***(0.00)	−0.01***(0,00)	−0.02***(0.00)
Mother with university degree	0.68***(0.00)	−0.28　(0.28)	0.12　(0.53)	0.28***(0.00)
Having children	−0.93** (0.05)	−0.95***(0.00)	−0.12***(0.00)	−0.70***(0.00)
Having parental support	0.60***(0.00)	0.26** (0.03)	−0.06　(0.76)	0.84***(0.00)
Months of unemployment	−0.004* (0.07)	−0.02***(0.01)	−0.03***(0.00)	−0.02***(0.00)
Past participation in training	−0.22***(0.03)	−0.48***(0.01)	0.55***(0.00)	−0.14***(0.02)
Active jobsearch	0.43***(0.01)	−0.06　(0.85)	0.15***(0.00)	0.10***(0.00)
Active political participation	0.04***(0.00)	0.03* (0.10)	0.14***(0.00)	0.11***(0.00)
Doing voluntary work	0.003 (0.99)	0.03　(0.90)	0.10　(0.56)	0.30***(0.00)
Number of observations for Y_i	276	229	405	2,647
Count-R^2 for every Y_i	0.28	0.49	0.18	0.31
Dependent variable	**Inactivity (Y = 4)**			
Constant	−0.72***(0.01)	0.05　(0.97)	−0.15***(0.00)	−0.12***(0.00)
Age	−0.0001 (0.80)	−0.15***(0.01)	0.0001 (0.80)	−0.0001 (0.50)
Women	0.10　(0.34)	−0.65***(0.01)	0.15　(0.12)	0.05　(0.26)
University education	0.10　(0.55)	−0.41　(0.79)	0.16　(0.38)	−0.04　(0.56)
High secondary education	−0.36** (0.04)	−0.27　(0.42)	−0.12　(0.29)	−0.09* (0.07)
Low secondary education	−0.43***(0.00)	0.56***(0.01)	−0.05　(0.65)	0.17***(0.00)
Months of work experience	−0.002　(0.31)	−0.03***(0.00)	−0.004**(0.05)	−0.004***(0.00)
Mother with university degree	0.25　(0.36)	0.19　(0.69)	−0.003 (0.98)	−0.01　(0.89)
Having children	0.10***(0.00)	0.20***(0.00)	0.12***(0.00)	0.12***(0.00)
Having parental support	−0.02　(0.83)	−0.14　(0.45)	−0.02　(0.88)	0.02　(0.65)
Months of unemployment	0.002　(0.31)	−0.02** (0.04)	−0.002　(0.59)	0.001　(0.27)
Past participation in training	0.13　(0.22)	−0.23　(0.37)	0.09　(0.31)	0.002　(0.96)
Active jobsearch	−0.04　(0.78)	0.21***(0.00)	0.50***(0.01)	0.15***(0.03)
Active political participation	−0.02　(0.12)	0.08***(0.00)	−0.01　(0.42)	0.001　(0.75)
Doing voluntary work	0.15　(0.39)	−0.46　(0.26)	−0.01　(0.92)	−0.02　(0.76)
Number of observations for Y_i	161	308	174	1,281
Count-R^2 for every Y_i	0.00	0.27	0.17	0.06

Source: authors' interpretation of YUSE data

Similar to the estimates relative to Italy carried out by Caroleo and Pastore (2001) on the same dataset, the predictive power of the model in the case of participation in training and inactivity is low with regard to Spain. In the case of training, this could be due, above all, to the low number of young people involved in training. As shown above, although double the value in 1985, the Spanish expenditure in ALMP was still very low in 2000 (see Figures 7.1 and 7.2) and especially low for young people (see Table 7.1). It is also important to recall that, in our sample, people in training account for only slightly more than 6%. These estimates confirm that the process of human capital formation is left only to a too rigid education system and to the market via temporary employment.

The individual variables

Not surprisingly, considering the homogeneity of the sample, the marginal effect of age is low in absolute value and almost generally insignificant. Only in Sweden does age significantly affect the probability of being unemployed and in training, whereas it reduces the probability of being in education and in inactivity. In Spain, age simply increases the probability of being in education, suggesting that, similar to Italy, education is a buffer against unemployment.

Confirming a general finding of the literature on youth unemployment (O'Higgins, 2001; Ryan, 2001), women have a lower probability of entering unemployment and a higher probability of being in training or in education within the EU. In Germany the female labour market appears to function better, as women have a significantly higher probability of being employed or in training and a lower probability of being unemployed or inactive than do men. Gender is not an issue when explaining the success in labour market participation early in a person's life, except in Spain. Here, being a woman increases the ceteris paribus probability to be unemployed.

Following expectations based on the human capital theory, having a university qualification significantly increases the probability of being employed and reduces the probability of being unemployed. Having high secondary school qualifications affects labour market participation in all the countries, except Sweden. As expected, individuals with high secondary school qualifications tend to continue their educational track by attending either university or training programmes, rather than being in the more typical statuses of employment, unemployment or inactivity.

The same applies also to young people possessing low secondary school qualifications who tend to continue education. The only exception of this group is Germany, where young people tend to be inactive. This could suggest that holding only low secondary school qualifications may result in social exclusion in Germany.

More generally, the educational variables significantly affect labour market participation in Germany and Spain, but not in Sweden. Moreover, in Germany there is little and insignificant difference between university and higher secondary education as a buffer against unemployment.

Having gained work experience affects the labour market participation of young people. It increases the probability of being employed and reduces the probability of being in other statuses. Spain and Sweden are the exceptions. Work experience positively affects the probability of being unemployed in Spain and the probability of being in education in Sweden. In Spain, this result could be explained by the high proportion of temporary employment and could be interpreted as a sign of precariousness of youth employment in that country.

Family background, proxied by mother's tertiary education, is an important factor influencing labour market participation, especially in Spain and in the sample as a whole. As expected, it increases the probability of being in education and reduces that of being employed. Again, the reason could be the higher unemployment rate of southern Mediterranean countries, coupled with a culture and welfare system based on the role of the family, as opposed to the state. In Germany and Sweden, this effect is not significant.

Having children represents an important factor in the low labour market participation of young people almost everywhere in Europe, but less so in Sweden, confirming the presence in this country of a solid welfare system. In turn, this could explain the low birth rate within the EU: if having children contributes to social exclusion, it is better to postpone it until after having attained satisfactory employment.

The third proxy of the reservation wage – parental support – is a significant factor influencing labour market participation, but with interesting cross-country differences. Looking at the entire sample, the lack of financial support from the family increases the probability of being unemployed and reduces the probability of being employed. This is evidence in favour of the hypothesis that receiving financial support from the family increases the job opportunities of young people. The coefficients are almost always significant and sizeable in the case of Spain.

Having parental support increases the probability of being out of employment, in unemployment, in training and especially in education. This holds true particularly in Spain, again confirming the important role of the family in this country. Conversely, parental support is less common in Sweden, where family support is not such an important factor in influencing labour market participation.

There was evidence of persistent unemployment in all the countries considered except Spain. In general, the longer the spell of unemployment, the higher the probability of being unemployed or in training, but the lower the probability of being employed or in education. The negative duration dependence observed in the case of Spain is quite surprising, considering that the OECD (2002, p 23) indicates long-term unemployment as one of the most remarkable features of youth unemployment in Spain even as recently as 2000[10]. Our result probably mirrors the increasingly high proportion of the youth workforce in temporary employment, which, in turn, increases turnover in the labour market.

The intensity of jobsearch negatively correlates with the probability of being unemployed and positively with the probability of being employed in the entire sample, with the exceptions of Spain and Germany, where it negatively correlates with the probability of being employed. As noted above, the used proxy – the number of adopted search methods – could measure different effects and the results should be read with caution. These findings could suggest that being employed in Germany and in Spain does not require the implementation of multiple strategies or methods of jobsearch for some individuals.

Less ambiguous is the positive correlation of active jobsearch with education in the case of Spain and the entire sample and with inactivity for all the countries except Spain, in which case the coefficient is statistically insignificant. The intensity of jobsearch by inactive workers confirms the conclusions of an extensive literature (see, for example, the seminal paper by Clark and Summers, 1990) which suggests that the line between unemployment and inactivity for young people is particularly fine. In fact, the inflow to employment from unemployment is equal to that from inactivity in the case of young people. Moreover, while involved in education, young people are also occasionally in search for jobs.

Past participation in training programmes increases the probability of being unemployed in all countries except Spain and, by a lower percentage, the probability of being employed in all countries except Germany. This, in turn, reduces the probability of remaining in education or training. This result is not surprising considering that our sample includes young people registered as unemployed, who are expected to be the least successful attendants of training programmes. Nonetheless, the overall performance of the variable suggests that, for the specific target group included in the survey, training reduces inactivity without remarkably increasing the chances of finding a job, except in the case of Sweden. This adds scepticism to the view that training is a successful substitute for the education system and the market in providing the human capital necessary for young people to find gainful employment.

Finally, we find that active political participation negatively correlates with the probability of actively participating in the workforce, either as employed or unemployed, but positively correlates with the probability of being in education. Germany is the exception, as active political participation significantly and positively correlates with inactivity, although by a small percentage. Similar results hold true for participation in voluntary work. Those who are actively seeking jobs or are employed are less active in voluntary work activities. And, vice versa, those in education or in training are bound to be more involved in voluntary work.

A picture of youth unemployment in Europe

The typical pattern of youth unemployment emerging from the estimates relative to Spain is women, especially those with children and with a low level of education attainment, who are trapped in precarious employment experiences that cause frequent unemployment spells. Moreover, these young unemployed women are often from poor family backgrounds and have no financial support from their families: workers with poor family backgrounds tend to leave education earlier in an unsuccessful search for a stable job. On a more positive note, due to the diffusion of temporary work, unemployment shows negative duration dependence.

Germany has a more typical profile comprising mainly of unemployment of men with low education attainment, little work experience and long unemployment spells. Unemployed people typically have not only low human capital but also low social capital, that is, they do not actively participate in social or political life. Having children increases the risk of unemployment; for these individuals, participating in a training programme has no effect on the employment probability.

Sweden's unemployment profile is not dissimilar from that of Germany. Unemployed young people are predominantly male with long unemployment spells and, to a lesser extent, with children. Unemployment correlates with little social and political participation. Active jobsearching among this group is lower than for people in education. Having participated in training schemes slightly increases the probability of being employed. As in Germany, Sweden's unemployment increases with age, but unlike Germany, with little difference across educational groups.

Concluding remarks

This chapter provides an analysis of the labour market participation decisions of young adults (aged 18-24) in a selection of European countries. The starting point of the analysis is that cross-country differences in youth labour markets depend conspicuously on the type of educational training system adopted. The analysis focuses on Spain and Sweden as examples of rigid and flexible sequential systems respectively, with training following education, and Germany as the best example of a dual educational and training system. Multinomial logit estimates of the probability of belonging to one of the five different labour market statuses – unemployment, employment, training, education and inactivity – provide a vivid picture of the features of youth labour markets in the countries considered.

Overall, the analysis suggests that in Spain, similar to other Mediterranean countries, the most important determinants of youth participation in the labour market are education and family background. Also, women fare worse than men. The recent increase in temporary employment has produced important changes in the behaviour of young people, as the probability of being unemployed is less duration-dependent and work experience a less important employment screening device than in the past. In fact, short employment experiences curtail their formative content.

In Germany, youth participation in the labour market appears to depend essentially on work experience and on the intensity of jobsearch. This could be interpreted as evidence of the fact that market mechanisms are more efficient in allocating jobs among workers. Labour market policy is still unable to affect employment probability, suggesting that the labour market be comparatively more efficient. The female labour market is also very efficient in Germany.

In Sweden, education and family background are less important factors of labour market participation. The small differences in the employment elasticity of workers with various educational qualifications could be taken as evidence of good matching between labour demand and supply. ALMP significantly increases the probability of finding employment and seems well targeted to long-term unemployed people. A more protective welfare system reduces the effect of social exclusion linked to having children in other countries.

Last but not least, we find little evidence for the positive role of training programmes in increasing the employability of young participants. Only in Sweden is the probability of being employed significantly dependent on participation in training programmes. The effect of ALMP on employment is quite weak in Spain and non-existent in Germany. This result could also be due to the policy's poor targeting to the weakest groups, especially in Spain and, to a lesser extent, in Germany. As is the case in Italy (Caroleo and Pastore, 2001), the variables included in the model appear unable to predict participation in training schemes in these countries, except Sweden. Our results raise the question of whether ALMP is a good instrument for tackling youth unemployment, considering that young people are at the age when capital formation is their most important objective. This issue would be better addressed by making the general education system more 'effective', that is, able to integrate the largest possible number of young people and to have closer links to the labour market, so as to produce the necessary qualifications.

Notes

[1] By 'stable' employment we mean a type of employment that is not short in duration, but is not necessarily the same permanent full-time job. The degree of labour turnover has increased everywhere, especially, perhaps, for young workers. However, stable employment is not inconsistent with job-to-job moves if these do not imply unemployment spells.

[2] Casmin stands for Comparative Analysis of Social Mobility in Industrial Nations.

[3] This variable is supposed to represent the family background better than the more traditional 'living with parents' or 'living alone', as these last variables seem to discriminate very little among young people, both across and within countries, reflecting more cultural

than economic factors (on this issue, see Bowers et al, 1999, p 9). Few respondents, especially if in training or inactive, had an unemployed father.

[4] The variable has been upper-truncated for unemployment spells longer than 108 months.

[5] It is based on question f17: 'Thinking about your current or last period of unemployment, can you indicate which methods you used to try to find a job?'. Overall, over 10 different search methods are considered, such as placing advertisements, consulting vacancy boards, contacting employers directly, using personal networks of family and friends, contacting unions, registering at private employment agencies or other institutions, replying to advertisements, preparing for public contests and attempting to start their own businesses. The used variable is more suited to capture how extensive, rather than how intensive, job search is, which is usually measured by the time spent seeking jobs. However, often in the relevant literature, the number of implemented search methods is used as a proxy for the intensity of job search. No attempt is made here to analyse the choice of the unemployed among the available job search actions.

[6] Various attempts to be more specific on the adopted policy failed. More specific variables include participation in on- or off-the-job training. Moreover, the questionnaire distinguishes the number of courses attended and months spent in training. Question 32 asks: 'How long have you spent on schemes during the past five years?'. Question f33 asks: 'Altogether, how many schemes have you been on?'. In fact, the two variables could represent different phenomena. Finally, it is possible to distinguish past from present participation. In all these cases, the number of those answering the questions was low.

[7] Three answers are possible in each case, which are coded from 1 to 3. The answer 'I would never do it' is coded 1; 'I would be prepared to do it' is coded 2; and 'I have already done it' is coded 3.

[8] Moreover, in the case of the logit with multiple outcomes, unlike the marginal and impact effects, the coefficients could have a different sign compared to the elasticity values.

[9] The McFadden (1974) pseudo-R^2 measures the goodness of fit of the model to the data. As shown in Maddala (1983), the usual R^2 would underestimate the goodness of fit of the model, as the maximum value it takes is lower than one and, ceteris paribus, depends inversely on the number of sample observations. McFadden's is a typical log-likelihood ratio test, where the restricted model is based on the assumption that all the coefficients are equal to zero, except for the constant term. It is defined as:

$$\text{McFadden Pseudo-}R^2 = 1 - \frac{\log L_U}{\log L_R}$$

where L_U and L_R are the values of the log likelihood at maximum with L_U including all the variables and with LR including only the constant term and assuming all the coefficients to be equal to zero. The McFadden test takes a value comprised between 0 and 1.

Count-R^2 is another statistic test of the overall significance level and measures the number of correct predictions as a percentage of the total number of observations.

[10] OECD (2002, Chart 1.3) shows that the average share of long-term youth unemployment has declined dramatically over the second half of the 1990s in Spain. In fact, the average share of long-term unemployment has declined from 50.3% to 34.1% for individuals aged 15-19 and from 57.9% to 46.6% for individuals aged 20-24 over the period 1983-90 and 1993-2000.

References

Barbieri, P. and Scherer, S. (2001) 'Logici e razionali? Comportamenti strategici dell'offerta di lavoro nella transizione scuola-lavoro: un confronto fra Nord e Sud Italia', Paper presented to AIEL Conference, Milan, 16 November.

Bohrman, J.R. and Rosenzweig, M.R. (1999) *Does increasing women's schooling raise the schooling of the next generation?*, PIER Working Paper 01-051, Penn Institute for Economic Research.

Booth, A.L. and Snower, D.J. (eds) (1995) *Acquiring skills: Market failures their symptoms and policy responses*, Cambridge: Cambridge University Press and CEPR.

Bowers, N., Sonnet, A. and Bardone, L. (1999) 'Giving young people a good start: the experience of OECD countries', in *Preparing youth for the 21st century: The transition from education to the labour market*, Proceeding of the Washington DC Conference, Paris: OECD, pp 7-80.

Calmfors, L. (1994) *Active labour policies and unemployment: A framework for the analysis of crucial design features*, OECD Economic Studies No 22, Paris: OECD, pp 7-47.

Calmfors, L., Forslung, A. and Hemström, M. (2002) *Does active labour market policy work? Lessons from the Swedish experiences*, IFAU Institute for Labour Market Policy Evaluation Working Paper No 4, IFAU.

Caroleo, F.E. and Pastore, F. (2001) *How fine targeted is active labour market policy to the youth long term unemployed in Italy?*, CELPE Discussion Paper No 62, University of Salerno.

Clark, K.B. and Summers, L.H. (1990) 'The dynamics of youth unemployment', in L.H. Summers (ed) *Understanding unemployment*, Cambridge, MA: MIT Press.

Esping-Andersen, G. (1990) *The three worlds of welfare capitalism*, Cambridge: Polity Press.

Greene, W.H. (2000) *Econometric analysis*, Baltimore, NJ: Prentice Hall.

Gregg, P. and Machin, S. (1999) 'Child development and success or failure in the youth labour market', *Luxembourg Income Study*, October.

ILO (International Labour Organization) (1999) *Employment youth: Promoting employment intensive growth*, Report for the Regional Symposium on Strategies to Combat Youth Unemployment and Marginalisation, Geneva: ILO.

Knack, S. and Kiefer, P. (1997) 'Does social capital have an economic payoff? A cross-country investigation', *Quarterly Journal of Economics*, vol 112, no 4, pp 1251-88.

Jimeno, J.F. and Rodriguez-Palenzuela, D. (2002) *Youth unemployment in the OECD: Demographic shifts, labour market institutions and macroeconomic shocks*, European Central Bank Working Paper No 155, June.

McFadden, D. (1974) 'The measurement of urban travel demand', *Journal of Public Economics*, no 3, pp 3003-328.

McFadden, D. (1984) 'Econometric analysis of qualitative response models', in Z. Griliches and M.D. Intriligator (eds) *Handbook of econometrics*, vol 2, Elsevier Science.

Maddala, G.S. (1983) *Limited dependent and qualitative variables in econometrics*, Cambridge: Cambridge University Press.

Meager, N. and Evans, C. (1998) *The evaluation of active labour market measures for the long-term unemployed*, ILO Employment and Training Papers No 16, Geneva: ILO.

Musella, M. (2002) 'Il contributo delle organizzazioni non-profit nei processi di accumulazione di capitale umano', in G. Antonelli (ed) *Istruzione: Economia e istituzioni*, Bologna: Il Mulino.

Nickell, S. (1997) 'Unemployment and labour market rigidities: Europe versus North America', *Journal of Economic Perspectives*, vol 11, no 3, pp 55-74.

OECD (Organisation for Economic Co-operation and Development) (various years) *Employment Outlook*, Paris: OECD.

O'Higgins, N. (2001) *Youth unemployment and employment policy: A global perspective*, Geneva: ILO.

Pierre, G. (1999) *A framework for active labour market policy evaluation*, ILO Employment and Training Papers No 49, Geneva: ILO.

Ryan, P. (2001) 'The school-to-work transition: a cross-national perspective', *Journal of Economic Literature*, vol 39, no 1.

Schmid, G., Büchtemann, C., O'Reilly, J. and Scömann, K. (eds) (1996) *International handbook of labour market policy and evaluation*, London: Edward Elgar.

EIGHT

Surviving unemployment: a question of money or families?

Torild Hammer and Ilse Julkunen

Introduction

Young people are at a stage in life when their financial situation is often strained. Setting up one's own home, getting established in the labour market, and having children and being on a low income are clearly related to financial problems. Young people tend not to have accumulated financial resources, and have therefore a high poverty risk (Julkunen, 2000). Long-term unemployment in this age group may accelerate a development towards poverty and welfare dependency. There is a need for comparative knowledge of contrasting policies and outcomes of different welfare models in Europe. The aim of this chapter is to analyse and compare the financial circumstances of young unemployed people in six different European countries – Denmark, Finland, Norway, Scotland, Spain and Italy – to study how different welfare arrangements influence the risk of financial marginalisation among unemployed youth. The countries represent three different clusters with similar welfare strategies: a Nordic model of advanced institutional welfare (Finland, Denmark and Norway); a model with moderate institutional and family arrangements in combination with corporate social protection (Scotland); and a southern European model with welfare strategies relying on the family as the prime source of welfare (Spain and Italy) (Vogel, 1997). How have young people survived unemployment? To what extent does financial deprivation prevail among them and are there different outcomes in countries with different strategies? The study draws on comparative surveys among representative samples of unemployed 18- to 24-year-olds who had been unemployed for at least three months continuously and were interviewed 12 months later in 10 countries across Europe.

Relative deprivation

Today, the young face a restructured labour market, an increased demand for qualifications and flexibility in the workplace, and cuts in social benefits that extend the period in which they remain dependent on their families. The changing structural context for the young can be seen in the way that the pattern of poverty has changed, as there has been a marked shift in the composition of the poor, away from older towards younger households. The pattern of higher poverty rates among young people appears to be a general trend all over Europe, (Vogel, 1997). The only exception seems to be the UK, where poverty rates are higher among middle-age groups. Deprivation is also an important concept in the analysis of social conditions and should be distinguished from poverty. Townsend (1988) defines deprivation as a state of observable and demonstrable disadvantage relative to the local community or to the wider society to which an individual belongs. People could be considered deprived if they lack food, clothing, housing, and social conditions and activities or facilities that are customary in their society. Many people may feel deprived of material or cultural conditions, but only if they lack or are denied resources to obtain these conditions can they be said to be in poverty (Julkunen, 2000). The first aspect depends on the level of conditions experienced, the second on the incomes and other resources (Townsend, 1993, pp 93-4).

The impact of poverty on young people and the transformation of the labour market have a fundamental effect on experiences of growing up. What happens during this transition is, according to many researchers, of significance to the paths that lie open to young people in the future (Silver, 1994). Other studies have claimed that exclusion and dependence at a young age are unlikely to be permanent generational problems, but rather problems related to different life-course stages (Wilska, 1999).

How people experience unemployment is dependent on the availability of financial resources, which make it possible to stabilise and maintain an established lifestyle, to uphold and extend social relations, and which are often a prerequisite for taking part in social activities. Financial resources also promote a feeling of control over the life situation and increase independence. Postmodern theories argue that consumption in contemporary society has become an integrating force (Bauman, 1998). It has a central role in the construction of identity. When the labour market ceases to offer the young a form of identity, the marketplace becomes a more important influence. Willis (1990) similarly argues that leisure and consumption have become the only arenas in which the young can realise and find their identities. As the supply of leisure time, goods and services increases, younger generations grow up in a new kind of consumer culture, and having access to necessary resources means that you are able to participate in youth cultures (Furlong and Cartmel, 1997; Wilska, 1999). Poverty among the unemployed is thus not only a question of being left outside of wage earning and experiencing financial misery. It also implies the incapacity to take part in leisure or free-time activities, because today nearly all such activities are dependent on having money (Julkunen, 2000).

Private or public transfer?

The different welfare models in Europe imply different unemployment protection systems and consequently different levels of deprivation and poverty among unemployed youth. In southern Europe young unemployed people rely heavily on their parents. Consequently, they often live with their parents until they reach their thirties. However, it is also important to stress that young people in employment or education often do so too (Vogel, 1997). One reason is the extremely high housing costs, especially in Italy and Spain, which makes it nearly impossible for young people to set up their own household (Miret-Gamundi, 1997; Russell and Barbieri, 2000). In other words, living much longer with parents in southern Europe than in northern Europe is not only an effect of unemployment. On the other hand, unemployment may make it even harder for young people as well as for their parents. No independent income will increase parental dependency, and may also increase the financial strain of the household. Youth unemployment may be related to financial deprivation in low-income families or in families where parents are unemployed or out of work. The concentration of unemployment in the household varies greatly across Europe. Data from LES (Luxembourg Employment Study) show that one half of unemployed people are heads of households in the UK, against a quarter in Spain (Lasaosa, 1997). According to the national labour force surveys provided by Eurostat for 1996, 35% of young unemployed people in Britain lived in a household where no other person was employed compared with 25% in Spain and about 20% in Italy (OECD, 1996). It seems that to rely on parents' financial support in Britain may create more problems than in Italy. Parental dependency may reinforce the process of inter-generational transmission of poverty. However, parental support may also be essential to the prevention of poverty among unemployed youth. Obviously, this would also be the case for unemployed youth in central or northern Europe. Even in Scandinavia, with its generous benefit system, many young unemployed people are not entitled to unemployment benefits because they lack work experience, and even if they receive such benefits, they can be low because of low previous income.

Still, in northern Europe, young people leave their parents much earlier than in the south, even if they are not yet established in the labour market. In northern Europe, young people leave home for education or employment, while in the south, leaving home is part of the process of family formation (Holdsworth, 2000).

Generally, young women leave home several years earlier than young men. This is also the case among unemployed youth, in fact even more so. Research from Britain and Scandinavia has found that unemployed young men stay longer in the parental home than those in employment, but young unemployed women often leave home in spite of unemployment (Wallace, 1986; Hammer, 1996). Most of them move in with a partner or husband who can support them. They also tend to have children earlier than those in employment. For young unemployed women, having children may solve their unemployment problem by withdrawing them from the labour market. Motherhood may also represent a shortcut to adulthood (Hammer, 1996). To be supported by a partner is another kind of private transfer which acts as a buffer against poverty and financial deprivation, especially for young unemployed women. However, this is dependent on the breadwinner's capacity as provider. If he is unemployed as well, financial deprivation may prevail. A number of young unemployed women also have children, but there are great variations across countries, also in northern Europe. Previous findings from our study show that in Iceland, about 70% had children compared with 50% in Norway and only 15% in Finland (Carle and Julkunen, 1998)[1]. They will be dependent on private transfer and to a lesser extent, public transfer to make ends meet. Unemployed single mothers face a more difficult situation. This is a very vulnerable group. Some countries have introduced special social benefit schemes for single parents, but the level of support varies greatly. In other countries they are not entitled to any social support. The poverty rate is much higher among single parents than other households (Saraceno, 1997), but varies a lot between countries (Pedersen et al, 2000). The differences can mainly be explained by the costs of paid childcare, the income support system and the participation of single parents in employment. Employment participation is related to the general female employment rate, where the EU average rate is 50%, but varies from 36% in Italy (28% in the south) to about 80% in Scandinavia.

When analysing the impact of different protection systems in different countries on financial deprivation of unemployed youth, it is important to consider the very complex mixture of private and public transfer. As discussed here, private support as a buffer against poverty among unemployed youth will always be related to family circumstances, such as low income in the family or unemployment among parents or a partner. Having children may increase the financial strain, in particular for lone mothers. However, in most countries unemployed youth will also be entitled to some kind of public support, even if the level of support and degree of coverage varies considerably between countries. As discussed in Chapter One, Gallie and Paugam (2000) have developed a typology of welfare regimes based on different protection systems for the unemployed in Europe. The sub-protective model is dominant in the south of Europe and implies very incomplete coverage and low level of support. The liberal/minimal model has an incomplete coverage and low level of support; the UK is an example. Unemployed youth will be entitled to a flat-rate benefit Jobseeker's Allowance. The employment-centred model dominant in France and Germany gives a higher level of support than the liberal/minimal model, but exclusively for those established in the labour market. The last regime is the universalistic model, with a high level of support and a high degree of coverage, which is dominant in Scandinavia.

Private and public transfer is important for unemployed young people. However, many of them will also have income from regular employment. Not all of them are continuously unemployed, but will find jobs interspersed with periods of unemployment, such as seasonal work, occasional jobs and so on.

Some will also have income from irregular employment in the illegal or informal economy. This is especially the case for unemployed youth in southern Europe. There are a lot of problems with this kind of employment, such as low pay, no rights to unemployment benefits or health insurance, dangerous working conditions and so on. Unemployed youth who work in the informal economy may end up in dead-end jobs with few prospects for the future. However, work in the underground economy, odd jobs or informal small-scale work may represent important additional income for unemployed youth attempting to survive long-term unemployment.

The level of unemployment

In this study, countries representing all the four welfare models of income support discussed previously are included. Here we will analyse the relationship between public and private support and reported financial deprivation among unemployed youth in three of the models. However, in order to do, so the unemployment career has to be taken into account. The long-term unemployed or those with successive periods of unemployment will clearly experience more financial hardship than those with only a short period of unemployment.

However, both the unemployment rate for young people and the proportion of long-term unemployed varies considerably between countries. In Italy, a total of 26% of young people were unemployed and unemployment is mainly concentrated in the south (45% in the age group 15-29 years) (Caroleo and Mozzotta, 1999). In the age group less than 24 years old, the unemployment rate is 30% higher in the south, and females have a higher rate than males (Caroleo, 2000). In total, 65% are long-term unemployed (for more than one year). Spain has a very high unemployment rate in young people, 42% among women and 29% among men in 1999, about 50% of whom were first-time jobseekers. In total 41% were long-term unemployed (Álvaro and Garrido, 2000). The unemployment rate in the UK (age less than 25 years) was 15.8% in 1997 and, unlike in the south of Europe, was higher for males (17%) than females (11.5%). About 30% were long-term unemployed. In Scandinavia, the unemployment rate has been at a much lower level than the rest of Europe, including that among young people. However, this changed in the 1990s and Finland was especially hit by very high youth unemployment (30% in 1996, of whom 36% were long-term unemployed). First-time jobseekers account for about 80% of the young unemployed in Finland, the same as in Italy and much higher than the proportion in Denmark (15%) or Germany (20%) (OECD, 1998). In Denmark and Norway the unemployment rate for young people in the same year was 10% and 12%, 14% of whom were long-term unemployed in both countries.

In summary, Italy, Spain and Finland had the highest youth unemployment, and Italy in particular had a very high rate of long-term unemployment. The UK was in the middle, and Denmark and Norway had the lowest levels, especially with regard to long-term unemployment.

Research questions

It is reasonable to assume that unemployment career will influence young people's experience of financial hardship. However, public and private transfer will, to different degrees, modify this effect depending on the welfare model of the respective countries. In this chapter we will answer the following research questions:

- What is the relationship between unemployment career and relative deprivation in each country?
- To what extent does private or public transfer act as a buffer against deprivation and poverty in each country, and does other income, such as irregular employment, also have a significant effect?
- How can such buffers against deprivation explain the different level of deprivation in the different countries?

Measurements

Unemployment career was constructed in much the same way as previously by the Scottish research team, Furlong and Cartmel (2000).

On the basis of information about previous employment and unemployment career and current situation, a measure of the unemployment career divided into four categories has been constructed:

1. *The included:* young people with less than six months' experience of unemployment and who at the time of the interview had been in full-time work or full-time education for more than six months.
2. *At risk:* young people with less than 12 months' experience of unemployment and who at the time of interview were in employment, education or stayed home to care for children.
3. *Vulnerable:* young people with less than 12 months' unemployment or a total unemployment experience of less than two years and who at the time of interview were unemployed or stayed home to care for children.
4. *Marginalised:* young people with more than one year of unemployment and a total unemployment experience of more than two years and who were unemployed at the time of interview.

Financial deprivation was measured by an 11-item scale, which covered both material and cultural deprivation:

During the past 12 months, which of the following have you had to give up due to lack of money?
- warm meals;
- essential clothes for yourself or your family;
- paying rent and bills on time;

- visiting the cinema, theatre or concerts;
- inviting friends to your home;
- visiting relatives or friends living in other towns;
- buying birthday or Christmas presents;
- holidays away;
- newspapers;
- hobbies or other recreational activities;
- visiting pubs or restaurants.

Scored from 1 (often) to 3 (never), the index is coded as a dummy for each question (often = 1) (range 0 to 1), Cronbach alpha = 0.85, mean = 0.20, sd (standard deviation) = 0.25. The distribution is very skewed, with 60% of the sample scoring less than the average value. Those who reported more than four items were defined as deprived (20% of the distribution).

Income the last month was measured by the following question: 'After tax and deductions, how much money did you receive last month?' (include money from all sources such as wages, grants and benefits).

Family risks was measured by:

- father's education coded as dummy variables and used as a proxy for parents' income;
- growing up in a single parent family is used as a measure of poverty in the family of origin;
- parents' unemployment: whether the mother or father are or have been unemployed for at least six months;
- husband's or cohabitee's unemployment: whether the partner is or has been unemployed for at least six months.

Income from employment

The respondents in all countries were asked about their main sources of income during the past year. The first alternative in all countries was income from regular employment. However, they were also asked about other income from irregular employment, such as income from odd/causal jobs and from employment in the informal economy. Irregular employment is measured in different ways in the different countries. It is a sensitive question and it was necessary to take the cultural context into account. In Scandinavia it took into account income from work in the black economy, and in Scotland and Germany, income from casual jobs or income from other activities. In Italy, France and Spain it included income from employment without contract, income from informal activities or work for a neighbour or a friend.

Results

Table 8.1 shows the distribution of unemployment career across countries.

The highest proportions of marginalised youth are found in Finland, Scotland and Italy. Finland has a much higher level of unemployment than Scotland, but the proportion of long-term unemployed is about the same in the two countries. Furthermore, very few (4%) in the Scottish sample have re-entered the education system compared with Finland and the other Nordic countries (20%) (Hammer, 2003). Spain has a very high unemployment level, and only 16% were involved in employment or education at the time of interview. The high proportion in Italy, in the included group, does not correspond with the extremely high level of long-term unemployment in this country. The reason is that so many were in full-time education that only 15% were in employment. Another reason is the system for registering unemployment in Italy. Many students register as jobseekers at the employment office because they are looking for work and because they also get other opportunities, such as admission to different courses and so on. Many people in Spain were in the 'at risk' group, as they were young people with temporary work contracts and employed for less than six months during the past year. This group also included young women in domestic work who did not report unemployment at the time of the interview.

Danish unemployed youth are well integrated in the labour market and only a small group can be characterised as marginalised.

Table 8.2 shows deprivation and mean income by unemployment career in the different countries. According to Table 8.2, both deprivation and income are clearly related to unemployment career. The marginalised group reports lower income and a higher level of deprivation and those included reported fewer problems.

Unemployed youth in Scotland experience more financial hardship than in all the other countries independent of unemployment career. Danish unemployed youth report a very low level of deprivation, and the deprivation score is nearly independent of the unemployment career. The results indicate that in Denmark, there are effective buffers against deprivation, probably because

Table 8.1: Unemployment career, by country (%)

	Included (*n* = 3,038)	At risk (*n* = 5,747)	Vulnerable (*n* = 2,312)	Marginalised (*n* = 1,551)
Finland	10	45	22	23
Norway	21	45	24	9
Denmark	33	40	21	6
Scotland	22	38	21	19
Italy	37	36	9	18
Spain	16	52	16	16

Source: Hammer (2003)

Table 8.2: Proportion deprived (%) and mean income (€) by unemployment career, by country

Country	Included	At risk	Vulnerable	Marginal	All
Finland	14	25	27	36	27
	€593	€435	€369	€351	€417
Norway	9	26	29	37	24
	€743	€542	€515	€468	€572
Denmark	5	12	12	15	10
	€893	€749	€710	€749	€789
Scotland	21	29	35	44	32
	€712	€482	€305	€287	€458
Italy	2	2	3	4	3
	€370	€420	€345	€287	€380
Spain	12	11	17	24	14
	€691	€606	€483	€347	€558

Note: Income is calculated by using purchase power parity (PPP) from 1998, correcting for a harmonised price consumption index.

of very generous benefits. The results could be caused by the biased sampling in Denmark, which only includes those insured. However, if we compare only those who receive unemployment benefits across countries, we get the same results. In Italy, reported deprivation is extremely low compared with the other countries. This is because virtually no one reported any material deprivation. The questions were not relevant for young people who lived with their parents. However, they also have low scores for cultural deprivation (range 8% to 14%), about the same level as Denmark.

The Italian youth population also has the lowest level of income in the included group. This is because most of them are students; those who are in work (only 15%) report the same level of income as in the other countries.

Interestingly, even among Scottish youth in employment (the included), every fifth reports deprivation. Scottish youth report the same average income as youth in Finland, but a higher degree of deprivation. It is possible that Scottish youth tend to report more problems as a kind of culturally determined reporting style. However, it is also possible that the higher deprivation score in Scotland is a result of a higher rate of deprivation among young people both in employment and unemployment compared with other countries. A higher level of deprivation could be explained by the higher concentration of poverty in the households compared with the other countries. Table 8.3 shows the proportion of unemployed youth reporting deprivation according to household composition.

In Scotland, 63% of unemployed young people live with their parents compared with one third in Finland and Norway and only 16% in Denmark, while in the southern countries most young unemployed people live with parents. Interestingly, even among those living alone in the south, the deprivation

Table 8.3: Proportion deprived (%) and household composition of the unemployed (% in brackets), by country

	Live with parents	Live with partner	Single	Have children
Finland	17	30	35	32
	(34)	(29)	(28)	(10)
Norway	16	29	32	24
	(33)	(19)	(26)	(28)
Denmark	5	8	13	11
	(16)	(35)	(30)	(20)
Scotland	24	35	48	47
	(63)	(8)	(24)	(10)
Italy	2	4	11	4
	(91)	(2)	(5)	(3)
Spain	13	13	17	35
	(78)	(8)	(8)	(7)

score is lower than in the other countries. It is possible that in these countries, young people who leave home still receive some economic support from their parents.

Among those who live with their parents in Scotland, a higher proportion report deprivation than in the other countries. In all countries, it seems that to live with parents is the best protection against deprivation, although this is less so in Scotland. As assumed, there are indeed higher levels of unemployment among families in Scotland. Fifty-two per cent of unemployed youth respondents reported that their parents had ever been unemployed for more than six months against 33% in Finland or 15% in Norway. Since so many unemployed young people in Scotland live with their parents, this may explain the higher level of deprivation among Scottish youth.

However, those who live alone are even more vulnerable. Nearly half of those in the Scottish sample report deprivation, which can be interpreted as the outcome of a very low level of benefits and no support from parents.

Lone parents are not specified as a category in the table because the numbers are too small. In total, 2% ($n = 188$) were lone parents and this group reported a much higher deprivation score than other households across countries.

If we look at income among young people in different households, we find clear differences between countries. In northern Europe, Danish youth have a much higher income, and Scottish and Finnish youth the lowest income compared with the other countries.

Italian unemployed young people report a low income, but they are supported by parents. There are not any great differences between households, even if we find the lowest income among Finnish and Scottish young people who live alone. Table 8.4 shows how private and public support influence income in the different countries.

The dependent variable is a measure of how much money the individual has received during past month, including both wage and benefits. Those who live

Table 8.4: The influence of private and public support and regular and irregular employment on income (€) controlled for unemployment career and family risks ($n = 8,773$, adjusted $R^2 = 0.25$)

	B	SE	Beta
Gender, female = 1	−67.3	7.2	−0.09***
Student	−190.7	10.0	−0.22***
Private support			
Single = Ref			
Partner	46.8	11.9	0.05***
Parents	−46.2	10.5	−0.06***
Public support			
Unemployment benefits	40.8	7.4	0.07***
Social assistance	−43.9	10.1	−0.05***
Housing benefits	30.0	13.1	0.03*
Family risks			
Unemployed parents	−18.2	7.6	−0.02
Unemployed partner	33.0	19.7	0.03ns
Having children	92.0	10.7	0.08***
Income employment			
Casual jobs	−40.4	10.3	−0.04***
Informal employment	62.5	15.8	0.06***
Unemployment career			
Included = Ref			
At risk	−114.8	8.6	−0.14***
Vulnerable	−200.4	10.6	−0.19***
Marginalised	−224.6	12.3	−0.18***
Veneto	143.8	20.1	0.07***
Norway = Ref			
Finland	−196.0	13.4	−0.17***
Denmark	368.5	26.3	0.27***
Scotland	−82.0	27.3	−0.05**
Italy	−343.4	23.1	−0.28***
Spain	−151.1	13.9	−0.15***
Scotland*unemployment benefits	−137.5	30.9	−0.07***
Denmark*unemployment benefits	157.1	17.9	0.09***
Finland*unemployment benefits	131.7	34.1	0.04***
Scotland*female	−124.9	28.8	−0.08***
Parents*informal employment	−66.2	20.8	−0.05**
Partner*partner unemployed	−79.9	25.1	−0.05**
Scotland*marginalised	−122.1	36.6	−0.03**
Constant	784.6	11.4	

Notes: SE = standard error; *** $p < 0.01$; ** $p < 0.05$; * $p < 0.10$, ns = not significant.

with parents have very little income of their own. The analysis gives no indication of wealthy unemployed youth in Spain and Italy, who are supported by parents and at the same time make good money in the underground economy. Quite the contrary, those who live with their parents and work in the informal economy have a lower income than other young people who work in this part of the labour market. On the other hand, jobs in the informal economy are more lucrative than casual jobs in the regular economy.

Those who have established their own households have a higher income than those who live alone, as long as the partner is not unemployed.

Receiving unemployment benefits boosts income for young people, especially in Denmark, although less so in Scotland where the benefits are very low. Receiving social assistance does not improve the economic situation for young people and receiving housing benefits has only a small effect.

According to Table 8.4, unemployed youth in Italy have the lowest income (but better in Veneto than Campania) and Danish unemployed youth the best economic situation. Females have lower incomes than males in all countries, particularly in Scotland. When controlled for private and public support, there are no significant differences between different unemployment careers, but those included have a better economic situation than all others.

How much money the individuals can dispose of does not tell us enough about how they experience their own situation, since many of them are dependent on private support from the family. Table 8.5, shows how public and private support influence deprivation.

According to Table 8.5, we can identify different buffers against deprivation. Most important are: being supported by parents (especially in Italy), income from regular employment, or living in Denmark with a generous income support system. However, to be supported by unemployed parents or a partner increases deprivation, in the same way as being supported by a single mother, which is an indication of poverty in the family. Those who are dependent on casual jobs or work in the informal economy do not experience less deprivation. Females experience more deprivation than males in all countries, and they also receive less money.

Deprivation is clearly related to unemployment career even after controlling for private and public transfer. Those with long previous and continuous unemployment experience higher levels of deprivation. Scottish unemployed youth report the highest levels of deprivation. Interestingly, Finnish youth are less deprived than the reference group (Norway), when controlling for private and public transfer and unemployment career. This is probably because the unemployment level was very low in Norway compared with Finland and the Norwegian unemployed youth may be a highly selected group, with more health and economic problems even before they become unemployed.

Table 8.5: The impact of private and public transfer on relative deprivation controlled for unemployment career and family risks (logistic regression, 1 = deprived)

	B	SE	OR
Gender, female = 1	0.53	0.05	1.7***
Private transfer			
Single = Ref			
Partner	−0.18	0.07	0.84**
Parents	−0.59	0.07	0.56***
Public transfer			
Unemployment benefits	0.13	0.05	1.1**
Social assistance	0.64	0.07	1.9***
Housing benefits	0.29	0.08	1.3***
Family risks			
Unemployed parents	0.36	0.05	1.4***
Unemployed partner	0.53	0.08	1.7***
Having children	0.11	0.07	1.1 ns
Growing up with single mother	0.40	0.06	1.5***
Income employment			
Regular employment	−0.22	0.05	0.81***
Casual jobs	−0.01	0.05	0.99 ns
Informal employment	0.26	0.09	1.3**
Unemployment career			
Included = Ref			
At risk	0.40	0.07	1.5***
Vulnerable	0.60	0.08	1.8***
Marginalised	0.92	0.09	2.5***
Norway = Ref			
Finland	−0.17	0.07	0.85*
Denmark	−1.1	0.11	0.34***
Scotland	0.52	0.11	1.7***
Italy	−3.0	0.22	0.05***
Spain	−0.60	0.11	0.55***
Constant	−1.8	0.09	

Chi-square 1,554.5 ***DF = 22

Discussion

The results presented here show that it is important to apply both measures of disposable income and the subjective experience of deprivation in order to measure poverty and deprivation among unemployed youth. Both measures are clearly related to the unemployment career of young people. Scottish and Finnish unemployed youth experience the highest levels of poverty and deprivation. In Scotland, more young people live with their parents (63%) than in Finland (33%); we would therefore have expected them to be in a better situation. However, the concentration of unemployment and deprivation in Scottish households implies that parental support is not an effective buffer against deprivation. The combination of high poverty in households and the low level of benefits makes Scottish unemployed youth a very vulnerable group. Previous research has found this to be the case also for other age groups (Gallie and Paugam, 2000). In Finland, the unemployment rate is very high for young people and at the same time there are strong social norms requiring young people to leave the parental home at a young age. Most unemployed youth are first-time jobseekers, so the coverage of unemployment benefits is rather low. In our sample, only 28% had received unemployment benefits during the past year (Hammer, 1999). This implies that they will only be eligible for social assistance or unemployment benefits for those not insured, which is about the same level as Jobseeker's Allowance in the UK. Consequently, according to the results presented here, young people who receive unemployment benefits in Finland have a higher disposable income, while Scottish youth receiving Jobseeker's Allowance have a lower disposable income than the reference group. However, the high level of deprivation among Scottish and Finnish unemployed youth shows that they fall between stools. They do not receive adequate public support and they are not supported by parents. Not even in Finland, with a universalistic nordic welfare model, are young unemployed youth entitled to more generous support.

Unemployed youth in Denmark are in the best situation by far. They have both the highest disposable incomes and the lowest deprivation scores. Higher income is due to the high coverage of very generous benefits, but also to a low unemployment rate, which implies that more young people had been included in the labour market. Furthermore, Danish unemployed youth had the opportunity to leave their parents and establish their own home. The results concur with previous studies, which also conclude that the Danish income support system is probably the most generous in Europe (Gallie and Paugam, 2000), compared with other universalistic models such as that in Sweden. Finland also has a universalistic welfare model, but as documented here, this model does not apply to Finnish unemployed youth. Social assistance does not act as an effective buffer against poverty and deprivation here.

In all countries, young women had lower income and higher levels of deprivation than unemployed young men. This may be the result of higher unemployment rates, lower wages and perhaps less 'pocket money' if they live with parents compared with young men. It is also possible that their access to income from other resources such as informal work and so on is more limited than for men.

In Italy 90% of unemployed youth lived with their parents, which is in accordance with previous studies that have found that about 80% of 15- to 30-year-olds live with their parents (Cavalli, 1995; Caroleo and Mazzotta, 1999). Unemployed youth report very low disposable incomes and very low levels of deprivation as a result of family support. In Spain, the situation is similar, but here more young people had left the parental home, resulting in a higher risk of deprivation. It is interesting, however, that even those who lived alone in Spain and Italy reported lower levels of deprivation than in the other countries, in spite of low level and coverage of benefits. According to previous research from Italy, those who leave home still receive support from parents (Carole and Mazzotta, 1999). Some of those who leave home are young women who marry a partner who can support them. However, some of those who leave home in Spain face a very difficult economic situation.

Previous research has found the highest poverty rates in UK and Spain. Italy is in an intermediate position, but rates are higher in the south (D'Andrea, 1998). In Italy, poverty is much higher for household heads in the age group 18-27 (Addabbo, 2000) and in Spain poverty rates are higher among younger households (Cordon, 1997). This has had a negative effect on the birth rate, which is very low in Spain and Italy with a persistent decline in fertility of young women in the age group 20-30. In Spain and Italy, leaving home is primarily a part of the process of family formation, and while young people postpone getting married, they also delay leaving home. Extremely high unemployment rates and high prices in the housing market make it nearly impossible for them to leave their parents and set up on their own (Holdsworth, 2000).

In this study of unemployed youth in Italy and Spain, it can be concluded that they do not appear to experience poverty and deprivation to a great extent. This is because they tend to receive support from their parents. They do not have much income from employment in the informal sector or from casual jobs. Actually, those who lived with parents and at the same time had jobs in the informal economy received less money than others did. The reason could be that these families have lower incomes, and young people try to find jobs to make some money for themselves. Spanish research has found that workers in the informal sector earn on average half as much as those working in the formal sector. Futhermore, individuals with higher education have easier access to the formal sector, and the probability of staying unemployed relative to working in the informal sector increases with education (Ahn and De la Rica, 1997). Low income in Spain and especially Italy among unemployed young people shows, however, that income from work in the informal sector is not very important. Moreover, income from casual jobs or work in the informal economy were not effective buffers against deprivation. Only regular employment gave young people an income level that prevented deprivation.

The results are in accordance with Bison and Esping-Andersen (2000), who also found very low market incomes among unemployed youth living with their parents.

Unemployed youth in Spain and Italy are well supported by their parents, in the same way as young people in education and even those in employment, which leads to a postponement of marriage and children. But what are the consequences of young adults living with their parents up to 30 years old? A survey carried out in Italy to investigate the process of leaving home (Cavalli, 1995) found no relation to social class, but the process of postponing had different meanings for young people from different social classes. The author concludes that, whereas lower down the social scale leaving home corresponds to the difficulty of finding employment, for those who are more comfortably off, delay implies the privilege of being able to hang on without assuming responsibility. "In the first case, postponement is endured in the second case it is chosen" (Cavalli, 1995, p 30). The study also tried to estimate the level of authority and control exercised by parents on their grown-up children. Such restrictions were placed only on the youngest age group and were harder on upper-middle-class boys than working-class boys. With regard to young women, it was the other way around. Working-class and lower-middle-class girls faced more restriction than upper-middle-class young women did. Beyond the age of 20, parents and children established a mutual pact of respect and non-interference (Cavalli, 1995).

It is clear that for Italian and Spanish working-class families, to support young adults up to the age of 30 must be hard, especially in the southern countries where poverty rates are much higher (D'Andrea, 1998). Young adults in these families have to endure living in the parental home because they are denied access to the labour market. Previous research has found that making a successful transition from unemployment to work and the time it takes to make that transition varies considerably between countries. The chances of finding a job are greatest in Denmark, France, the UK and Portugal and are worst in Spain, Greece and Italy (Russell and O'Connell, 2001). In other words, the postponement of adulthood experienced by unemployed youth in Italy and Spain is not necessarily voluntary.

Unemployed youth in Spain and Italy reported a low income and low levels of deprivation. A problem with the relative concept of deprivation is that it is measured relative to the local community or to the wider society to which an individual belongs. This is both a strength and a weakness in comparative research. The strength is that it will result in a greater awareness about living conditions in different countries. The weakness is that disparities in cultural patterns and lifestyles create differences that are reflected in how young people answer questions. Low or high levels of deprivation could thus reflect a generally low or high standards of living in the community and not necessarily an individual condition.

Youth, as a life phase, ends with adult integration into society, when the young person achieves the economic and social independence that guarantees not only recognition of adult rights but also the capacity to exercise them. In other words, they acquire citizenship implying rights and duties. Feminist research has criticised welfare research that uses theories of welfare systems based on the male-breadwinner models and neglect female participants as citizens (Lister, 1999). In this way, Esping-Andersen's welfare models based on theories of decommodification basically apply to males integrated into the labour market (Esping-Andersen, 1990). According to feminist critiques, welfare theories should also include women's responsibilities and work in the private sphere. For females not integrated into the labour market, access to citizenship rights and welfare provision is not a question of decommodification but a question of 'defamilialisation'. Full citizenship implies access to welfare provision independent of integration in the labour market. The same criticism may apply to young people, who are no longer youth but young adults. Even in a universalistic welfare model such as Finland, young unemployed people are not granted full citizenship implying independence of parents, access to employment and adequate welfare provision for the unemployed. In the southern countries, where young people are denied access to adulthood and citizenship for longer, the demand for 'defamilialisation' is even stronger. They are not poor or deprived, but many of them remain dependants when most young people in Europe have gained adulthood and full citizenship.

Acknowledgements

This chapter is based on a paper presented at the conference funded by the European Science Foundation and the European Commission in Helsinki, 15-20 April, 2001, entitled 'Changing Labour Market, Unemployment and Citizenship'. We would like to thank Dr Brendan J. Burchell and Professor Duncan Gallie for comments.

Note

[1] However, it is hard to tell whether these are in fact country-specific differences or differences in registration procedures. We have a sample of unemployed youth registered as unemployed by labour market authorities. In some countries unemployed young mothers may have no incentive to register as unemployed, so hidden unemployment may be higher in this group.

References

Addabbo, T. (2000) 'Poverty dynamics: analysis of household incomes in Italy', *LABOUR*, vol 14, no 1, pp 119-44.

Ahn, N. and De La Rica, N. (1997) 'The underground economy in Spain: an alternative to unemployment', *Applied Economics*, no 29, pp 733-43.

Álvaro, J.L. and Garrido, A. (2000) *Background report, Spain*, Working Paper.

Bauman, Z. (1998) *Work, consumerism and the new poor*, Buckingham: Open University Press.

Bison, I. and Esping-Andersen, G. (2000) 'Unemployment, welfare regime, and income packaging', in D. Gallie and S. Paugam (eds) *Welfare regimes and the experience of unemployment in Europe*, Oxford/New York: Oxford University Press.

Carle, J. and Julkunen, I. (eds) (1998) 'Young and unemployed in Scandinavia – a Nordic comparative study', *Nord 1998*, no 14, Copenhagen: The Nordic Council of Ministeries.

Caroleo, F.E. (2000) *Background report, Italy*, Working Paper.

Caroleo, F.E. and Mazzotta, F. (1999) *Youth unemployment and youth unemployment policies in Italy*, ILO Employment and Training Paper No 42, Geneva: ILO.

Cavalli, A. (1995) 'Prolonging youth in Italy: being in no hurry', in A. Cavalli and O. Galland (eds) *Youth in Europe*, London/New York: Pinter, St Martin Press.

Cordon, J.A.F. (1997) 'Youth residential independence and autonomy: a comparative study", *Journal of Family Issues*, vol 18, no 6, pp 576-607.

D'Andrea, S.S. (1998) 'Italian quality of life', *Social Indicators Research*, vol 44, no 1, pp 5-39.

Esping-Andersen, G. (1990) *The three worlds of welfare capitalism*, Cambridge: Polity Press.

Furlong, A. and Cartmel, F. (1997) *Young people and social change: Individualisation and risk in the age of high modernity*, Buckingham: Open University Press.

Furlong, A. and Cartmel, F. (2000) 'Does long-term youth unemployment lead to social and economic exclusion? Evidence from six European countries', in B. Furaker (ed) *Employment and unemployment and marginalisation: Studies in contemporary labour markets*, Gothenburg: Gothenburg University Press.

Gallie, D. and Paugam, S. (eds) (2000) *Welfare regimes and the experience of unemployment in Europe*, Oxford/New York: Oxford University Press.

Hammer, T. (1996) 'Consequences of unemployment from youth to adulthood in a life course perspective', *Youth and Society*, vol 27, no 4, pp 450-68.

Hammer, T. (1999) 'The influence of different compensation level of unemployment benefit on job chances among unemployed youth: a comparative study of the Nordic countries', *Acta Sociologica*, no 2, pp 123-34.

Hammer, T. (2000) 'Mental health and social exclusion among unemployed youth in Scandinavia: a comparative study', *International Journal of Social Welfare*, no 9, pp 53-63.

Hammer, T. (2003) 'The probability for unemployed young people to re-enter education or employment: a comparative study in six northern European countries', *British Journal of Sociology of Education*, vol 24, no 2, pp 209-23.

Holdsworth, C. (2000) 'Leaving home in Britain and Spain', *European Sociological Review*, vol 16, no 2, pp 201-22.

Julkunen, I. (2000) 'Social and material deprivation among unemployed youth in Northern Europe', *Social Policy and Administration*, vol 36, no 3, pp 235-53.

Lasaosa, A. (1997) *Job search behaviour in Spain: A comparative perspective*, Luxembourg Employment Study No 8.

Miret-Gamundi, P. (1997) 'Nuptiality patterns in Spain in the eighties', *Genus*, vol 53, nos 3-4, pp 183-98.

OECD (Organisation for Economic Co-operation and Development) (1996) *Employment outlook*, Paris: OECD.

OECD (1998) *Employment outlook*, Paris: OECD.

Pedersen, L., Weise, H., Jacobs, S. and White, M. (2000) 'Lone mothers' poverty and employment', in D. Gallie and S. Paugam (eds) *Welfare regimes and the experience of unemployment in Europe*, Oxford/New York: Oxford University Press.

Russell, H. and Barbieri, P. (2000) 'Gender and the experience of unemployment: a comparative analysis', in D. Gallie and S. Paugam (eds) *Welfare regimes and the experience of unemployment in Europe,* Oxford/New York: Oxford University Press.

Russell, H. and O'Connell, P. (2001) 'Getting a job in Europe: the transition from unemployment to employment among young people in nine European countries', *Work, Employment & Society*, vol 15, no 1, pp 1-24.

Saraceno, C. (1997) 'Family change, family policies and the restructuring of welfare', in OECD, *Family market and community*, OECD Social Policy Studies No 21, Paris: OECD, pp 81-100.

Silver, H. (1994) 'Social exclusion and social solidarity: three paradigms', *International Labour Review*, vol 133, nos 5-6, pp 531-78.

Townsend, P. (1988) 'Deprivation', *Journal of Social Policy*, vol 16, no 2, pp 125-46.

Townsend, P. (1993) *The international analysis of poverty*, London: Harvester Wheatsheaf.

Vogel, J. (1997) *Living conditions and inequality in the European Union*, Eurostat Working Papers E/1997-3.

Wallace, C. (1986) 'From girls and boys to women and men: the social reproduction of gender roles in the transition from school to (un)employment', in S. Walker and L. Barton (eds) *Youth, unemployment and schooling*, London: Open University Press.

Willis, P. (1990) *Common culture*, Buckingham: Open University Press.

Wilska, T-A. (1999) *Survival with dignity? The consumption of young adults during economic depression: A comparative study of Finland and Britain, 1990-1994*, Series A-3:1999, Turku: Turku School of Economics and Business Administration.

NINE

Buffers and predictors of mental health problems among unemployed young women in countries with different breadwinner models

Ilse Julkunen and Ira Malmberg-Heimonen

Introduction

There is a vast body of knowledge regarding the interrelation between mental health and unemployment, which predominantly shows that mental health problems increase during states of unemployment. A high level of work commitment and frequent states of jobseeking increase the risk for mental health problems among the unemployed (Warr and Jackson, 1985; Winefield and Tiggerman, 1994; Hanish, 1998; Kessler et al, 1998; Nordenmark, 1999). Generally, studies have demonstrated that women tend to adjust to unemployment better than men, and this has been explained by lower levels of work commitment, an increased commitment to the domestic role, more extensive social networks and the higher levels of activity that women have when they are unemployed (Lahelma, 1989; Mannila, 1993; Gershuny, 1994; Vähätalo, 1998). Nevertheless, recent studies have also shown that unemployed women value work as highly as men do, and that they have more negative experiences when they are unemployed compared with young unemployed men. The experiences however, have been shown to vary cross-culturally (Gallie and Alm, 2000; Russell and Barbieri, 2000; Julkunen, 2001; Malmberg-Heimonen and Julkunen, 2002).

In recent years, a growing number of studies have focused on comparing the situation of women's employment across countries (see Stier and Lewin-Epstein, 2001). These studies document cross-country variations and emphasise the importance of the institutional context within which women operate, for the purpose of understanding gender differences in labour market outcomes on an individual and societal level. Traditionally, there has been a distinction made between the male-breadwinner and the dual-breadwinner models. Lewis (1992), for instance, distinguishes between strong, weak and modified breadwinner welfare state systems, in order to highlight the extent to which policies encourage or inhibit women in terms of working when they are wives or mothers.

Scandinavian countries are prominent examples of weak male–breadwinner models, where the majority of adults of working age are employed or seeking a job. Taxation and benefit systems are individually based in the Scandinavian countries, although welfare benefits involve household means-testing, once an individual's entitlements are exhausted. The various forms of family support have dramatically transformed family life, and very few women are entirely dependent on their husband's incomes anymore (Palme, 1999). Lewis selects Sweden as typifying a weak male–breadwinner model, but argues that the Norwegian system has continued to treat women primarily as wives and mothers. Finland, on the other hand, may perhaps be regarded as the other extreme, where a large proportion of women work full-time. This state of gender parity in the workforce has a long history, and can be explained by the importance of the agricultural sector, which has been a more important employer than elsewhere in the Nordic countries, for both women and men (Melkas and Anker, 1998). Spain, as well as Germany, may be regarded as strong male–breadwinner models. In Germany, there is a heavy reliance on the social insurance system – welfare is strongly linked to labour market participation – in other words, the risks covered are mainly male risks, while women's entitlement within the system is primarily as the dependants of men, and care is largely privatised. It has been argued (Rubery and Fagan, 1999) that the male–breadwinner arrangement has taken a particular form in Germany for instance, where mothers have shifted to engaging in part-time employment. In Spain, on the other hand, fewer mothers are involved in paid employment, but full-time employment is the norm for those who are.

This chapter focuses on young women's experiences of unemployment in four different European countries: Finland, Sweden, Germany and Spain. It draws on a comparative study of youth unemployment in Europe (Hammer, 1999). The countries included in this study represent different welfare gender models: the weak breadwinner model (Finland and Sweden), and the strong breadwinner model (Germany and Spain). In this study, the different buffers and predictors of mental health problems among unemployed young women are examined. What is the impact of work commitment, family context, financial and social support? To what extent can experiences of unemployment be related to different welfare strategies or to certain gendered cultures? Can we find differences between different breadwinner models, or are there inconsistencies within these models?

This chapter is organised in three sections. The first part compares the labour market context of women and cross-country differences regarding welfare arrangements. The second part consists of a short overview of research concerning unemployment and wellbeing among women. The empirical research is reported in the final section, which covers a comparison of mental health problems among young unemployed women and men, and further analyses the influence of different buffers and predictors of mental health problems among women in countries with different breadwinner models.

Gender, employment and welfare strategies

Women's participation in working life increased across Europe during the 1990s. In 1997, the employment rate for women rose to 51%, and the gender gap was 20%, compared with 26% in 1990. Although women's overall participation in working life has increased, the unemployment rate among women in Europe remains high. This varies among different countries, and contemporary statistics from 1997 show that young women's unemployment is higher than young men's in Finland, Spain and Germany, whereas in Sweden women's unemployment is lower than men's (OECD, 1998). In all of the studied countries, the labour force participation of young men is higher than that of young women. The labour force participation rates of women, however, are only slightly lower than those of men in Sweden (74.5%) and Finland (71.1%) while the female participation rate is much lower in Germany (61.4%) and in Spain (48.0%). The unemployment rate of young women is particularly high in Finland and in Spain, whereas we can see relatively low unemployment rates in Sweden and Germany. This is partly related to the overall unemployment rate, but it also reflects the high proportion of temporary jobs among women in both Spain and Finland (Julkunen and Nätti, 1999; Lázaro et al, 2000).

Various social institutions are often said to influence employment in general, and women's employment in particular. The role of the family, the educational system and the labour market all mediate processes of labour market integration. Some researchers have emphasised the importance of labour market regulations and the interaction between the market and the welfare state (Esping-Andersen, 1990; Lewis, 1992; Rubery and Fagan, 1999). There is a continuing debate about the most appropriate means of categorising welfare regimes in relation to their impact on gender relations. This is partly due to internal contradictions within welfare regimes as the breadwinner regime principle is more strongly adhered to in some policy areas than in others (Rubery and Fagan, 1999).

Nevertheless, welfare regimes promote women's employment to a different degree, and thus play a major part in explaining international differences. The most well-used categorisation of welfare regimes is Esping-Andersen's (1990) typology of three ideal types of welfare states: the social democratic, the liberal and the conservative. The social democratic welfare states promote principals of equality and universalism. Women, regardless of their family status, are engaged to participate in work for wages, which is made possible through the state-provided childcare system. The conservative welfare regime supports a traditional division of labour between genders, both normatively and institutionally. Childcare is provided to some extent, but only for a part of the day, which increases women's financial dependency on their partners (Bianchi et al, 1999). In the liberal welfare state, gender equality is valued, but not pursued through public policies, which makes women's participation in wage-earning work difficult. Although Esping-Andersen's typology has been criticised for not adequately addressing the family and the gendered division of labour, in his latest writings (2001) he has introduced the concepts of 'familialisation' and 'defamilialisation' to differentiate between countries in which more traditional family dependencies still prevail and those in which defamilialisation is strong. If we then divide the studied countries according to these characteristics, we achieve two very broad categories. Finland and Sweden are portrayed as belonging to a more defamilialised (non-traditional) gender model, while Germany and Spain are seen as belonging to a more familialised (traditional) model. There are internal differences, however, regarding welfare arrangements. Table 9.1 summarises the main categorisations of the gender models on the one hand, and the main distinctions of the welfare arrangements within these aforementioned countries.

As can be seen from this table, there are clear distinctions between Finland and Sweden on the one hand, and between Germany and Spain on the other, as regards gender norms and culture. In addition, there are clearer distinctions between Germany and Spain with regard to welfare arrangements, as opposed to Finland and Sweden. Interestingly, full-time involvement unifies Finland and Spain, whereas part-time involvement is distinctive of both Sweden and Germany. How gender norms on the one hand and welfare arrangement on the other have an influence on female participation in employment is not altogether clear. Comparative studies (Almqvist and Boje, 1999) have suggested that there is a clear connection between high levels of female labour market participation and a generous welfare regime. Russell and Gallie (1999), however, have also highlighted other factors that may lead to marked differences between countries. These consist of the unemployment level and the cultural importance that is attached to work. A comparative study by Gallie and Alm (2000, p 126) showed that where gender norms were traditional, a high level of benefit compensation was associated with a lower level of employment commitment among women, while the reverse was true among the group of non-traditional countries.

The institutional differences in societies as regards promoting the reconciliation of work and family may also affect young women when they are planning for

Table 9.1: Gender arrangements by country

Country	Gender model	Welfare arrangements
Finland	Gender equality	Universalism
Sweden	Dual-breadwinner model High involvement in employment Defamilialisation	State-provided childcare Full-time involvement (Finland) Part-time involvement (Sweden)
Germany	Traditional gender norms	Employment-centred support (Germany)
Spain	Male-breadwinner model Reduced involvement in employment Familialisation	Low support (Spain) Privatised childcare (Germany) High family support (Spain) Full-time involvement (Spain) Part-time involvement (Germany)

Source: Lewis (1992); Rubery and Fagan (1999); Gallie and Paugam (2000); Esping-Andersen (2001)

their future life. If reconciling motherhood and working life is difficult, the decision to start a family might be postponed, or the number of children visibly reduced. Declining fertility rates, increasing activity rates and a higher mean age at childbirth indicate such a development. In Spain, for instance, the total fertility rate dropped from a level of approximately three children per woman in the 1970s, which was among the highest in Europe, to 1.15 children per woman in 1990s, which is the lowest in the world (Ahn and Mira, 2002). Furthermore, in countries where strong cultural expectations decree that mothers should stay at home and there are practical difficulties in reconciling work with family, some groups of women may choose to have no children at all in order to compete in the labour market. This kind of 'children or work' phenomenon can be found especially in Italy and in Spain, but also within several other European societies (Rubery et al, 1999, p 110).

Buffers and predictors of mental health among women

Most comparative studies thus far have focused on explaining the relationship between welfare arrangements and employment outcomes. How welfare arrangements and gender norms influence the ways in which women experience unemployment, however, is not clear. How does gender equality, for instance, affect the way that women experience unemployment? Would women who live in countries with job equity feel more stressed or less stressed than women who live in a country with more traditional gender norms?

Generally, it has been shown that unemployment increases mental distress, which is reversed when satisfactorily employed (Warr and Jackson, 1985; Hanish, 1998; Kessler et al, 1998). Nevertheless, research has demonstrated that women generally tend to adjust to unemployment better than men (Lahelma, 1989; Mannila, 1993; Gershuny, 1994). There are different explanations for this assumption. One explanation is that women in general enjoy more extensive social networks, which offer support during times of unemployment (Gershuny, 1994; Vähätalo, 1998). It has also been revealed that purposeful use of spare time acts as a buffer in coping with the stresses of unemployment (Winefield et al, 1992). Another explanation is that women have lower salaries and fewer career opportunities, and thus view employment as less important than men do (Gallie and Marsh, 1994). De Witte and Wets' (1996) study of unemployed women, for instance, showed that the availability of an alternative role, such as being at home with children, served as a buffer for women's negative experiences of unemployment. Hence, traditional gender norms may serve as a buffer for women.

Recently, the importance of financial support and state policies has also been addressed through research. Generally, the level of financial support during unemployment has been shown to moderate mental distress during unemployment (Rodriquez, 2001; Strandh, 2001) but also to have an impact on work commitment and future re-employment opportunities (Hammer, 1999). Women, however, are often in a more vulnerable situation than men. Due to restrictions in criteria for receiving insurance unemployment benefits, limited work experience and caring responsibilities, unemployed young women are often left to rely solely on means-tested benefits, increasing their financial dependency on their spouses (Russell and Barbieri, 2000).

Studies have generally shown that rating work commitment highly increases the risk for mental health problems among the unemployed (Nordenmark, 1999), and that an unemployed person who rates getting a job as relatively important shows a greater susceptibility to depressive symptoms than those who report that having a job is less important to them (Winefield and Tiggerman, 1994). Furthermore, the study by Nordenmark (1999) showed that the age of respondents is another important factor mediating employment commitment among women and men in Sweden. Older women, for example, had lower levels of employment commitment than older men. On the contrary, levels of employment commitment among young women were even higher than those among both young men and older men. In all, the study showed that both women and men with high levels of work commitment sustained higher risks of poor mental wellbeing compared with those with lower levels. This relationship, however, may vary between countries.

Negative experiences of unemployment and high levels of work commitment among unemployed young women have also been examined in studies including Scandinavian countries (Julkunen, 2001; Malmberg-Heimonen and Julkunen, 2002). These studies, based partly on the same data that is used in this study, showed that Swedish and Finnish women had both the most negative experiences of unemployment and the highest level of work commitment. The determining factor explaining these gender differences was the family situation. The study showed that having children generally increases work commitment and job opportunities among men, while the reverse was the case among women. The experiences of unemployment were less negative for women with children than for those without children. Russell and Barbieri (2000), however, showed in their cross-national study that employment deprivation was still significantly higher among unemployed women with pre-school children than among full-time housewives.

All in all, women's better adjustment to unemployment has been explained by more extensive social networks, and a higher level of activity and commitment to the domestic role. All these factors can be said to serve as buffers that decrease mental health problems among unemployed young women (Jahoda, 1982; Lahelma, 1989; Mannila, 1993; Gallie and Marsh, 1994; Gershuny, 1994; Vähätalo, 1998). On the other hand, high levels of work commitment and financial dependency may well predict mental health problems among women. Both buffers and predictors, however, may vary in countries that have different breadwinner models. It can be argued that in countries with a more traditional gender norm, unemployment may not be as problematic to individuals as in countries where the gender norm is more equal. Thus, the domestic role would serve as a buffer in countries with strong male-breadwinner models. In countries with a weak breadwinner model, on the other hand, a high level of work commitment and financial dependency could predict mental health problems better than in countries with a strong breadwinner model.

Research question and hypothesis

The aim of this study is to analyse buffers and predictors of mental health problems for unemployed young women in countries with different breadwinner models. What are the different buffers and predictors, and how do they vary across different gender culture models? The hypothesis is as follows:

Hypothesis 1: In countries with a male-breadwinner model (Spain, Germany), the domestic role, social support and level of activity function *to a higher degree as a buffer* against mental health problems among young unemployed women, as opposed to countries with a dual-breadwinner model (Sweden, Finland).

Hypothesis 2: In countries with a dual-breadwinner model (Sweden, Finland), mental health problems of young unemployed women are to a higher degree predicted by work commitment, jobseeking, and financial dependency, compared with countries with a male-breadwinner model (Spain, Germany).

Measures

Demographics were obtained by asking standard survey questions as regards reporting age, gender, cohabitation, children, education, residence and duration of unemployment.

Symptoms of mental health problems were assessed by a measure according to responses to 10 questions from Hopkin's Symptoms Checklist (HSCL) on anxiety and depression (1 = no problems to 4 = heavy problems). The scale for mental health problems varied between 10 and 40 and the internal consistency of the scale was good (Cronbach alpha 0.88). The risk group for mental health problems consisted of one third of the studied group, including all those with >19 on the scale measuring mental health problems.

Receiving an *unemployment insurance benefit* was coded as a dummy variable. Those in the studied group who had received unemployment insurance benefit during the past 12 months were coded as '1', while the others were coded as '0'.

Helping and visiting friends and relatives were assessed by two measures: 'In a normal week how often have you been helping your relatives/friends?' and 'In a normal week how often have you been visiting your relatives?'. Respondents rated their answers on a five-point scale which included: 'not at all', 'less than once a week', 'once a week', 'several times a week' and 'daily'.

Domestic work was measured by three different measures: 'In a normal week how often have you been doing housework (cleaning, cooking)?', 'In a normal week how often have you been working in the house or garden?' and 'In a normal week how often have you been shopping?'. Respondents rated their answers on a five-point scale, which included: 'not at all', 'less than once a week', 'once a week', 'several times a week' and 'daily'.

Spending time with friends was assessed by three different measures: 'In a normal week, how often have you been going to the pub, restaurant or cinema?', 'In a normal week, how often have you been going to the cinema, theatre or a concert?' and 'In a normal week, how often have you been with friends?'. Respondents rated their answers on a five-point scale, which included: 'not at all', 'less than once a week', 'once a week', 'several times a week' and 'daily'.

Social support was assessed by one question: 'During the latest two weeks, how often have your friends talked to you about personal matters?'. Respondents rated their answers on a five-point scale from 1 = never to 5 = very often.

Jobseeking was studied by asking the respondent if he or she had used the following methods for jobsearch: 'looking at the vacancy boards at the employment office', 'contacting local employers', 'asked friends about job vacancies', 'asked relatives about job vacancies', 'looked at advertisements in the newspaper', 'replied to advertisements' and 'other'. The options for answers were 'no' or 'yes' and the answers were used to create an index measuring jobseeking. In all, the index varied between 0 and 7, and the Cronbach alpha measure for the index was 0.86.

Work commitment was measured by utilising a six-item version of the Work Involvement Scale, which is a known index measuring work involvement (Warr et al, 1979). The following items were included: 'It is very important for me to have a job'; 'If I won lots of money I would want to work'; 'I hate being unemployed'; 'I feel restless if I do not have a job'; 'Work is one of the most important things in my life'; 'I would prefer to work even if unemployment benefits were generous'. Respondents rated their answers from 1 = strongly disagree to 5 = strongly agree, and the measures were used as an index to establish levels of work commitment. The internal consistency of the scale was good, and the Cronbach alpha measure for the work involvement scale was 0.89.

Financial dependency was assessed by a single question: 'In relation to your own experience of unemployment, how strongly do you agree or disagree with the statement that when you are unemployed you are financially dependent on others?'. Respondents rated their answers on a five-point scale rating from 1 = strongly disagree to 5 = strongly agree.

Results

In this study we have focused our analysis on those young people who were unemployed at the time of the interview, which altogether consisted of 1,407 men and 1,270 women. These individuals came from Finland, Sweden, Germany and Spain, all of which support differing models of encouraging women's participation in working life.

At the time of the interview, 33% of the young persons had found employment, 12% were in training, 14% in education or in some other occupation (military service, maternity leave, sick leave). When interviewed, 31% of the young persons were still unemployed. The proportion of unemployed young people was highest in Finland (42%), followed by Sweden (31%), Spain (27%) and Germany (25%). In Finland and Sweden, the number of unemployed men was higher than unemployed women, whereas the opposite was the case in Spain. In Germany, there were no significant gender differences in relation to the number of unemployed at the time of the interview.

All in all, it was shown that on a national level young people in Spain had the highest occurrence of mental health problems when unemployed, whereas young people in Germany had the lowest occurrence of mental health problems. Finland and Sweden came in between. Nevertheless, there are marked gender differences, as can be seen from the results displayed in Figure 9.1, between men and women in Finland ($p<0.001$) and men and women in Sweden ($p<0.001$), whereas no gender differences were found in Spain and Germany. When comparing mental health problems among women in all countries, we found that German women experience fewer mental health problems when compared with women in the other studied countries ($p<0.001$), whereas young Swedish women experienced the most mental health problems.

Further analysis shows that the main contributing factor to the high mean level of mental health problems among Finnish and Swedish unemployed women is explained by the fact that there is a high percentage of women who are in the high-risk group for having mental health problems[1]. The Finnish high-risk group comprises 40% of the unemployed women studied, while the Swedish figure is 44%, whereas only 22% of Finnish unemployed men and 24% of the Swedish unemployed men belong to the high-risk group. In Spain and Germany, the gender differences were non-significant.

Figure 9.1: Mental health problems among young unemployed women and men

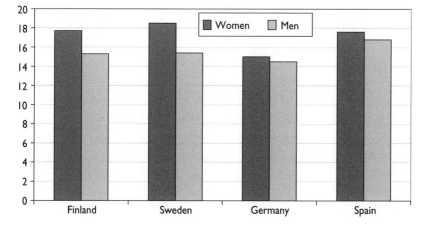

Before testing the hypotheses, it was important to study whether unemployed women have more mental health problems than women who are employed, in training, involved in education or who are doing something else (for example, on maternity leave or sick leave) at the time of the interview. The results are displayed in Table 9.2. Unemployed women in all the countries generally have a higher degree of mental health problems compared with women in other occupations. Differences between the occupations vary between the countries, however. In Finland, unemployed women report higher levels of mental health problems than women who are getting an education ($p<0.05$), whereas there are no significant differences in relation to the other occupational groups. In Sweden, unemployed women report significantly higher levels of mental health problems than do employed women ($p<0.001$) and women in the group 'other' ($p<0.01$). In Germany, unemployed women report more mental health problems than women who are in education ($p<0.05$). In Spain, unemployed women report higher values on the HSCL scale, but only when compared with women who are working ($p<0.05$).

In Table 9.3, we have displayed descriptive statistics of factors that can be regarded as buffers and predictors of mental health problems. With regard to buffers, comparisons between the countries show that the percentage of women with children is highest in Germany ($p<0.001$), followed by Sweden, Spain and Finland. Spanish women do the most domestic work, while Finnish women do the least domestic work ($p<0.05$). Women in the other countries do not differ substantially in relation to the frequency of housework. Spanish and German unemployed women ($p<0.001$) visit relatives most frequently, whereas the frequency of Finnish and Swedish women helping and visiting relatives does not differ significantly. Spanish women socialise with friends most often, while German women socialise with friends most seldom. Finnish and Swedish women do not differ significantly in relation to spending time with friends. On the contrary, Finnish and Swedish women have personal discussions with their friends more often than do Spanish ($p<0.001$) and German women ($p<0.05$). All in all, it seems as if women in Germany and Spain are more oriented towards family.

Table 9.2: Mental health problems among young unemployed women by country and occupation (mean values of mental health index)

	Finland	Sweden	Germany	Spain
Unemployed	17.7	18.5	15.0	17.6
Employed	16.3	16.0	14.2	16.3
Labour market training	17.4	17.7	13.9	17.0
Education	15.6	17.1	13.0	16.9
Other	15.6	15.8	14.9	15.6
n	748	1,247	1,557	832

Table 9.3: Buffers and predictors of depressive symptoms among unemployed young women, a country comparison

	Finland	Sweden	Germany	Spain
Buffers				
Children (%)	10.8	19.2	31.1	14.6
Domestic work (mean on scale)	11.1	10.6	11.2	11.6
Helping and visiting relatives (mean on scale)	5.6	5.8	6.7	8.3
Spending time with friends (mean on scale)	7.3	7.4	6.6	8.5
Personal discussions with friends (% often/very often)	67.7	66.9	49.7	54.3
Unemployment insurance benefit (%)	35.9	59.9	64.2	19.8
Predictors				
Work commitment (mean on scale)	23.0	25.0	25.0	24.9
Jobseeking (mean on scale)	3.8	4.4	3.8	4.7
Financial dependency (% agree)	52.8	60.2	64	73.3

The country comparisons also demonstrate that Finnish women have the lowest level of work commitment ($p<0.001$), and thus differ significantly from women in all other countries. Spanish and Swedish women have searched for a job using very different methods ($p<0.05$), whereas German and Finnish women do not differ significantly in relation to the methods used for jobsearch. The experience of financial dependency is the lowest among women in Finland, while it is the highest among women in Spain.

In all, the results in Table 9.3 show that Finnish and Swedish women are similar in relation to their buffering factors. They differ, however, in relation to predicting variables (when it comes to jobsearch and work commitment) as young unemployed women in Finland had the lowest levels of work commitment and jobsearch activity. This is probably because they are somewhat younger, first-time jobseekers, and thus have less work experience. Furthermore, the extremely high unemployment level in Finland may partly explain these results.

Buffers of mental health problems among young unemployed women in countries with differing breadwinner models (Hypothesis 1)

The results from the regression analyses displayed in Table 9.4 illustrate that the buffers of mental health problems among young women differ between countries. In Finland and Sweden, helping and visiting relatives acts as a buffer against mental health problems, whereas the social support from friends serves as a buffer against mental health problems in Germany and Spain. In Sweden in particular, the explanatory power of the buffering variables is low, whereas it is

Table 9.4: Buffers and predictors of mental health problems among unemployed young women in countries with differing breadwinner models (standardised beta coefficients)

	Finland		Sweden		Germany		Spain	
	I	2	I	2	I	2	I	2
Background								
Age	−0.09	−0.09	−0.09	−0.07	−0.14	−0.13	−0.04	−0.03
Living with parents	−0.06	−0.04	−0.15*	−0.14*	−0.04	−0.04	−0.22	−0.20
Cohabitation	0.06	0.06	−0.09	−0.13	0.07	0.09	−0.24	−0.18
Education	−0.12	−0.12	−0.01	−0.02	0.07	0.08	−0.04	−0.04
Unemployment duration	0.09	0.06	0.13	0.08	0.09	0.10	0.04	0.04
Buffers								
Children	−0.07	−0.01	−0.02	−0.05	−0.03	−0.03	−0.08	−0.07
Unemployment insurance benefit	−0.06	−0.03	−0.11	−0.07	−0.05	−0.05	0.07	0.10
Helping and visiting relatives	**−0.22****	**−0.25*****	**−0.16***	**−0.12***	−0.13	−0.13	−0.10	−0.10
Domestic work	−0.11	−0.08	0.05	0.10	0.03	0.02	**0.14***	0.13
Spending time with friends	−0.03	−0.02	0.02	−0.02	**−0.22***	**−0.19***	**−0.16***	**−0.15***
Social support	−0.02	0.02	0.01	0.00	**−0.21***	**−0.18***	**−0.24****	**−0.22****
Predictors								
Jobseeking		0.05		0.02		0.00		0.11
Work commitment		0.03		0.10		0.08		0.07
Financial dependency		**0.33*****		**0.39*****		0.11		**0.16***
Overall R^2	0.11	0.23	0.07	0.23	0.14	0.16	0.11	0.16
n	218	218	259	259	169	169	245	245

*** $p<0.001$, ** $p<0.01$, * $p<0.05$

much higher in the other studied countries. In none of the studied countries did having children, the domestic role or receiving an unemployment insurance benefit serve as a buffer for mental health problems. On the contrary, the results show that frequent domestic work is associated with increases in mental health problems among Spanish unemployed women.

Predictors of mental health problems among young unemployed women in countries with differing breadwinner models (Hypothesis 2)

Adding predictors of depressive symptoms to the model gives us a better picture of the cross-country differences. In Finland, Sweden and Spain, financial dependency predicts mental health problems among unemployed young women. In Germany, no substantial effects are found in relation to the predicting variables.

Jobseeking and work commitment does not substantially increase mental distress among women in any of the countries. In all, the explanatory power of the predicting variables is strongest in Sweden, followed by Finland, Spain and Germany. Adding the predictors to the model only marginally changes their explanatory power in Germany.

Discussion

The results partly supported the initial hypotheses in showing that the buffers and predictors of mental health problems among unemployed women vary between dual and male breadwinner-model countries. Nevertheless, similar trends between the different breadwinner models were also found.

We found a significant relationship between financial dependency and mental health problems, which was significant in all countries, except Germany. According to Esping-Andersen's welfare models (1990), Germany belongs to a conservative welfare state, which discourages women's labour force participation in order to 'preserve' the family. The consequence of this is an increase in women's financial dependency on their partners (Bianchi et al, 1999). When a state of financial dependency is the norm, however, it might be experienced as less distressing. Nevertheless, financial dependency and mental health problems were clearly interrelated among young Spanish women, indicating that in countries where the strong cultural expectations are that mothers should stay at home and in countries where there are practical difficulties in reconciling work and family, some groups of women may choose to have no children at all in order to compete in the labour markets (see Rubery et al, 1999, p 110). The results also indicate that it may be the group of work-oriented women who experience financial dependency as distressing when they are unemployed. This interpretation of the results is also supported by the fact that the frequency of domestic work is associated with increased mental health problems among Spanish unemployed women. In addition, the explanatory power of the predictive independent variable also supports this conclusion, as it is much higher in Spain than in Germany, where the explanatory power of the predictive variables is marginal. In Finland and Sweden there is a strong connection between financial dependency and mental health problems, as was expected.

Furthermore, it was initially expected that jobsearch activity and work commitment would predict mental health problems to a higher degree in countries with a dual-breadwinner model as opposed to those with a male-breadwinner model. The results, however, did not support our hypothesis. This was true even though previous findings from our project have found that Swedish women in particular have a high level of work commitment, and report high levels of mental distress when unemployed (Julkunen and Malmberg-Heimonen, 1998; Malmberg-Heimonen and Julkunen, 2002). Still, the analysis demonstrated a positive non-substantial correlation among all surveyed countries, indicating that level of work commitment is generally related to mental health problems among unemployed women.

The role of social networks also seemed to form an important buffer against mental health problems among unemployed women in Germany and Spain, but not for unemployed women in Finland and Sweden. This result is in line with a previous study (Julkunen and Malmberg-Heimonen, 1998), which found that feelings of social isolation were high among unemployed women in the Nordic countries. This result may be explained by the norm of high female labour force participation, thereby decreasing the buffering effects of friends and social activities on mental health problems among unemployed women in these countries.

Interestingly, raising children does not serve as a buffer in any of the studied countries, although previous studies have shown that childrearing buffers negative experiences that arise from a state of unemployment. The explanation may be that the measure of mental health problems was a better measure than the measure of negative experiences of unemployment, which might also explain the lack of the buffering effect of children observed in this study. In fact, this study found no buffering effect on mental health problems related to the frequency of engagement in domestic activities generally, but did find that frequent domestic activity is associated with an increase in mental health problems among Spanish women. This parallels the results of the study conducted by Russell and Barbieri (2000), which suggests that only women with the most demanding domestic roles, such as raising pre-school children, felt their joblessness to be less problematic than for other women. Our study complemented the previous results by emphasising that neither attitudes related to one's domestic role, nor the frequency of activities related to such a domestic role, adequately serve as a buffer against mental health problems among young unemployed women.

Accordingly, we found there to be no positive effect linked to receiving unemployment insurance benefits. This contradicts the results of Strandh (2001) and Rodriquez (2001), which both demonstrate that receiving an unemployment insurance benefit clearly diminishes the negative effects of unemployment on mental health. The lack of the buffering effects of an unemployment insurance benefit can rather be explained by the low level of state-based financial support for women due to stringent rules, limited work experience and caring responsibilities, particularly as regards part-time work (Russell and Barbieri, 2000). Another explanation is that our study sample consists of young people who have less work experience and hence lower wages, which results in lower unemployment insurance benefit levels compared with those found in similar studies of the entire labour force.

Our study clearly shows that both social institutions and cultural norms do influence the degree to which young women experience their unemployment as distressing. This can be seen in the extent to which financial dependency serves as a stress factor among women in countries with a dual-breadwinner model. In Germany, however, traditional norms still seem to influence the way in which young women experience unemployment. Still, converging trends can also be found in Spain, which show that young women may also act according to new cultural orientations. In all, the Spanish results were similar to the results from Sweden and Finland, which were the countries that represented the dual-breadwinner model in the study.

Interestingly, Finland differs from Sweden, especially as regards the lower level of work commitment and jobsearch activity among unemployed women. This result may well be explained by the Finnish full-time work culture, as this seems to discourage unemployed young women from entering the labour market. On the other hand, the more flexible dual breadwinner and part-time work culture found in Sweden supports, to a higher degree, unemployed young women's integration into the labour market (Malmberg-Heimonen and Julkunen, 2002). These controversial results show that engagement in part-time arrangements and full-time work is a more complex issue. Part-time arrangements can, on the one hand, be advantageous for young mothers as they allow young mothers to combine work and motherhood better. On the other hand, if the consequence of this flexibility regarding working time goes along with low pay and poor welfare support, this may be a trap for young women, which may also have a negative effect on the mental health of young unemployed women. In Sweden, the employment conditions for part-time workers are usually similar to those for women engaged in full-time work in terms of social rights and employment protection (Almqvist and Boje, 1999). The policies appear to encourage women with children to enter the labour market after a period of unemployment.

In summary, the results from this study demonstrate that the buffers and predictors of mental health problems among unemployed women vary between dual and male breadwinner model countries. Nevertheless, similar trends between the different breadwinner models were also found. Whereas the German results still correspond with the expectations of a male-breadwinner country, contemporary trends are found in Spain. Spanish unemployed women generally experience their unemployment in a similar way to the women in the Scandinavian countries, although the countries represent diverse breadwinner models. Our results demonstrate how cultural values are also changing in the southern European countries and it seems that where there are difficulties reconciling work and family, some young women prefer to choose the status of worker rather than the status of wife and mother.

Note

[1] The risk group for mental health problems was measured as those who scored >19 on the scale measuring mental health problems. All in all, one third of the young people studied were included.

References

Ahn, M. and Mira, P. (2002) 'Job bust, baby bust? Evidence from Spain', *Journal of Population Economics*, no 3, pp 505-22.

Almqvist, A.-L. and Boje, T. (1999) 'Who cares, who pays and how is care for children provided? Comparing family life and work in different European welfare systems', in *Comparing social welfare systems in Nordic Europe and France*, Nantes: Mire 4.

Bianchi, S., Casper, L. and Peltola, P. (1999) 'A cross-national look at married women's earning dependency', *Gender Issues*, no 2, pp 4-43.

de Witte, H. and Wets, J. (1996) 'On the heterogeneity of the experience of long-term unemployment among women', in M. de Goede, P. de Klaver, J. van Ophem, C. Verhaar and A. de Vries (eds) *Youth: Unemployment, identity and policy*, Avebury: Fryske Academy.

Esping-Andersen, G. (1990) *The three worlds of welfare capitalism*, Cambridge: Polity Press.

Esping-Andersen, G. (2001) 'A welfare state for the 21st century', Paper presented at the seminar 'The Nordic alternative', Stockholm, 12 March.

Gallie, D. and Alm, S. (2000) 'Unemployment, gender and attitudes towards work', in D. Gallie and S. Paugam (eds) *Welfare regimes and the experience of unemployment in Europe*, New York: Oxford University Press, pp 109-34.

Gallie, D. and Marsh, C. (1994) 'The experience of unemployment', in D. Gallie, C. Marsh and C. Volger (eds) *Social change and the experience of unemployment*, Oxford: Oxford University Press.

Gallie, D. and Paugam, S. (2000) 'The experience of unemployment in Europe: the debate', in D. Gallie and S. Paugam (eds) *Welfare regimes and the experience of unemployment in Europe*, New York: Oxford University Press.

Gershuny, J. (1994) 'The psychological consequences of unemployment: an assessment to the Jahoda thesis', in D. Gallie, C. Marsh and C. Volger (eds) *Social change and the experience of unemployment*, Oxford: Oxford University Press.

Hammer, T. (1999) 'The influence of different compensation levels of unemployment benefits on job chances among young unemployed', *Acta Sociologica*, no 2, pp 123-35.

Hanish, K. (1998) 'Job loss and unemployment research from 1994 to 1998: a review and recommendations for research and intervention', *Journal of Vocational Behavior*, no 55, pp 188-220.

Jahoda, M. (1982) *Employment and unemployment: A socialpsychological analysis*, Cambridge: Cambridge University Press.

Julkunen, I. (2001) 'Coping and mental wellbeing among unemployed youth – a northern European perspective', *Journal of Youth Studies*, no 4, pp 261-78.

Julkunen, I. and Malmberg-Heimonen I. (1998) *The encounter of high unemployment among youth – A Nordic perspective*, Labour Market Policy Studies 188, Helsinki.

Julkunen, R. and Nätti, J. (1999) *The modernization of working times: Flexibility and work sharing in Finland*, Jyväskylä: Sophi.

Kessler, R., Turner, B. and House, J. (1998) 'Effects of unemployment on health in a community survey: main, modifying and mediating effects', *Journal of Social Issues*, no 44, pp 69-85.

Lahelma, E. (1989) *Unemployment, re-employment and mental wellbeing: A panel study of industrial jobseekers in Finland*, Eripainoksia 70, Helsinki: Kuntoutussäätiö.

Lázaro, V., Moltó, M. and Sánchez, R. (2000) 'Unemployment determinants for women in Spain', *Review of Labour Economics and Industrial Relations*, no 1, pp 53-78.

Lewis, J. (1992) 'Gender and the development of welfare regimes', *Journal of European Social Policy*, no 2, pp 59-73.

Malmberg-Heimonen, I. and Julkunen, I. (2002) 'Equal opportunities, true options or hidden unemployment? A comparative perspective on labour market marginality', *International Journal of Social Welfare*, no 2, pp 120-31.

Mannila, S. (1993) *Työhistoria ja syrjäytyminen (Work history and marginalisation)*. Työpoliiittinen tutkimus 58, Helsinki: Työministeriö.

Melkas, H. and Anker, R. (1998) *Gender equality and occupational segregation in the Nordic labour markets*, Geneva: International Labour Office.

Nordenmark, M. (1999) 'Employment commitment and psychological wellbeing among unemployed men and women', *Acta Sociologica*, no 2, pp 135-47.

OECD (Organisation for Economic Co-operation and Development) (1998) *Employment outlook*, Paris: OECD.

Palme, J. (1999) *The Nordic model and the modernisation of social protection in Europe*, Copenhagen: Nordic Council of Ministers.

Rodriquez, E. (2001) 'Keeping the unemployed healthy: the effects of means-tested and entitlement benefits in Britain, Germany and the United States', *American Journal of Public Health*, no 9, pp 1403-11.

Rubery, J. and Fagan, C. (1999) 'Gender and labour markets in EU', Paper presented at the COST workshop 'Gender labour markets and citizenship', Vienna, Austria, 19-20 March.

Rubery J., Smith, M. and Fagan, C. (1999) *Women's employment in Europe – Trends and prospects*, London: Routledge.

Russell, H. and Barbieri, P. (2000) 'Gender and the experience of unemployment: a comparative analysis', in D. Gallie and S. Paugam (eds) *Welfare regimes and the experience of unemployment in Europe*, Oxford/New York: Oxford University Press.

Stier, H. and Lewin-Epstein, N. (2001) 'Welfare regimes, family-supportive policies and women's employment along the life-course', *American Journal of Sociology*, no 106, pp 1731-60.

Strandh, M. (2001) 'State intervention, mental wellbeing and the unemployed', *Journal of Social Policy*, no 1, pp 57-79.

Vähätalo, K. (1998) *Työttömyys ja suomalainen yhteiskunta (Unemployment and the Finnish society)*, Tampere: Tammer-paino.

Warr, P. and Jackson, P. (1985) 'Factors influencing the psychosocial impact of prolonged unemployment and of re-employment', *Psychological Medicine*, no 15, pp 759-807.

Warr, P., Cook, J. and Wall, T. (1979) 'Scales for the measurement of some work attitudes and aspects of psychological well-being', *Journal of Occupational Psychology*, vol 52, pp 129-48.

Winefield, A. and Tiggerman, M. (1994) 'Affective reactions to employment and unemployment as a function of prior expectations and motivation', *Psychological Reports*, no 75, pp 243-47.

Winefield, A., Tiggermann, M. and Winefield, H. (1992) 'Spare time use and psychological wellbeing in employed and unemployed young people', *Journal of Occupational and Organizational Psychology*, no 65, pp 307-13.

TEN

Economic hardship, employment status and psychological wellbeing of young people in Europe

José Luis Álvaro and Alicia Garrido

Introduction

Since the first studies on the psychosocial effects of unemployment were carried out in the 1930s (Jahoda et al, 1933; Eisenberg and Lazarsfeld, 1938), one of the most closely studied aspects of unemployment has been its influence on mental health. In general, research has shown that, while unemployment does not cause serious alterations in mental health, it is associated with reduced levels of psychological wellbeing. In the case of young people there are numerous studies showing that unemployment is associated with lower levels of general psychological wellbeing (Banks and Jackson, 1982; Álvaro, 1989), with a higher frequency of depressive feelings (Feather, 1982; Feather and Bond, 1983; Blanch, 1986), with an increase in anxiety symptoms (Donovan and Oddy, 1982; Banks and Ullah, 1987), with a lower degree of satisfaction with life (Breakwell, 1985) and with a reduction in self-esteem (Donovan and Oddy, 1982; Feather, 1982; Breakwell, 1985).

Obviously, unemployed young people do not constitute a homogeneous group, and a great deal of psychosocial research on the effects of unemployment has been aimed at identifying factors that might help to explain the variability in the response to unemployment. Among the factors most frequently used in explanations of the emotional impact of unemployment are duration of the period of unemployment, social support and the economic hardship experienced by the unemployed person. However, the analysis of these factors and of their relationship to the emotional impact of unemployment has largely ignored the social and cultural context of the unemployed person. In general, and with some exceptions (Jahoda, 1982/87; Kelvin and Jarret, 1985; Feather, 1990; Marsh and Álvaro, 1990; Hammer, 1999; Julkunen, 2002), psychosocial research on youth unemployment has ignored the fact that unemployment is a social problem, and that when analysing the response to unemployment it is necessary to bear in mind the context in which the person lives. However, it is evident that the experience of unemployment and the way in which an individual responds to such a situation depends to a large extent on the support offered by his or her society.

The aim of this chapter is to compare the emotional impact of unemployment in different countries, analysing the extent to which the emotional wellbeing of the unemployed person is affected by the characteristics of the context in which the unemployment is experienced. The data that will be presented here have been drawn from a comparative study on youth unemployment in Europe (Hammer, 1999). The results of previous analysis comparing mental health in different northern European countries have already been presented (Hammer, 1999; Julkunen, 2002). This analysis will be continued here and will include three more countries: Germany, Italy and Spain.

One of the factors to be taken into account when comparing the psychological wellbeing of young people in different countries is their situation with regard to the labour market. The unemployment rate, the percentage of long-term unemployed and the stability of occupations are structural factors that affect the person's probability of achieving successful integration in the labour market, which in turn has an influence on his or her psychological wellbeing. The countries in this particular comparison differ considerably in this aspect. The youth unemployment rate is much higher in southern European countries than in northern Europe. Italy, for example, recorded in 1999 a youth unemployment rate of 26%, and 65% of young unemployed people had been looking for work for more than one year. The situation was similar in Spain, where the unemployment rate was 29% for those aged 20-24 and 41% for those under 20 years old. The proportion of long-term unemployed was 43% and 32%, respectively. The situation of the Mediterranean countries contrasts markedly with that of the Scandinavian countries, where the unemployment rate is much lower. The only exception in this regard is Finland, where youth unemployment, despite being a relatively new phenomenon, has reached considerable levels (30%). In the rest of the Scandinavian countries, the youth unemployment rate is low. Finally, both the UK and Germany occupy intermediate positions. It is to be expected that these structural differences give rise to variations in the way unemployment is experienced in each country, not only because they affect the probabilities of success in the labour market, but also because they influence young people's expectations with regard to the future. One of the aims of this chapter will be to analyse the extent to which both the objective position within the labour market and the subjective perception of this position, assessed by means of future expectations, affect the wellbeing of young people.

Another factor to be taken into account in any explanation of the emotional impact of unemployment is the precarious economic situation in which it places the person. Some researchers suggest that it is the lack of economic resources and not the lack of a job that explains the psychological deterioration of unemployed young people (see Álvaro, 1992). If this were true, unemployment would have negative effects on mental health only in those cases where it placed the person in a situation of severe economic deprivation. Other researchers, however, without denying the negative effect of loss of income on mental health, question whether this is the factor that explains the psychological deterioration of the unemployed. Jahoda (1982/87), for example, points out that employment does not simply fulfil the function of providing economic resources necessary for subsistence, but that it also facilitates access to a number of experiential categories that cover certain basic psychological needs: interpersonal relationships, structuring of time, achievement of collective goals and social position and identity. According to Jahoda, it is the loss of these types of experience, more than the loss of income, that causes the psychological deterioration of unemployed people. Psychosocial research on the effects of unemployment has not provided conclusive information about the role played by unemployment in the mental health of unemployed people. Indeed, one of the criticisms levelled at psychosocial research on unemployment is that the economic factor has frequently been overlooked. It seems that the conclusion to be drawn from the studies that considered this factor is that if the lack of a job is in itself associated with a deterioration in mental health, such deterioration is exacerbated when, as a result, the person is faced with a high degree of economic hardship (Álvaro, 1992). Thus, it seems logical to expect the emotional impact of unemployment to be lower in countries where there are mechanisms to alleviate the economic precariousness of the unemployed.

One of the main mechanisms for alleviating the economic effects of unemployment is the system of social protection offered to unemployed people. In this respect there are clear differences between the countries compared in this study. Following Gallie and Paugam (2000), there are four social welfare models, differentiated by the degree of generalisation of aid, the level of compensation provided and public expenditure on employment policies: (a) the universalistic model of Nordic countries; (b) the liberal model of the UK; (c) the sub-protective model characteristic of southern European countries; and (d) the employment-centred model of France and Germany. Although the Nordic countries are not homogeneous in their approach (see Hammer, 1999; Julkunen, 2002), it can be said that public aid to the unemployed is highly generalised, and that the level of compensation is very high, ranging from 60% in Finland and Norway to 90% in Denmark (Hammer, 1999). This is in marked contrast to the situation in southern European countries. In Spain, for example, very few young people have access to unemployment insurance (12%) or welfare benefits (10%), and in Italy the situation is even worse. In both countries the deficiencies in public aid systems are counterbalanced by the existence of more extensive black economies and the family's assumption of responsibility for the economic sustenance of unemployed people. Both in Spain and in Italy the majority of young people continue living with their parents even after finding their first job, since starting salaries often make economic independence impossible. The situation is different in the Scandinavian countries, where young people leave the family home relatively early. This is also the case, albeit to a lesser extent, in Scotland and Germany.

The differences between some countries and others in the living situation or household type of young people is another factor that may give rise to differences in the emotional response to unemployment. The nature of the living situation of unemployed people not only influences their economic circumstances, but is also indicative of their degree of social and family integration. Given that social support is one of the factors that influences the psychological wellbeing of the unemployed, it seems pertinent to consider whether the different living situations of young people imply different degrees of family support, and whether this, in turn, has an influence on their mental health. The concept of social support refers to the different types of help received from other people. The relationship between the psychological wellbeing of young unemployed people and the degree of social support received has been analysed in previous studies of this project. More specifically, in the Nordic countries social support has been considered an important variable that contributes to explaining the psychological deterioration associated with unemployment (Hammer, 2000; Sigurdardottir and Bjarnason, 2000). These studies found a significant effect of social support on mental health. However, contrary to what was expected, an increase in parental social support was related to a decrease in mental health: the young people who reported a greater degree of social support were those who showed more symptoms of depression and anxiety. This apparently contradictory result can be explained in different ways. On the one hand, it is possible that social support received from parents is significantly related to the degree of control they exert. If this is the case, one could expect parents who provide most social support to be those who also impose the greatest degree of control over young people. From this perspective, the negative effects of social control on mental health could be explained by the fact that parental social support is associated with an increase in the degree of dependency experienced by young people. Another possible explanation is that not all forms of social support have the same effect on psychological wellbeing. Some researchers have emphasised the need to distinguish between different types of help. A frequent distinction made is that between emotional support, such as understanding, acceptance and affection, and instrumental support, which provides practical help in the solution of everyday problems (Thoits, 1982; Cohen and Wills, 1985). This classification was enlarged by Veiel (1985), who proposed two dimensions for differentiating between types of support. The first dimension, which refers to the type of help received by the person, allows a distinction to be made between psychological support (emotional/cognitive) and instrumental support (practical/instrumental). The second dimension, referring to the situation in which support is received, establishes a distinction between support received in crisis situations and that which is received on an everyday basis. Some studies on the effect of social support on the mental health of unemployed young people indicate that the young people with the greatest psychological wellbeing are those that have someone to help them economically, someone to suggest interesting things to do and someone to provide practical support in the search for employment (Ullah et al, 1985; Banks and Ullah, 1987). Lastly, some researchers have suggested that it is useful to distinguish between different types of support on the basis of the social context in which it is received. This suggestion is supported by the results of studies showing that the effects of social support are particularly noticeable when such support comes from groups with which the person has strong emotional attachments, such as the family or friends (Gore, 1978; Álvaro, 1992).

In conclusion, there are many factors that may contribute to differences and similarities in the experience of unemployment, depending on each social and cultural context. The labour market situation in each country determines the expectations and probabilities of finding a job; the degree of social and family protection received affects the economic situation of young people; and the social and family integration of youth may influence the degree of emotional and instrumental support they receive. All of these factors, which can determine the emotional effects of unemployment, may explain the differences and similarities among countries. The main objective of this chapter is to analyse the relationship between the above-mentioned factors and mental health in the different countries.

Measures

In order to evaluate mental health, 10 statements from the Hopkins Symptoms Checklist (HSCL) (Derogatis et al, 1974) were used. These are used to determine whether in the previous two weeks the person has experienced different symptoms related to depression and anxiety. Response to the statements is based on a scale of 1 (no problems) to 4 (many problems). The total score was based on the mean obtained for the 10 statements. The internal reliability alpha coefficient was 0.87. Mean for the total sample was 1.57 and the standard deviation was 0.55. Of the total sample, 59% scored below the mean.

The experience of both employment and unemployment was measured by means of the total number of months the interviewee had been employed and unemployed, respectively, throughout his or her life.

In order to assess parental support, interviewees were asked about the frequency with which, in the previous two weeks, their parents had provided them with money, given advice regarding study or work, spoken to them about personal matters, given advice about economic matters, provided help in practical matters, done them favours and shown affection. Possible answers ranged from 1 (very often) to 5 (never). To obtain the total score for the scale the responses were re-coded as dummy variables (1 = very often and often; 0 = 3,4,5). Total score on the scale indicates the number of aspects in which the young people claimed to have parental support. The range is from 1 to 7. The alpha coefficient was 0.82. The mean score for the sample was 2.75 and the standard deviation (sd) 2.05.

The same scale was used to evaluate the support of friends. In this case, the alpha coefficient was 0.78. The mean score was 1.86 and the standard deviation 1.72.

The degree of contact with family, friends and partner was evaluated by means of three separate questions about the quantity of time normally spent with each in the course of a normal week. Possible responses were: no time (1); less than once a week (2); once a week (3); several times a week (4); and every day (5). For contact with the family, a mean score of 3.66 (sd = 1.26) was obtained. For contact with friends, the mean was 3.83 (sd = 1), while for contact with the partner, the mean was 3.75 (sd = 1.59).

The degree of economic deprivation experienced by the young people was evaluated by means of a scale of 11 statements asking if the person in the previous year had had to deprive himself or herself, due to lack of money, of any of the following: main meals, clothes, payments of bills, going to the cinema, theatre or concerts, inviting friends home, visiting friends or relatives in other cities, buying birthday or Christmas presents, going on holiday, buying the newspaper, practising hobbies, or going to bars and restaurants. Possible responses were 1 (often), 2 (sometimes) and 3 (never). After carrying out a factorial analysis it was observed that the scale was made up of two factors. The first, which explained 46% of the variance, was composed of the first three statements. The second factor, which explained 10% of the variance, was made up of the rest of the statements. The results of the factorial analysis led to the scale being divided in two. One was a scale of material deprivation and the other of social deprivation. The total score on the scale is the mean number of activities the person has had to forgo.

Expectations about the future were evaluated by means of a question about what the person thought he/she would be doing in a year's time. Possible responses were working, studying or unemployed.

Results

Situation of young people in the labour market: differences between countries

Table 10.1 gives information about periods of employment and unemployment experienced by young people in each of the countries compared. By and large, these data show that the position of young people in the labour market is more fragile in southern European countries than in the rest of the countries studied.

If the longest period of time in which the person has been continuously unemployed is analysed, the conclusion that long-term unemployment is much more frequent in Spain and Italy than in northern European countries is reached. For 40% of young Spaniards, the longest period of unemployment has been more than one year, whereas only 16% of Danes have experienced such a long period of unemployment. The mean duration in number of months of the longest period of continuous unemployment is in fact twice as long in Spain (19.7 months) as it is in Denmark (9.2 months). Both in Finland (13.8 months) and in Norway (13.7 months), the mean length of the period of continuous unemployment is greater than one year, and in this respect they are more similar to countries such as Scotland (15.5 months) than to their neighbouring countries. Finally, Italy (24.6 months) is without doubt the country in which young people experience the longest periods of continuous unemployment.

Table 10.1: Differences between countries in economic deprivation, labour market and social integration

	Finland	Norway	Sweden	Denmark	Scotland	Italy	Spain	Germany
Labour market position								
% unemployment	42.1	28.5	31.1	28.6	43.1	29.9	27.9	25.0
% employment	17.5	29.9	26.5	43.4	41.9	19.4	44.0	28.1
Total time employed (mean)	13.0	23.7	22.9	43.7	21.5	20.1	23.4	14.0
Total time unemployed (mean)	22.2	21.0	16.5	14.4	21.8	30.9	29.3	16.4
Longest period of unemployment (mean)	13.8	13.7	09.4	09.2	15.5	24.6	19.7	10.8
% more than one year of continuous unemployment	39.1	30.7	15.3	16.4	37.3	33.3	40.2	29.9
% more than two years of total unemployment	36.2	31.2	26.4	15.8	35.4	64.4	53.9	27.7
% more than two years in paid employment	17.3	34.2	35.4	74.8	33.0	27.8	36.9	20.1
% without labour experience	38.1	21.8	20.4	05.0	24.1	22.2	18.3	24.3
% think they will be working in a year's time	46.5	56.0	54.8	53.4	65.7	48.1	72.5	54.6
% think they will be unemployed in a year's time	18.8	7.3	8.6	0.4	5.5	2.7	5.7	1.5
Deprivation								
% high material deprivation[a]	12.2	15.5	7.9	3.2	11.0	0.2	3.1	6.5
Material deprivation (mean)	0.5	0.6	0.4	0.2	0.5	0.2	0.1	0.3
% high social deprivation[b]	29.0	23.6	28.3	11.7	34.3	4.0	17.8	21.6
Social deprivation (mean)	2.2	2.0	2.1	1.1	2.6	0.5	1.53	1.8
Social and family integration								
Living with parents	33.8	32.9	24.8	16.2	62.8	90.7	78.1	50.7
Living with partner	37.8	38.3	42.6	51.7	12.3	4.0	13.6	26.9
Living with friends	5.0	7.3	5.0	8.6	11.5	3.3	6.4	8.0
Living alone	23.4	21.5	27.6	23.5	13.4	2.0	2.0	14.4
Social relations								
% high contact with family[c]	27.0	49.0	34.0	37.0	66.0	87.0	88.0	63.0
Time spent with family	2.8	3.3	3.3	3.1	3.7	4.4	4.4	3.6
% high contact with friends[c]	68.0	75.0	73.0	59.0	72.0	85.0	72.0	66.0
Time spent with friends	3.8	3.9	3.9	3.5	3.9	4.2	3.9	3.6
% high contact with partner[c]	60.0	60.0	61.0	61.0	56.0	56.0	66.0	60.0
Time spent with partner	3.9	4.1	4.3	4.1	3.2	3.2	3.5	3.2
Social support								
Parents' support	2.1	1.8	2.6	2.8	2.5	2.8	3.4	2.5
Friends' support	1.7	1.3	1.8	2.0	1.7	1.7	2.0	2.0

Notes: [a] High material deprivation = deprivation in more than two aspects. [b] High social deprivation = deprivation in more than four aspects. [c] High contact = several times a week or daily.

If all unemployment periods experienced by young people from the time of completing their studies are considered as a whole, quite similar conclusions are reached. The country in which young people spend least time unemployed is Denmark, where only 16% of young people in the sample have an accumulated experience of unemployment of more than 24 months. In the rest of the countries it is more common for the period of accumulated unemployment to exceed two years. The most extreme cases are to be found in Italy and Spain, where more than 50% of young people experience accumulated unemployment of more than two years. For young Spaniards, the mean duration of the period of accumulated unemployment is 29 months, twice that of young people in Denmark, where the figure is 14 months. The figures for Sweden and Germany are similar to those of Denmark, while Finland and Norway occupy intermediate positions.

The data provided by this study indicate that Denmark is where young unemployed people have the greatest probability of finding a job, and that this probability is lowest in Italy. At the time when the study was completed, 43% of young Danes had a job, whereas only 19% of young Italians were working. Finland, where only 17% of young people were working when the study ended, was more similar in this respect to Italy than to its neighbouring countries. In Spain, 44% of young people had a job, a figure quite similar to that observed in Scotland. Germany, Norway and Sweden occupied intermediate positions.

Within the Nordic context, Finland stands out, not just for being the country with the least probability of finding a job, but also because it seems to offer the least job stability. While in other Nordic countries almost half of the young people employed had had their current job for longer than six months, most young Finns had been working for a shorter period. Scotland was the only country in which lower stability could be observed. It is worth mentioning the case of Italy and Spain, since despite being the countries with the highest unemployment duration periods, they are also those in which the highest percentage of young people seem to have stable employment. In Spain, for example, 80% of young people had spent more than six months in their current job, and 50% more than a year. This result is maintained even after controlling for the effect of age, which is higher in the Spanish sample. This high percentage of young people with relatively stable employment may be a result of employment policies adopted in recent years, which, unlike those of the past, have aimed to reduce job instability and encourage the hiring of young people on a long-term basis. It must be pointed out, however, that the increase in the number of long-term contracts has been achieved at the expense of making redundancies cheaper. Therefore, obtaining a long-term contract is no longer a total guarantee of stability.

Another interesting finding, with respect to the situation of young people in the labour market, concerns the work experience accumulated since leaving the educational system. In this respect, Denmark is once again the country in which young people are in the best situation. Three quarters of young Danes have accumulated work experience of more than two years. This contrasts with Finland and Germany, which are among the countries where young people have had the shortest periods of employment. Spain occupies an intermediate position, with 36.9 % of young people having worked for more than two years. The country with the highest percentage of young people without work experience is Finland (38%), and the country with fewest young people in this situation is Denmark. In the other countries the percentage of young people that have never had any experience of work is between 20% and 25%.

With regard to expectations about the future situation, Finland again stands out (within the Scandinavian context) as being the country in which young people perceive their future in the most negative way; this is reflected not only in the lower percentage of young people that believe they will be working within a year, but also in the higher percentage of young people who think they will be unemployed. The data obtained for Spain are also noteworthy, since, despite it being one of the countries in which the labour market situation is poorest in objective terms, it is the one where young people have the highest expectations with regard to the future: almost three quarters of young Spaniards think they will be working within a year, while just 6% think they will be unemployed.

The economic situation of young people

The percentage of young unemployed people receiving some kind of state assistance for their situation is much higher in northern European countries than in southern Europe. The situation in Denmark, Finland and Sweden, where more than three quarters of young people receive some kind of state assistance, contrasts sharply with that of Italy and Spain, where only 1% and 10% of young people, respectively, receive assistance.

The results of this study show that it is in southern European countries that the young unemployed claim to have lower levels of both social and material deprivation. As can be seen in Table 10.1, the percentage of young people who say they feel a high degree of material deprivation is four times higher in Norway and Finland than in Spain. In Spain, the percentage of young people in great economic difficulty is similar to that observed in Denmark, despite the obvious differences in income levels to be found in young people from the two countries. In countries such as Sweden and Germany, material deprivation levels occupy an intermediate position, and it is Italy where young people claim to suffer least in terms of material necessities. Similar results are observed when analysing the difficulties experienced by young people in participating in leisure-related activities and the satisfaction of social and cultural needs. In all the countries, the level of social deprivation is greater than the level of material deprivation, indicating that economic difficulties arising from unemployment basically affect the satisfaction of social and cultural needs. Once again, Denmark and Italy are the countries in which people claim to have the lowest levels of deprivation, while in Finland, Norway, Sweden and Scotland the difficulty in satisfying these types of need is greater. Spain, like Germany, occupies an intermediate position.

Despite the greater generosity of the social welfare system in northern European countries, the results of this study show that the economic difficulties experienced by young people in these countries are greater than those found in southern European countries. Denmark is the only exception in this regard. The fact that in Spain and Italy the levels of deprivation observed are similar to those of Denmark is surprising, given that young Danes have significantly higher incomes than their Spanish counterparts and that the system of social protection for the unemployed is clearly superior in Denmark. It is also surprising that economic difficulties are less important in Spain than in countries such as Norway and Sweden, where the income levels of young people are similar, or Germany, where they are even higher. The fact that the majority of young Spaniards still live with their parents, and therefore do not have economic responsibilities, may explain these results.

Social and family integration: differences between countries

Table 10.1 shows some data that provide information on the degree of family and social integration of young people in each of the countries studied.

As can be seen, there are notable differences between countries with respect to the type of home in which young people live. The percentage of young people who continue to live with their parents reflects the quite different social realities of each country. While in the Nordic countries it is very common for young people to have left the family nucleus, in the other countries studied, the majority of young people continue to live with one or both parents. The two most extreme cases in this respect are Denmark, where only 16% of young people continue living with their parents, and Italy, where the figure is 91%. In all the countries, the majority of those who have left the family home have done so in order to live with a partner, and this is the most common type of living situation. The only exception in this respect is Scotland, where the percentage of young people living with a partner is similar to that of those living alone or with friends. The percentage of young people living alone is higher in Nordic countries than in other countries included in the study. Sweden has the highest percentage of young people living alone, while both Spain and Italy are at the other extreme, with just 2% of the young living alone.

It is in southern Europe that young people claim to spend most time with their families, which makes sense given that a higher percentage of young people here remain in the family unit. More than 85% of young Spaniards and Italians claim to see their families at least several times a week. The Nordic countries are those in which the young devote least time to being with the family, while both Scotland and Germany occupy the middle ground in this respect. Obviously, frequency of contact is not in itself an indicator of the degree of family integration of young people: a high level of integration cannot be assumed simply because a lot of time is spent with the family, and neither can it be concluded that family links are weaker if contact with the family is less frequent. It is therefore important to complement this type of information with some sort of measure of the degree to which young people feel they have their parents' support. In Denmark, for example, the support young people claim to receive from their parents is high, even though it is among the countries where there is least contact with the family. In fact, young Danes are more similar in this respect to young Spaniards and Italians than to young people from neighbouring countries, such as Finland and Norway, where young people feel least supported.

In all the countries, parental support is greater than that received from friends, despite the fact that more time is spent with the latter. Italy is the country where most time is devoted to being with friends, while the least contact with friends is to be found in Denmark and Germany. There are no significant differences in this respect among the other countries included in the study. Young Spaniards attach the greatest importance to the support received from friends, but they do not differ significantly in this respect from young people in countries such as Germany, Denmark or Sweden. It is in Norway where young people claim to receive least support from friends. Although it may be unwise to draw conclusions from this data about the degree of family and social integration of young people in the different countries, the information provided by the study does allow us to appreciate sharply contrasting social realities, with each possibly having different consequences for the person's psychological wellbeing. The family links maintained by young people from southern European countries appear to be greater than those in Nordic countries, where young people spend less time with the family and claim to receive less parental support. In principle, neither of the situations is better or worse for the psychological wellbeing of the young person. The higher degree of separation from the family in the case of young Nordic people may help to reinforce their personal identity in the transition to adult life, in the sense that this separation strengthens feelings of independence. However, it is equally true that continuing strong links with the family unit may contribute to reducing the emotional impact of negative situations such as unemployment, despite the risk of hindering the full integration of young people into adult society.

Differences in mental health

Figure 10.1 shows mean scores obtained in the Hopkins scale by young people from each of the countries included in the study. Hopkins scale measures the experience of symptoms related to depression and anxiety in the past two weeks. The higher the score the lower the mental health. In general terms, the mean scores obtained indicate that the level of psychological wellbeing of young people is high in all the countries compared. An analysis of variance reveals significant differences from country to country with respect to the mental health of young people ($F = 77.305$; $p<0.001$). Germany and Italy, followed by Denmark, are the countries where young people are found to have similar levels of mental health. The other Nordic countries, along with Spain and Scotland, have the lowest levels of mental health.

Figure 10.1: Differences between countries in mental health

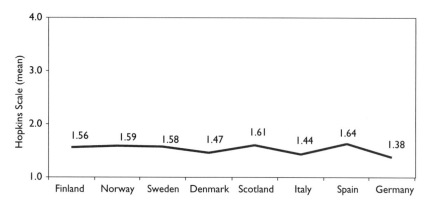

Note: Figure shows mean scores in the Hopkins Scale. Scores vary from 1 to 4.

Table 10.2 summarises the results of a regression analysis that included all the previously analysed variables. Gender is a predictor variable in terms of mental health, with women showing lower levels of psychological wellbeing than men. This result confirms those obtained in previous studies in which women were found to present more symptoms of depression and anxiety. The explanations offered for the difference in vulnerability between men and women vary, and it would appear to be due to a series of factors, among which are differences in role between the sexes, abuse received in childhood, socialisation differences and contrasting coping strategies in the face of stressful life events (Cochrane, 1992).

Age, on the other hand, does not have any effect on the psychological wellbeing of young people. Only in Denmark was there found to be a significant association between age and mental health, with symptoms of depression and anxiety being less marked for the youngest. Level of education did not have a significant influence on mental health in any of the countries considered, though lack of educational achievement was found to be associated with an increase in depression in all countries except Finland, Italy and Germany. All in all, the sociodemographic variables explained a very low percentage of the variance in all countries.

Variables related to social and family integration had a different effect depending on each national context. Household type does appear to have a slight effect on mental health. Living with a partner had a positive impact in Sweden. Nevertheless, this factor explains only a small percentage of the variance. Social support also had a small influence on mental health. As one of the objectives of this research was to analyse the effects of different forms of social support on the mental health of young people, no global measure was used, and all the items of the social support scale were included in the analysis.

Table 10.2: Factors influencing mental health (regression analysis)

	Finland	Norway	Sweden	Denmark	Scotland	Italy	Spain	Germany
Gender (female = 1)	0.205***	0.130***	0.224***	0.243***	0.184***	0.210***	0.133***	0.107***
Age				−0.082**				
Failed course		0.107***	0.090***		0.103***		0.079***	0.070***
Education (Ref = university)								0.059**
Compulsory								
Secondary								
Vocational								
Current situation								
Employment					−0.081**			
Ocassional work					0.072*			
Education	−0.065**							
Training scheme								
Total time in paid job (Ref = no experience)								
<6 months								
6-12 months								
13-24 months								
>24 months					0.073*	0.081**		
Total time unemployed (Ref = <6 months)								
6-12 months								
13-24 months				0.114**	0.073*	0.063*		0.061**
> 24 months				0.094**				
Economic situation								
Monthly income (*)								
Material deprivation	0.157***	0.096**	0.127***	0.087**	0.181***		0.081***	0.168***
Social deprivation	0.170***	0.205***	0.192***	0.248***	0.159***	0.189***	0.260***	0.194***
Living with... (Ref = parents)								
Alone								
Partner			−0.073***					
Friends								
Parental support								
Warmth/ affection	0.121***						0.066***	
Lent money		−0.145***					−0.048*	−0.078***
Work/study advice	−0.079***		−0.046*	−0.060*		−0.088***	−0.069***	−0.120***
Talk about personal matters								
Economic advice								
Help in practical matters								
Other favours		0.114***		−0.066*				0.054*
Support to education				−0.083***	−0.142***	−0.084**	−0.067***	−0.114***

/continued

Table 10.2: contd.../

	Finland	Norway	Sweden	Denmark	Scotland	Italy	Spain	Germany
Friends' support								
Warmth/ affection			0.077***	0.120***		0.069*		
Lent money	−0.103***		−0.59**					
Work/study advice			−0.065**	−0.088**		−0.079**	−0.078***	−0.074***
Talk about personal matters						−0.123***		−0.070**
Economic advice					−0.099**			
Help in practical matters			0.071***			0.071**		
Other favours								
Social relations: contact with...								
Family	−0.061**		−0.036*	−0.066*	−0.067*		−0.057**	
Friends	−0.060**		−0.060**				−0.108***	−0.064**
Girl/boyfriend					−0.102***			
Expectations								
Working	−0.101		−0.078***	−0.070**	−0.083**	−0.179***	−0.062**	−0.056**
Unemployed	0.061**		0.065**				0.041*	
Education								
R^2	0.225	0.183	0.241	0.231	0.274	0.152	0.225	0.257

* $p<0.05$, ** $p<0.01$, *** $p<0.001$.

Note: Only significant variables are reported.

In this way it was possible to evaluate the effect of each form of social support on psychological wellbeing. As can be observed, economic support offered by parents had a positive influence on the mental health of young people in some countries. Those respondents who say that they had received financial support from their parents present fewer symptoms of psychological deterioration. The same effect is observed when this form of support is given by friends. Another result that deserves comment is that for the effects of emotional support on mental health. In contrast to the consequences observed for financial support, emotional support is negatively associated with psychological wellbeing. Those young people that report more emotional support from parents show greater psychological deterioration. This apparently negative effect could be explained by this form of social support being associated with a high degree of parental control. However, the results obtained do not confirm this hypothesis. If social control had a negative impact on mental health, then negative effects should correspond to frequency of contact with the family, and our results show that the more frequent the family contact, the better the mental health of young people. Moreover, our data indicate that emotional support received from friends has negative effects comparable to those for parental support, and it is highly improbable that support given by friends is associated with social control. What our data suggest is that the causal relationship between social support and mental health should be reversed. Receiving emotional social support from parents and friends may be the consequence of trying to cope with the effects of a deterioration in mental health, rather than the cause of a decrease in psychological wellbeing. Taking into account that the questions included to measure the degree of social support received referred to the previous two weeks, it is probable that those young people who experienced symptoms of depression and anxiety sought this form of support to a greater extent than those who did not have these types of problem. In any case, the effect of these variables on mental health is weak.

In all of the countries, the most important factor for predicting mental health among the young was economic hardship. The degree of deprivation, be it social or material, had a significant effect on mental health in every country. It was the introduction of these variables that gave rise to the greatest increases in R^2, and once they had been taken into account, the explanatory power of the other variables fell considerably.

Once economic precariousness had been taken into account, then, the employment status of the young people at the time of the interview had little effect on mental health. Scotland was the only country in which employed young people presented higher levels of mental health than those who were unemployed. On the other hand, doing casual or seasonal work, without continuity, had a negative effect on the mental health of young Scots.

The experience of unemployment accumulated by young people throughout their working life had a greater effect on mental health than their employment situation at the end of the study, though this result was not obtained in all countries. Young people that had accumulated unemployment experience of more than a year presented lower levels of mental health in countries such as Scotland, Italy, Germany and Denmark.

It should be emphasised that the subjective perception of one's position within the labour market had more impact on young people's psychological wellbeing than did their objective situation at the time of the interview. In general, those young people who expected to be working within a year showed higher levels of psychological wellbeing than those who expected to be jobless.

In sum, the results of the regression analysis indicate that the principal determinant of young people's psychological wellbeing is the degree of economic deprivation, both social and material, to which they are subjected. Once this factor is taken into account, other variables, such as social support or employment status, have a slight influence on their mental health. The extent of financial hardship experienced by young people is significantly associated with depression and anxiety. Financial difficulties or non-availability of financial support is significantly predictive of greater deterioration in affective wellbeing after controlling for other variables.

Summary and discussion

This study has compared the level of mental health of unemployed young people in different countries, identifying some of the variables that help to explain the differences observed. The employment situation of young people, the accumulated experience of employment and unemployment, subjective perception of the future employment situation, economic difficulties, and the degree of social support received are some of the factors that have been taken into account in describing the emotional response to unemployment in each country.

One of the main differences between the countries studied is the level of social protection offered to unemployed people. In the Nordic countries there is a generous model of social welfare offering generalised aid to the unemployed. On the other hand, it is uncommon for young unemployed people from southern European countries to benefit from such support, and where people do have access to this type of help it is usually insufficient in itself to guarantee proper satisfaction of their needs. The data obtained in this study reflect these differences to some extent, though they also indicate that the economic situation of the unemployed person and the hardship suffered is not solely dependent on the social welfare model of the country in question. Despite enjoying less social protection, young people from Mediterranean countries claim to feel less deprivation than their counterparts from northern European countries. Young Spaniards and Italians experience as many economic difficulties as the Danes and fewer than the Scots, Finns, Norwegians and Germans. These results can mainly be put down to the fact that the majority of young people from Mediterranean countries still live in the parental home, a highly uncommon situation in Scandinavian countries.

The results of this study also show that where and how young people live is not indicative of their degree of family and social integration. The fact that most young people from Mediterranean countries continue to live in the family home does not mean that the family support received is greater in southern European countries than in those of northern Europe. If we compare the level of parental support received in the different countries, we can see the similarity between Denmark and the southern European countries in this respect. Although young Italians and Spaniards spend more time with their families than their Danish counterparts, the support received from parents is quite similar in the three countries. It can be affirmed that in this respect, Denmark is more similar to the countries of southern Europe than to its neighbours, among whom Finland and Norway stand out as being the countries where young people have least parental support. The influence of social support on mental health is small. As found in previous studies (Ullah et al, 1985; Banks and Ullah, 1987), among all forms of social support, it is the financial support received by young unemployed people that has the greatest influence on their mental health. Those young unemployed people who experience a greater degree of financial support from parents or friends show better mental health;

emotional support does not have such a strong effect. Contrary to what might be expected, emotional support has a negative influence on the mental health of young unemployed people. Young people with a lower degree of emotional support have better mental health. The explanation for this result can be found in the fact that in the presence of psychological problems, such as symptoms of depression and anxiety, young people tend to seek and obtain emotional support from parents and friends. According to this explanation, certain forms of emotional support may be associated with depression and at the same time have a positive impact on mental health.

Another result that should be underlined is the small influence of employment status at the time of the interview on the affective wellbeing of young people. However, this does not mean that being unemployed has no effect on mental health. In fact, young people's expectations about their employment situation did have an influence on the psychological wellbeing scores in the different countries analysed. Those young people who expected to be unemployed in a year's time showed higher levels of deterioration than those who thought they would be working. These data suggest that for this age group, in a transitional phase with respect to the labour market, it is necessary to take into account not just the present situation but also their working-life history and their employment expectations for the future.

Taking into account all the variables considered, we can conclude that it is in Denmark where young people are in the best situation. In addition to living in one of the countries where least economic difficulty is experienced by the young unemployed, young Danish people have a more solid position within the labour market. Young Danes experience the shortest periods of unemployment, have spent most time in paid employment and have the highest probability of re-employment. In addition, they receive a high degree of support from parents, and their situation in this respect is more similar to that of young people in Mediterranean countries than that of young people in their neighbouring countries. Bearing this in mind, it is hardly surprising that Denmark is one of the countries with the highest level of mental health among young people.

The data obtained in this study show that the economic instability associated with unemployment is a basic factor affecting the mental health of the unemployed. In all the countries studied, the psychological wellbeing of young people was more closely linked to social and material deprivation than to their work situation. This leads us to highlight the role of economic hardship in determining the mental health of the unemployed, a role that has been largely ignored in psychosocial research on the effects of unemployment. Although the first studies in which the effects of unemployment on mental health were assessed (Jahoda et al, 1933) concluded that the impact of unemployment was greater when it went hand in hand with high levels of economic difficulty, subsequent research has placed little emphasis on the economic factor. This is, in fact, one of the main focuses of criticism of psychosocial research on the effects of unemployment. One of the reasons for this oversight may be the erroneous interpretation of Jahoda's approach (1979), one of the most widely-used theoretical explanations of the effects of unemployment. Jahoda's hypothesis (1979), derived from Merton's functionalist theory, is that employment, in addition to fulfilling the obvious function of providing the individual with economic subsistence, has a series of latent functions – it imposes a time structure, it facilitates personal relationships outside the family environment, it provides social prestige, it enables participation in the achievement of collective objectives and it helps the development of an identity. According to Jahoda, it is the lack of access to such experiences, and not just the loss of income, that explains emotional deterioration among the unemployed. Although the author never denied the influence of economic difficulty on mental health, it is a fact that the use of this conception of employment has led to the underestimation of this factor, giving rise to criticism by a number of researchers (Fraser, 1980; Kelvin and Jarret, 1985; Álvaro, 1992).

In conclusion, it can be said that this study has shown how, in the current European context, (at least with regard to the countries analysed) unemployment is related to psychological deterioration and to processes of social exclusion when associated with a situation of economic hardship. Given the social protection system established in the Nordic countries and the economic support from the family characteristic of southern European countries, such as Spain and Italy, situations of economic deprivation are scarce; this may help to understand the high levels of psychological wellbeing observed among young people in the different European countries analysed. However, the conclusion here should not be interpreted in the sense that unemployment is not a risk factor for the affective wellbeing of young people. The most appropriate interpretation is that unemployment will provoke emotional destabilisation insofar as it contributes to a significant reduction in young people's economic and sociocultural resources. The fact that economic hardship and financial support are two variables that significantly contribute to explaining psychological wellbeing in young people confirms the importance of income for mental health.

Finally, it should be stressed that these results refer to young people in the countries analysed, and cannot be generalised to other age groups or contexts other than those described here.

References

Álvaro, J.L. (1989) 'Desempleo juvenil y salud mental' ('Youth unemployment and mental health'), in J.R. Torregrosa, J. Bergere and J.L. Álvaro (eds) *Juventud, trabajo y desempleo: Un análisis psicosociológico (Youth, work and unemployment: A psychological analysis)*, Madrid: Ministerio de Trabajo.

Álvaro, J.L. (1992) *Desempleo y bienestar psicológico (Unemployment and psychological wellbeing)*, Madrid: Siglo XXI.

Banks, M.H. and Jackson, P. (1982) 'Unemployment and risk of minor psychiatric disorders in young people: cross-sectional and longitudinal evidence', *Psychological Medicine*, no 12, pp 789-98.

Banks, M.H. and Ullah, P. (1987) *Youth unemployment: Social and psychological perspectives*, Department of Employment Research Paper no 61, London: HMSO.

Blanch, J. M. (1986) *Desempleo juvenil y salud psicosocial (Youth unemployment and psychological health)*, Documentos de Psicología Social Serie Monografías 2, Barcelona: Universidad Autónoma de Barcelona.

Breakwell, G.M. (1985) 'Young people in and out of work', in B. Roberts, R. Finnegan and D. Gallie (eds) *New directions in economic life*, Manchester: Manchester University Press.

Cochrane, R. (1992) 'Incidencia de la depresión en hombres y mujeres' ('Incidences of depression in men and women'), in J.L. Álvaro, J.R. Torregrosa and A. Garrido (eds) *Influencias sociales y psicológicas en la salud mental (Social and psychological influences on mental health)*, Madrid: Siglo XXI.

Cohen, S. and Wills, T.A. (1985) 'Stress, social support and the buffering hyypothesis', *Psychological Bulletin*, no 98, pp 310-57.

Derogatis, L.R., Lipman, R.S., Uhlenhut, E.H. and Cori, L. (1974) 'The Hopkins Symptom Checklist: a self report symptom inventory', *Behavioural Science*, no 19, pp 1-15.

Donovan, A. and Oddy, M. (1982) 'Psychological aspects of unemployed: an investigation into the emotional and social adjustment of school-leavers', *Journal of Adolescence*, no 5, pp 15-30.

Eisenberg, P. and Lazarsfeld, P.F. (1938) 'The psychological effects of unemployment', *Psychological Bulletin*, no 35, pp 358-90.

Feather, N.T. (1982) 'Unemployment and its psychological correlates: a study of depressive symptoms, self-esteem, protestant ethic values, attributional style and apathy', *Australian Journal of Psychology*, vol 34, no 3, pp 309-23.

Feather, N.T. (1990) *The psychological impact of unemployment*, New York, NY: Springer-Verlag.

Feather, N.T. and Bond, M.J. (1983) 'Time structure and purposeful activity among employed and unemployed university graduates', *Journal of Occupational Psychology*, no 56, pp 241-54.

Fraser, C. (1980) 'The social psychology of unemployment', in M. Jeeves (ed) *Psychology survey*, London: Allen and Unwin.

Gallie, D. and Paugam, S. (2000) 'The experience of unemployment in Europe: the debate', in D. Gallie and S. Paugam (eds) *Welfare regimes and the experience of unemployment in Europe*, Oxford: Oxford University Press.

Gore, S. (1978) 'The effect of social support in moderating the health consequences of unemployment', *Journal of Health and Social Behaviour*, no 19, pp 157-65.

Hammer, T. (1999) 'The influence of different compensation levels of unemployment benefits on job chances among unemployed youth: a comparative study of the Nordic countries', *Acta Sociologica*, vol 42, no 2, pp 123-34.

Hammer, T. (2000) 'Mental health and social exclusion among unemployed youth in Scandinavia: a comparative study', *International Journal of Social Welfare*, no 9, pp 53-63.

Jahoda, M. (1979) 'The impact of unemployment in the 1930s and 1970s', *Bulletin of the British Psychological Society*, no 32, pp 309-14.

Jahoda, M. (1982/87) *Empleo y desempleo: Un análisis sociopsicológico (Employment and unemployment: A sociopsychologial analysis)*, Madrid: Morata.

Jahoda, M., Lazarsfeld, P. and Zeisel, H. (1933) *Mariethal: The sociography of an unemployment community*, New York, NY: Aldine-Atherton.

Julkunen, I. (2002) *Being young and unemployed: Reactions and actions in northern Europe,* Helsinki: University of Helsinki.

Kelvin, P. and Jarret, J. (1985) *Unemployment: Its social and psychological effects*, Cambridge: Cambridge University Press.

Marsh, C. and Álvaro, J.L. (1990) 'A cross-cultural perspective on the psychological distress caused by unemployment: a comparison of Spain and the United Kingdom', *European Journal of Sociology*, no 6, pp 237-55.

Sigurdardottir, T. and Bjarnason, N.T. (2000) 'Psychological distress among youth during unemployment and beyond', in A. Furlong and T. Hammer (eds) *Youth unemployment and marginalisation in northern Europe*, NOVA Report 18/00, Oslo: Norwegian Social Research.

Thoits, P.A. (1982) 'Conceptual, methodological and theoretical problems in studying social support as a buffer against life stress', *Journal of Health and Social Behavior*, no 23, pp 145-59.

Ullah, P., Banks, M.H. and Warr, P.B. (1985) 'Social support, social pressures and phychological distress during unemployment', *Psychological Medicine*, no 15, pp 283-95.

Veiel, H.O. (1985) 'Dimensions of social support: a conceptual framework for research', *Social Psychiatry*, no 20, pp 156-62.

ELEVEN

Welfare regimes and political activity among unemployed young people

Jan Carle

A great deal of discussion has emphasised the fact that there are differences in political behaviour (voting rates and so on) and attitudes (for example, support for left- and right-wing politics) between groups of young people in different social positions (Clark, 1985; Banks and Ullah, 1987; De Witte, 1992; Ashford, 1994; Riepel and Wintersberg, 1999). Research describing country-specific differences in political behaviour is also available. These differences might be interpreted as political styles within groups of countries (Franklin et al, 1992; France, 1996; Wallace and Kovatcheva, 1998). It might be the case that political behaviour reflects different political cultures, within as well as between countries. The reasons for these differences and similarities, however, are not very often the focus of research that deals with youth. Research on youth in general, as well as research on different subcultures, tends to describe segments of 'youth society', such as different segments of unemployed young people compared to the employed, skinheads versus punks, young people living with parents and those who do not (Dancis, 1978; Elterman, 1988; Decker, 1993; Lusane, 1993; Eyerman and Jamison, 1995; Dalhouse and Frideres, 1996). In research on youth unemployment it is common to stress that periods of unemployment are important in explaining different types of political behaviour among young people in general, as well as among those who are unemployed. This is to say that youth unemployment in itself could be the basis of a different and specific political subculture, rather than living within a different subculture. Moreover, unemployed people may have a situation in common that goes beyond the diverse aspects of the lives of young people in different countries. A great deal of research reflects this empirically, but much empirical research reflects uncertainty in this respect (Furlong and Cartmel, 1997; Wallace and Kovatcheva, 1998; Carle, 2000; Hammer, 2002). This kind of issue also enters the debate on postmodernisation and the supposed blurred relations between different social positions and social and cultural activity (Crook et al, 1992; Griffin, 1992; Jones and Wallace, 1992; Eyerman and Jamison, 1995; Marshall and Bottomore, 1997).

It may be that political behaviour and attitudes still embody much deeper social and cultural experiences going beyond what could be influenced even by long-term unemployment. Perhaps there are, among young unemployed people, some visions of a future society that incorporate certain inherent political strategies and imbedded cultural patterns. Moreover, perhaps these inherited visions are partly understandable in the light of the concept of welfare regimes. To use the concept in this context is a way of exploring the phenomena of youth unemployment and political behaviour in terms of different political cultures, rather than different subcultures among groups of young people. It is a way of believing in the existence of a national context.

Welfare regimes

I would like to use a model presented by Gallie and Paugam (2000) that could be described as the 'unemployment welfare regime model'. The model, introduced in Chapter One, has been constructed as a way of comparing countries according to strategies for combating unemployment. In the model – directly or indirectly – is imbedded the idea that a strategy for combating unemployment is a political choice and, therefore, the ultimate sign of different and similar political strategies within and between countries. The assumption within the model is therefore that welfare regimes are characterised by something related to the fact that people create specific strategies suitable for the situation in the particular country in which they live. My argument is that since the concept of welfare regimes tries to deal with the idea of political strategies one has to assume that political leaders plan these political strategies. Different regimes therefore reflect national and different political cultures. If not, then the model would be a simple reification, an empty concept not usable in social sciences.

According to Gallie and Paugam, the 'unemployment welfare regime model' deals with:

> those aspects of welfare regimes that provide protection from misfortunes in the labour market, primarily through the system of financial support for the unemployed and the institutional arrangements for intervention in the process of job allocation. (Gallie and Paugam, 2000, p 4)

Gallie and Paugam argue that it is possible to distinguish four regimes, based on three criteria:

> the degree of coverage is likely to be a critical factor for the way the welfare state affects the experience of unemployment [...] the level of compensation is also likely to have an important effect on experience of unemployment [...] the extent of development of active employment policies is likely to have an effect on the experience of unemployment, given that these can reduce the risk of long-term marginalisation from the labour market. (Gallie and Paugam, 2000, pp 4-5)

As described and analysed in previous chapters of this book Gallie and Paugam distinguish between four unemployment welfare regimes in Europe: the sub-protective regime, the liberal/minimal regime, the employment-centered regime and the universalistic regime.

This model can be criticised for not explicitly dealing with the social and cultural consequences of youth unemployment. It deals with welfare regimes in a more general sense, even if unemployment is the focus. One aim of this chapter is therefore to discuss this problem using this model to describe and analyse the relations between political behaviour and youth unemployment. Is it possible to distinguish any differences in political behaviour and youth unemployment that attest 'unemployment cultures' or 'cultures of unemployment'? What if looking at young people within different welfare regimes generates greater differences in political behaviour than experiences of unemployment? The general issue to be raised is: are there any differences in political behaviour if one takes into consideration that young people live in different welfare regimes? Are the similarities or differences of the same magnitude compared to experiences of unemployment?

In this study, three indicators of political activity are analysed. These indicators are: attitudes toward future society; the type of political activity in which young people have participated; and, finally, political attitudes measured on the commonly used scale of left and right. This chapter will focus on two themes: differences between the countries (in this case, country will be treated as a variable mainly by using the concept of welfare regimes) and differences among the young (concentrating on differences concerning gender, occupation and experience of unemployment).

It is important to stress some methodological problems. It is problematic to try to use the number of countries included in this study in a common analysis. One strategy would be to use only some of the countries, for example three or four, in order to maximise some expected differences. The argument is that when dealing with such a complex question as political culture it is very difficult to compare how young people actually interpret, for example, the concept of left and right. Nevertheless, having taken into consideration the concept of political activity and attitudes, the analyses have to be more general in order to be able to make comparisons. This is one of the essential problems in all comparative research. The variables that are available for comparison are very limited if you want to take into consideration more than hard facts such as income or age distribution. Attitudes and behaviour are indeed difficult to compare within different cultural and political contexts, which may be why studies on political behaviour among unemployed young people (at least in the opinion of this author) seem to be based on speculations and extrapolations made from small studies within specific subcultures, or simply assumptions derived from signs within other areas of society.

Political views on society

In the questionnaire we asked the respondents about their views of what kind of society they wanted in the future with the question: 'What kind of society do you think we should be working for?'. Seven different types of societies were listed and respondents marked on a five-point scale how strongly they agreed (5) or disagreed (1) with each type:

- a society of private enterprise and market economy;
- an environmentally friendly society, even if economic growth will be low;
- a society that utilises advanced technology such as computers and robots;
- a society of law and order;
- a society of equality with small income differences;
- a society with equality between men and women;
- a society of equality between ethnic groups.

The above question was used to map respondents' attitudes to society and to speculate about any relationships between these views and the political behaviour in different countries, as well as between occupational status, experience of unemployment and welfare regimes.

The results are shown in Table 11.1, where a higher mean (value) implies stronger agreement with working towards this kind of society. One can see that the variance, which is explained, is quite low. No more than 13% of the differences in the views on a future society with law and order, and 12% of the differences in the views on a future society with equality between ethnic groups, are explained by differences between countries. Less than 11% of the variation of opinion on the others types of future societies is explained by country. There are, however, some interesting features to comment upon in this table.

Unemployed youth in all countries appear to agree that a future society must have equality between men and women as a central goal. In contrast, the young people in this study are not as supportive of a society with more private enterprise and market economy or advanced technology.

However, it might be that these differences actually obscure other interesting aspects. With regard to the attitudes towards a future society with more law and order, the opinion in all the different countries is roughly the same, except for in Finland, France and Germany where young people are less positive.

Looking at equality for ethnic groups, we find that the countries are roughly divided into three groups: Finland, Norway and Denmark (with more disagreement); Iceland, Sweden, and Germany (with a little more agreement); and Scotland, Italy, Spain and France (where more young people agree). These groupings of countries do not correspond with Gallie and Paugam's models of different welfare regimes.

Women have a more positive attitude towards the three types of future society that imply equality, while men support those future societies that imply more private enterprise and advanced technology.

Very little of the variation is explained by occupation and experience of unemployment. However, it is possible to note a difference between young people in education and those who are unemployed. Those in education are

Table 11.1: Mean scores on attitudes towards future society, by country

	All	Finland	Iceland	Norway	Sweden	Denmark	Scotland	Italy	Spain	France	Germany
Private enterprise	0.091	3.9	3.6	3.5	3.6	3.6	3.0	3.3	3.8	2.8	2.8
Environment-friendly	0.035	3.5	3.2	3.5	3.5	3.7	3.5	3.8	3.9	3.4	3.5
Advanced technology	0.061	2.9	3.1	2.9	3.1	3	3.2	3.6	3.5	3.3	2.6
Law and order	0.132	2.8	3.9	4	4	4.1	3.9	3.9	4.1	3.2	3.4
Equal income	0.039	3.9	3.9	3.9	4.0	3.4	3.6	3.7	3.8	3.8	3.3
Equal men and women	0.040	4.4	4.6	4.1	4.5	4.4	4.2	4.3	4.7	4.2	4.2
Equal ethnic groups	0.117	3.2	3.7	3.3	3.9	3.1	4.1	4.2	4.3	4.2	3.7

Note: Eta-squared is the proportion of variance in the dependent variable (views on society) that is explained by differences among groups (countries). It is the ratio of the between-groups sum of squares and the total sum of squares.

more in favour of a future society with equality between ethnic groups, as well as a society with more advanced technology.

These views on a future society appear to have little to do with young people's current activity or experience of unemployment, which indicates that neither the experience of unemployment nor the country's welfare arrangements have a significant influence on young unemployed people's political attitudes.

To further investigate the attitudes on types of future society, a factor analysis was carried out in order to reduce the information and to be able to use it in other analyses[1]. The analysis identifies two factors, which explain 43% of the total variance in the variables. The first factor combines all the questions dealing with attitudes on more equality and attitudes on a more environmentally friendly society. The second factor combines society with more private enterprise, advanced technology and a society with more law and order. Based on this information, two variables were constructed as an index (total mean) of the two sets of variables. The two new variables were called *equality* and *technology*. It is important to stress that these factors are strictly statistical, that is, it is based on which combinations of variables individuals gave high scores. The reason for choosing these factors must also be interpreted theoretically. It can be assumed that these two different factors actually deal with well-known political differences between left and right, as well as between different views on the role of the state and on political strategies within the welfare state. It has also been assumed that there is a gender difference, as women are assumed to rate equality more highly than are men.

The factor *equality* scores higher (analysis based on comparisons between means, Anova test with significant differences) in the sub-protective regime (4.1) and about the same in the other regimes (3.8). There is hardly any difference at all according to current activity. Females are more positive about equality (4) than men (3.8). There are no differences at all in the attitudes on equality if we consider time spent unemployed (between one and six months [3.9] compared to more than 36 months [3.9]).

The most positive attitudes towards *technology* were found among young people living in *sub-protective regimes* (3.7), and the least positive attitudes among young people living in *employment-centred regimes* (3.1). Unemployed young people are less positive about technology (3.4) than young people who are in education (3.5). There are no differences at all in the attitudes on technology if we consider time spent as unemployed (between one and six months [3.5], compared to more than 36 months [3.5]).

To conclude, the differences in views on future society have very little to do with experience of unemployment or current activity. However, the differences are higher if we consider welfare regimes and, in some cases, age and gender as well. It is possible to find a pattern in these attitudes. We find either a group that foresees a society with diverse aspects of equality, or one that foresees a society with more advanced technology and market economy. The similarities in attitudes are slightly more homogeneous towards *equality* than towards *technology*. Young people living in sub-protective regimes are more positive about both *technology* and *equality* than those in other regimes. Moreover, these differences suggest something else – a well-known variation in political orientations towards the left and the right. The validity of this assumption is examined in the next section.

Political attitudes

The differences in political attitudes are measured on a left–right scale. This type of scale is widely used in comparative studies. What is generally known about political sympathy measured with such a scale is that, among many other social characteristics, there are also differences between adults and young people, as well as between countries. It is possible to examine the data in at least two ways: by placing those who have said that they are definitely somewhat to the left and right in the scale's two categories and using the middle alternative as political indifference, and by analysing means. According to the data, the general picture is the same when using either of these two types of measurement. In the following section, both measures are used.

Eight countries were compared in this case. The findings are as follows, in terms of sympathy with the left: Italy (54%), Sweden (43%), Scotland (43%), Denmark (36%), Iceland (29%), Norway (25%), Germany (20%) and Finland (15%). The young unemployed in Italy, Sweden and Scotland lean more to the left, while young people in Finland and Germany do not have leftist sympathies. These figures are close to what is known about random samples of young people in Europe. The proportion of young people who place themselves on the left ranges from nearly 60% in Spain to nearly 30% in Denmark and 10% in Poland (Wallace and Kovatcheva, 1998).

Looking at current activity, we find that there is hardly any difference at all between different activities, except that the unemployed have slightly less sympathy with the left than young people in other activity groups. If we then look at welfare regimes, the following pattern according to support for the left can be found: sub-protective (54%), liberal/minimal (43%), universalistic (32%), and employment-centred (20%). The main result is that young people who live in universalistic and employment-centred welfare regimes have political attitudes that are less on the left than do the young unemployed in the other regimes.

It is also interesting to discuss the number of young people who lean to the right. Whether there is rising support for right-wing parties is an often-debated question among youth researchers today, especially in the context of unemployment. In fact, there is a fear of the consequences of increased right-wing support (rather than increased left-wing support), which probably dates back to the events in Europe that preceded the Second World War. The presidential election in France in 2002, where the extreme right-wing candidate Jean Marie le Pen gained considerable support before losing in the second round is one example of increasing right-wing support in Europe. Others are Silvio Berlusconi in Italy and Pia Kjersgaard in Denmark, leaders representing a new right-wing political movement. In the debate, a combination of general economic decline, high unemployment among uneducated young men in urban areas, and the proportion of immigrants in these countries explain much of the 'success' of right-wing politics.

In Sweden, however, there is very little support for right-wing parties. During the economic decline in the 1990s, Sweden had a right-wing government rather than a socialist one, as was the case in several other European countries with strong right-wing parties today, such as Denmark, Norway, Italy (with a partly socialist government previously) and France. In the election in Sweden during autumn 2002, the Social Democratic Party remained in power and the Conservative Party suffered its greatest loss in modern times. However, in the local elections in the municipalities and especially in the south of Sweden (close to Denmark) extreme right-wing parties won victories.

The results show that the young unemployed people in Scotland and Germany clearly do not have sympathies with the right, while at least in Denmark, Norway, Finland and Italy about one third of the young unemployed have such sympathies. It is also in Denmark, Norway and Italy that we find right-wing parties represented in both national and local parliaments. Of course, one has to take into consideration the fact that left and right could actually mean slightly different things within different countries. It is therefore important to stress that these similarities and differences should not be interpreted as absolute differences, but rather as relative and understood within the specific context of this study.

Finally, what do we know about current activity? Young people who were unemployed at the time of the study, together with those in education, are generally more to the left. In addition, however, those in employment have the highest proportion of sympathy with the right, and this pattern is the same in each country. These results indicate that there are differences between countries when it comes to political interests and attitudes, which seem concerned with different political cultures. This is particularly significant if we compare the general impact of experience of unemployment and sympathy for the right. What we find is that sympathy for the right decreases with experience of unemployment, up to an experience of over 37 months, but after that, the figure increases. Support for the left increases somewhat, but decreases slightly after more than 37 months of unemployment.

However, the main impact of unemployment has to do with neither left nor right. This pattern prevails in every country, although at different levels. The most striking finding is in Germany, where two thirds of the unemployed young people are neither to the political left or right, and this figure hardly changes with experience of unemployment. This result, too, reflects general research on political behaviour, which shows that the best political supporters to recruit are those who have not yet taken a political stand. It is much harder to convince a person who knows their position already.

This result might be taken to mean that unemployment goes hand in hand with political apathy, or that such political standpoints do not seem very important when one has much experience of unemployment. However, the experience of unemployment is not comparable with the far stronger influence of country or welfare regime. Political attitudes vary between countries independent of unemployment status.

The above results show two distinct but important things about youth unemployment and political attitudes. First, the time spent in unemployment does seem to have some influence on political attitudes, and in at least two ways. There is more political support for the left, but in some cases, a swing towards the right occurs after a very long experience of unemployment. There is also a growing tendency of young people to support neither left nor right, which actually means that experience of unemployment goes hand in hand with not taking a political standpoint.

Political actions

In this study, questions were asked about participation in political actions and attitudes towards willingness to participate. The respondents were asked about their involvement in several pre-specified political actions on three illustrative levels: whether they had engaged in a stated political action; whether they could imagine carrying out a stated action; or whether they could not imagine carrying out a stated action. The following actions were covered in this study:

- signing a petition;
- taking part in boycotts;
- taking part in legal demonstrations;
- taking part in wildcat/illegal strikes;
- occupying buildings or factories;
- wearing a pin to show support for a cause;
- voting;
- attending meetings organised by a political party;
- attending meetings organised by a union organisation;
- attending meetings organised by other organisations.

This type of technique has also been used in international studies (for example, Eurobarometre 37.0, 1992). Table 11.2 shows the percentage of young people who said that they had participated in any of these kinds of political actions, by country.

The most common political activity among the participants was voting in elections, although on a lower level in Scotland and Germany. These figures also highlight a well-known pattern: the percentage of those who vote in elections increases with age. Looking at current activity, the voting rate is lowest among unemployed (77%) and highest among those in education (88%),

Table 11.2: Participation in political action, by country (%/total scale mean of all actions)

	All	Finland	Iceland	Norway	Sweden	Denmark	Scotland	Italy	Spain	Germany
Signed a petition	55	46	61	63	74	59	60	30	63	38
Taken part in boycott or strike	14	11	19	16	26	22	14	10	7	5
Taken part in demonstration	12	6	12	15	15	14	11	36	31	5
Taken part in unofficial strike	15	1	2	3	2	2	2	47	39	21
Occupied factories and so on	5	1	1	2	1	1	4	37	3	1
Carried badge	19	9	34	26	15	21	43	10	24	6
Voted in elections	82	80	86	83	85	89	68	87	86	70
Attended political meetings	14	4	19	14	12	13	11	20	21	14
Attended union meetings	12	5	15	16	17	27	8	6	10	9
Attended organisation meetings[a]	18	11	26	18	18	19	18	30	22	4
Total scale mean of all actions	2.5	1.7	2.7	2.5	2.6	2.6	2.3	3.1	2.9	1.7

Note: [a] Other than a union or political meeting.

and this pattern holds even when taking age into account. The longer young people were unemployed the less likely they were to vote, but the differences are not very large. Of those who had been unemployed for up to six months, 85% voted in elections, compared to 80% of those unemployed for more than 37 months.

Besides voting, the young people have, in ranked order, signed a petition, carried a badge, attended other organisations' meetings, taken part in unofficial strikes, attended political meetings, taken part in boycotts or strikes, taken part in demonstrations and attended union meetings, and lastly, occupied factories or buildings. The figures are in some senses striking. The figures for taking part in unofficial strikes are high in Italy, Spain and Germany compared with all the other countries. The same goes for taking part in demonstrations and attending political meetings, where the figures are high in Italy and Spain compared with all the other countries.

The general impression is that participation in political actions in general is higher in Sweden and lower in Finland and Scotland, except for participation in demonstrations, unofficial strikes, and political meetings and other organisations' meetings, where the activity is higher in Spain and Italy. To check this impression in a more simple way, a total index was made, which is a mean of all the different actions (index value from minimum 1 to maximum 10).

This comparison shows another picture. The countries divide into three groups: Finland and Germany clearly below the overall mean, Italy and Spain above it, and the rest of the countries close to it. These differences might be correlated with welfare regimes. Political activity is lowest in employment-centred regimes (1.7), slightly higher in liberal/minimal (2.3) and universalistic regimes (2.4), and highest in sub-protective regimes (3).

From the research available, one might expect the unemployed to participate to a lesser extent in political actions, and men and women to engage in different political activities (Griffin, 1992; Furlong and Cartmel, 1997; Wallace and Kovatcheva, 1998). Women are in general more politically active than men, but men are more engaged in what could be called militant activities (demonstrations, occupations and so on). In general, there are three different levels of participation, according to current activity. Looking at the total mean value, we find differences between those who are unemployed and others (below the overall mean) compared to those who are in education (above the overall mean), while the differences between the other groups are quite small (close to the overall mean). The total time spent in unemployment does affect political participation negatively. Participation decreases up to a total experience of 36 months of unemployment, but after more than 37 months, there is a slight increase in activity. It is interesting to find the increase in participation in unofficial strikes, demonstrations, political meetings and other organisations' meetings that comes with more than 37 months of unemployment experience. The fact is that time spent in unemployment has an impact on political participation in two directions – a decrease as well as an increase.

It is also interesting to see the relationship between views on a future society and political activity. Political activity (as a number of counted activities) is generally higher among those who support a future society with equality and lower among those who support a future society with technology. The activity is also related to political attitudes. Those with sympathies to the left are at the same time more politically active. There is also a significant positive correlation between sympathies to the left and a future society with equality. This indicates that political activity, views on a future society, political attitudes, and living in different unemployment welfare regimes go hand in hand.

If we then look at attitudes toward the statement that one is not prepared to take part in any political action, we find differences between the countries. Young unemployed people in Germany (with some exceptions) seem to be most reluctant to participate in any of these stated actions except to vote in elections. The young people in Scotland, together with those in Sweden, are in some cases much less reluctant to participate in actions, especially signing a petition, taking part in boycotts or strikes and occupying factories (together with Finland) and demonstrations, and carrying a badge (together with Iceland).

In the same way, we can look at welfare regimes, age, gender, occupational status and experience of unemployment, and the reluctance to participate in political actions. Age correlates with reluctance to participate: younger unemployed people are more reluctant. Men are also more reluctant. The unemployed are more reluctant to participate than those in training or especially those in education, therefore experience of unemployment correlates with reluctance to participate.

Concluding remarks

From a Nordic point of view, it is often said that the Nordic welfare state model (a universalistic regime) goes hand in hand with both political awareness and activity. This is not clearly borne out by the young people in this study. Those who live within the universalistic welfare regimes are in many ways living in a society with a better system of social protection. This does not necessarily result in more political activity and less reluctance to participate in it. It appears that welfare regime did not have an important influence on the political behaviour of young unemployed people.

However, there were some main differences between countries. Rates of political activity such as voting in elections were clearly lower in Scotland, Finland and Germany, compared with the other countries. The general participation rate in all political actions was also very low in Finland and Germany, but was higher in Scotland for some actions.

A striking result is the great similarity between young people in different countries, especially when it comes to their views on what type of society is worth fighting for in the future. The opinions of young people in this study have indicated that European society should be based on equality more than one based on technology and market economy. This is an interesting point to bear in mind when considering the future of the European Union.

Note

[1] "Factor analysis attempts to identify underlying variables, or factors, that explain the pattern of correlations within a set of observed variables. Factor analysis is often used in data reduction, by identifying a small number of factors that explain most of the variance observed in a much larger number of manifest variables. Factor analysis can also be used to generate hypotheses regarding causal mechanisms or to screen variables for subsequent analysis" (SPSS, from help-file within program).

References

Ashford, S. (1994) 'Politics and participation – some antecedents of young people's attitudes to the political system and political activity', *European Journal of Social Psychology*, vol 24, no 2, pp 223-36.

Banks, M. and Ullah, P. (1987) 'Political attitudes and voting among unemployed youth', *Journal of Adolescence*, vol 10, no 2, June, pp 201-16.

Carle, J. (2000) 'Political activity in the context of youth unemployment – experiences from young people in six northern European countries', *YOUNG*, vol 8, no 4.

Clark, A. (1985) 'The effects of unemployment on political attitudes', *Australian and New Zealand Journal of Sociology*, vol 21, no 1, March, pp 100-8.

Crook, S., Pakulski, J. and Waters, M. (1992) *Post-modernization: Change in advanced society*, London: Sage Publications.

Dalhouse, M. and Frideres, J.S. (1996) 'Intergenerational congruency – the role of the family in political attitudes of youth', *Journal of Family Issues*, vol 17, no 2, pp 227-48.

Dancis, B. (1978) 'Safety pins and class struggle: punk rock and the left', *Socialist Review*, vol 8, no 3, pp 58-83.

Decker, J.-L. (1993) 'The state of the rap: time and place in hip hop nationalism', *Social Text*, vol 34, pp 53-84.

De Witte, H. (1992) 'Unemployment, political attitudes and voting behaviour', *Politics and the Individual*, vol 2, no 1, pp 29-41.

Elterman, H. (1988) 'The politics of music and the protest song: a case study of antiwar songs of the 1960s', *Sociological Viewpoints*, vol 4, no 1, pp 63-81.

Eurobarometre 37.0 (1992) *Europeans and the environment*, Brussels: European Commission, INRA.

Eyerman, R. and Jamison, A. (1995) 'Social movements and cultural transformation: popular music in the 1960s', *Media, Culture and Society*, vol 17, no 3, pp 449-68.

France, A. (1996) 'Youth and citizenship in the 1990s', *Youth and Policy*, vol 53, pp 28-43.

Franklin, M.N., Mackie, T. and Valen, H. (eds) (1992) *Electoral change: Responses to evolving social and attitudinal structures in Western countries*, Cambridge: Cambridge University Press.

Furlong, A. and Cartmel, F. (1997) *Young people and social change*, Buckingham: Open University Press.

Gallie, D. and Paugam S. (eds) (2000) *Welfare regimes and the experience of unemployment in Europe*, Oxford: Oxford University Press.

Griffin, C. (1992) *Representations of youth: The study of youth and adolescence in Britain and America*, Cambridge: Polity Press.

Hammer, T. (2002) 'Youth unemployment, welfare and political participation: a comparative study of six countries', in J. Goul Andersen and P. Jensen (eds) *Changing labour markets, welfare policies and citizenship*, Bristol: The Policy Press, pp 129-48.

Jones, G. and Wallace, C. (1992) *Youth, family and citizenship*, Buckingham: Open University Press.

Lusane, C. (1993) 'Rhapsodic aspirations: rap, race and power politics', *Black Scholar*, vol 23, no 2, pp 37-51.

Marshall, T.H. and Bottomore, T. (1997) *Citizenship and social class*, London: Pluto Press.

Riepel, B. and Wintersberg, H. (1999) *Political participation of youth below voting age*, Eurosocial 66/99, Vienna: European Centre.

Wallace, C. and Kovatcheva, S. (1998) *Youth in society: The construction and deconstruction of youth in east and west Europe*, London: Macmillan Press.

TWELVE

Concluding remarks

Torild Hammer

The main finding of this study is that few young unemployed people were socially excluded, even in countries such as Italy and Spain with extremely high unemployment. We identified vulnerable and marginalised groups, but not groups that were socially excluded in the sense that they were marginalised according to all dimensions (see Chapter One). However, it must be stressed that our study encompasses only young people who were registered as unemployed. It is possible that those who do not register as unemployed face worse situations than those who do register.

Nonetheless, the study found that young unemployed people, particularly those who have experienced financial deprivation, have a higher risk of marginalisation in some areas. The results of the study showed that Scottish and Finnish unemployed youth face a particularly difficult situation. Even though the unemployment rate is high in southern Europe, young people there are well supported by their parents. Although the unemployment rate is much lower in Scotland, the proportion of long-term unemployed people was nearly as high in Scotland as in Finland and southern Europe – countries with much higher unemployment rates overall. Further, the high unemployment rate among parents of unemployed Scottish youth indicates that unemployment tends to hit Scottish households and marginal groups, suggesting a cumulative disadvantage over time.

Scottish and Finnish unemployed youth are not as well supported by their parents as are their counterparts in Italy and Spain, and at the same time they receive a relatively low level of benefits. The universalistic welfare regime of Finland entitles young people without unemployment benefits to flat-rate benefits such as social assistance or benefits for the uninsured. However, the level of support is about the same as those who receive Jobseeker's Allowance in Scotland. In Finland, there are strong social norms about leaving the parental home at a young age to seek independence. In Scotland, more young people live with their parents than in Finland. However, unemployment and deprivation in Scottish households make the situation difficult for Scottish unemployed youth. This situation is also evident if we examine the subjective dimensions of social exclusion.

It was found that Scottish and Finnish unemployed youth reported lower levels of wellbeing than their counterparts in the other countries. We also found lower levels of political activity in Scotland and Finland compared with the other countries, in particular among the long-term unemployed. Danish unemployed youth enjoyed by far the best situation. Generous unemployment benefits and high coverage allowed them to leave home independent of unemployment. They reported low levels of financial deprivation, better mental health, better coping with unemployment, and a higher level of wellbeing than their counterparts in the other countries.

It is important to note that Scottish and Finnish unemployed youth did not experience social marginalisation. However, those with careers dominated by unemployment received low scores on the sociability scale, which was developed from information on the frequency of participation in a range of social activities. Seven activities were included in the scale. However, even those unemployed young people who were passive, it seems, were not isolated, and their social networks seemed to be intact, with emotional and instrumental social support from parents and friends.

Given the arguments about the disincentive effects of high levels of benefits, we would have expected particularly high levels of work commitment among Scottish and Finnish youth. However, contrary to expectations, the results indicated lower levels of work commitment among the long-term unemployed in these countries than, for instance, in Sweden or Spain, where unemployed youth enjoyed a better financial situation.

This project highlights some pressing questions that are important for a comparative perspective on youth policy. Such a perspective has been missing in most previous studies because of lack of data. Because most policies to combat youth unemployment and social exclusion are instituted at the national level, there is a pressing need to locate variations in such policies. Without variation, it is difficult to investigate if and why some policies are more successful than others.

The findings clearly illustrate how complicated for the young unemployed the transition from youth to adulthood is. Their unemployment renders them financially vulnerable if they are not financially supported by their families or through sufficient benefits. The political debate has, to a great extent, focused on the need to cut benefits for young people and to introduce workfare. Many people would argue that the withdrawl of benefits for young people is a withdrawal of citizenship rights. The results here show that Danish unemployed youth, with their high levels and broad coverage of benefits, were enjoying by far the best situation and that, in spite of this, they were returning to employment. They were also better integrated into employment than were the unemployed youth in the other countries. Unemployed youth in Spain and Italy were also far better off than young people in Finland and Scotland, although their integration into the labour market was heavily dominated by temporary contracts and informal employment. The low level of support in Finland implies that this country does not represent a universalistic welfare regime for unemployed youth. Even though the unemployment rate has dropped in the past three years, 25% of young people were still unemployed in 2000. The results of this study demonstrate that this group, the majority of whom are first-time jobseekers, face an extremely difficult situation.

During the past decade, there have been many debates about creating a common framework for social policies in the European Union (EU) countries. Such policies should be based on the social values and attitudes that the countries in the EU have in common: the European social model. The decision taken by the EU leaders at the European Council held in December 2000 in Nice to initiate new National Action Plans for social inclusion was in accordance with such a framework. There have also been several calls for a 'Social Europe' to complement 'Economic Europe' (Begg and Berghman, 2002). Social exclusion and long-term unemployment is evident throughout the EU, but varies markedly between countries. There are also systematic differences among countries in the degree to which their welfare systems succeed in forestalling social exclusion. It is one thing to create a common framework for an identified European social model, but quite another to implement welfare policies in the different countries. There are clearly very different welfare regimes and protection systems in the member states. Social protection systems are often politically sensitive because they represent national agreements that have been carefully constructed over generations. They are not easy to change.

Previous research about unemployment and social exclusion has found that the protection against social exclusion varies according to different welfare regimes. Most previous research differentiates between the universalistic, social democratic model represented by the Nordic welfare states; the continental sub-protective model; and the liberal/minimal model (Ireland/UK and southern Europe). These welfare regimes vary according to protection systems (Gallie and Paugam, 2000). The Nordic model offers generous social protection, whereas the sub-protective model in Spain and Italy gives little public support, and protection is primarily based on family support. Previous research has found that in the south, full-time employment of the male breadwinner is the most important barrier against social exclusion.

The EXSPRO research (Begg and Berghman, 2002) found that the Nordic model performs best in attaining a high level of labour market flexibility while providing income and employment security. At the other end of the scale, southern Europe appears to deliver the worst combination of flexicurity, with a combination of little public support, while relying heavily on a traditional male-breadwinner model with a rigid labour market. Denmark represents the opposite: a flexible labour market combined with high levels of public protection and strong coverage of public protection. The Anglo-Saxon regime, based on a liberal/minimal model, represents a flexible labour market with little protection. The sub-protective regime lies between the two others.

However, none of these previous studies has focused especially on unemployed youth. The results from our study show that the relationship between unemployment and social exclusion is different in this age group.

Italy, in particular, represents a rigid labour market with high long-term unemployment among youth. However, our study shows that Italian unemployed youth do not experience financial deprivation and do, in fact, enjoy high levels of wellbeing. They tend to be sociable, with high levels of support and good mental health. However, even though unemployment in their households is low, they are dependent on the breadwinner of the family. Few (15%) were integrated in employment. In other words, the situation for young unemployed people in Italy is a combination of high levels of support and a rigid labour market with insiders and outsiders. They are excluded from the labour market, but not from other areas of life. Such a situation may create disincentive problems: first, they are highly dependent on their families, which may discourage geographical mobility; second, the economic incentives for jobsearch may be a problem, not because of generous benefits but because of extensive family support. Danish young people are in much the same situation. However, the flexibility of the Danish labour market may explain why so many of the previously unemployed young people in Denmark were integrated into employment at the time of the interview, even compared with other countries such as Norway, with the same unemployment level. In any case, the Danish political situation has changed since the year of our data collection (1996/97), by introducing workfare and a more active labour market policy to counteract disincentive effects among unemployed youth.

The Nordic model is the most generous, but not for unemployed youth in Finland, where the structure of unemployment hit young people in particular. Even if the sample of unemployed youth was drawn on the basis of the same criteria in all countries, the Finnish sample is much younger than the Swedish and Norwegian samples. In Norway and Sweden, the governments guarantee that everyone under 20 years of age will receive an offer of either education or employment. This guarantee has been implemented, and explains the difference between countries. In addition, mass unemployment in Finland occurred suddenly, and there was no established family culture such as exists in the south that would place responsibility for providing for the young unemployed on the shoulders of the family.

It is difficult to identify a policy to combat youth unemployment that can be applied equally well in all countries, for a successful policy in one country can be difficult to transfer to a different labour market situation and a different welfare regime. However, it is possible to identify some dilemmas that politicians must acknowledge in order to implement new policy.

One such dilemma is the level of benefits that young people should be entitled to. Our results indicate that young people in a difficult financial situation often face many other problems that can inhibit effective jobsearch and consequently reduce the probability of employment. This is particularly so in Britain, where unemployment is more concentrated within households and benefits have been withdrawn for anyone under the age of 18. The current policy recommended by the Organisation for Economic Co-operation and Development (OECD) is to reduce benefits. It seems that at a certain level, and given certain national labour market conditions, such a policy could actually reduce employment opportunities.

———

In any case, in many countries, such as Italy and Spain, the question of benefits is irrelevant because the family's dependency on the employment of its male breadwinner is the most important barrier to social exclusion. This reality constitutes the second dilemma. Most young people in Spain and Italy are well supported by their families. However, this situation in itself constitutes its own set of problems, particularly in low-income families, because many young people are denied access to the labour market and therefore full citizenship at an age when most of their counterparts in Europe are well established on their own. These are indeed difficult problems – problems that we believe must be faced at the national level if solutions are to be found.

We also learned that Finnish and Scottish youth faced a particularly difficult situation and were marginalised along several dimensions. Moreover, we found that the age of the first spell of unemployment was an important predictor of successive unemployment. The situation in Scandinavia (Norway, Sweden and Denmark) was much better than in the other countries studied in this project. The youth guarantee implemented in these countries implies that all young people should have an offer of either education or employment. Our recommendation is that such a guarantee should also be implemented at a European level or at least as a policy recommendation for the member countries. This is particularly important in Britain and Finland. In Britain nearly 30% of the age cohort leaves school at 16 years old, often without any alternatives; the situation is also difficult in Finland. Such a guarantee would at least postpone some of the problems faced by young unemployed people in Europe and make the situation easier for them and their families.

References

Begg, I. and Berghman, J. (2002) 'Introduction: social (exclusion) policy revisited?', *Journal of European Social Policy*, vol 12, no 3, pp 179-94.

Gallie, D. and Paugam, S. (eds) (2000) *Welfare regimes and the experience of unemployment in Europe*, Oxford/New York: Oxford University Press.

Samples and attrition

Finland

Sample

The criteria for the sampling procedure were the same as in the research design. The statistical representativeness was controlled on the basis of region, unemployment level, unemployment duration, gender and education. The sample was drawn from national unemployment registers, and included young people who were receiving either flat-rate benefits or unemployment insurance payments. The following criteria must be fulfilled in order to be included in the register:

- 17-64 years of age;
- capable of work;
- a jobseeker at the employment office;
- looking for full-time work.

Attrition analysis

The Finnish register material comprises information concerning the age, residence, education, employment and unemployment of the young people in the study, as well as the municipal unemployment level. It also gives information on spells of unemployment and employment of the young people from 1992 to 1995.

The Finnish sample consisted of 2,386 people. A total of 1,736 young people responded to the questionnaire, which gives a response rate of 73%. Seven age classes were included, the oldest subjects being born in 1970 and therefore being 24 years old at the time of the sample. The youngest were born in 1976 and were therefore 18 years old at the time of the sample. The 19- and 20-year-olds were the groups with proportionately the highest response rate – nearly 80% – whereas the response rate was 70% for the 18- and 23-year-olds. The response rate was lowest among the 24-year-olds: 62%. The overall response rate was 78% for women and 69% for men; women were, therefore, somewhat over-represented in the data. As regards variables such as education and duration of unemployment, the analysis showed that there were no significant differences between the entire sample and the respondents. The attrition analysis on the local unemployment level showed that young people from average unemployment areas (17-22%) were slightly under-represented, whereas those from high unemployment areas (>22%) were slightly over-represented (see Julkunen and Malmberg-Heimonen, 1998).

Iceland

Sample

The sample was selected from the same age groups as in the other Nordic countries, but there were some different sampling procedures. The questionnaire was sent to those who were registered as unemployed at the 20 different unemployment offices throughout Iceland. The sample consisted of young unemployed people who had undergone at least two months of unemployment during the first half of 1995. The total number of unemployed young people is relatively small in Iceland, particularly in comparison with the other Nordic countries (the population of Iceland is approximately 270,000, which corresponds to the population of Bergen). Due to the small numbers of unemployed, and particularly long-term unemployed young people in Iceland, the research was conducted as a total study in which virtually every person who was unemployed at the time of the sampling was included. This strategy created some problems in the statistical analysis, which assumes random sampling. The following rules are applicable for being registered as unemployed in Iceland:

• The person must be a wage-earner who has worked at least 425 hours during the previous 12 months before becoming unemployed (and also has the right to receive compensation from the unemployment insurance fund).
• The person must be looking for work, older than 16 years but younger than 70 years, and live in Iceland or in another EEC country.
• The person must be able to provide certification from an employment office that he or she been unemployed for at least three whole days at the beginning of the period for which the unemployment compensation is applied.

Private entrepreneurs have the same rights as wage-earners, provided that they fulfil all the basic criteria and can prove that their business has been closed down. The questionnaire was answered by 1,290 persons, which gave a response rate of 60%. The sample was 53% male and 47% female, with 70% of the women and 61% of the men answering the questionnaire. Thus, women are slightly over-represented in the material.

Norway

Sample

A total of 97,934 young people aged 18-24 years were registered as unemployed at some time during the first half of 1995, and 19% of these fit the definition of long-term unemployed (>3 months). The sample was selected from among those who had had at least three months of continuous unemployment during the period 1 January to 30 June 1995, and who were looking for full-time work. The group consisted of 39,020 persons, of whom 17,909 were unemployed at the time of the sample. From this population 2,000 people were selected. The sample seems to be representative of the population (39,020) in terms of key characteristics that can be controlled through the register. When it comes to age there was a slight over-representation of the older age groups in the sample.

Attrition analysis

Altogether 1,106 people answered the questionnaire, yielding a response rate of 56%. The register data were coupled with information about those young people in our study who had given their permission (85%; $n = 944$). It is possible to use register information of the whole sample ($n = 2,000$) to analyse eventual skewness that may affect the possibility of making generalisations from the sample.

In the attrition analysis we compared the sample with the respondents on an extensive set of register information. There were no differences between the sample and the respondents with regard to proportion who had received benefits, length of the unemployment period, total experience of unemployment, dropout from compulsory schooling, previous work experience, proportion without any relevant work experience or education, and place of residence. The only difference was that 22.9% of the sample had only compulsory school education or had no qualifications, compared with 16.1% among the respondents. The difference is statistically significant ($z = 4.47$). However, a larger proportion of the respondents had only one or two years of vocational education, compared with the overall sample, in which a greater proportion had completed a full vocational education. There were no differences with regard to other educational categories. Contrary to expectations and despite a low response rate, the attrition cannot be considered skewed.

Sweden

Sample

The criteria applied to the sample were the same as in the research as a whole. The sample was selected through the AMS (the Labour Market Board), which created a random sample among people registered as unemployed in HÄNDEL, the database on people actively seeking work. There are no formal limitations to being included in the register, other than attending an employment office to report looking for a job. The next phase consisted of coding the different categories, for example, student, working, unemployed. The sample therefore consisted of people registered as unemployed (which excludes full-time students and retired persons).

Attrition analysis

There was a total of 801,093 young people aged 18-24 in Sweden in 1995. During the first half of the year there was an average of 82,000 unemployed people per month aged 16-24 (Labour Force Survey), yielding a sample of 1.2% of the unemployed young people during the sample period.

The sample comprised 4,000 people (two people were excluded because of technical problems, and the net sample was therefore 3,998). There were altogether 1,853 women (46%) and 2,147 men (54%). The questionnaire was answered by 2,534 persons (1,247 women and 1,287 men), yielding a response rate of 63%. The questionnaire was answered by 49% of women and 51% men. The response rate among the women was 67% and 60% among the men.

The attrition consists of 1,084 persons. An attrition analysis was carried out on the basis of information from the register material. Due to technical problems, however, a comparison between the sample and the respondents could not be completed for all cases. Information on 191 respondents (97 women and 94 men) was not included in the attrition analysis.

The attrition analysis showed that there were no statistical differences in citizenship, work handicaps and place of residence. Men turned out to have been unemployed for an average of 22.8 weeks compared with 20.9 weeks among the respondents. Unemployment among women averaged 8.9 weeks in the attrition group and 9.7 weeks among the respondents.

Denmark

Sample

The sample was randomly drawn from the Central Unemployment Register (CRAM), in which all unemployed are currently registered. Most unemployed people (about 85%) and the main part of the labour force (about 80%) are members of an unemployment insurance fund. Both insured and non-insured are registered. The non-insured unemployed are those receiving social assistance from the local authorities. However, many people receiving social assistance are not registered as unemployed in the Central Unemployment Register. This means that some non-insured young people without employment are not registered as unemployed. Therefore, and because of the limited size of sample, it was decided only to include insured young unemployed people in the study.

The population from which the Danish sample was drawn was defined in the following way:

• Insured people of age 19-24 years (at 1 January 1995) with a total of less than three months' unemployment in the second half of 1994, and with more than 13 weeks of unemployment in the last 26 weeks before weeks 1-26 in 1995.

Consequently, the population consists of young insured people with more than three months of unemployment in the last 26 weeks before weeks 1-26 in the first half of 1995. Or put more simply, the Danish population consists of young insured persons having been unemployed more than three months. From this population (about 12,000 persons) a simple random sample of 1,500 persons was drawn. Of these, 19 persons had invalid person identification numbers.

Consequently, the effective sample consisted of 1,481 persons to whom the questionnaire was sent. Those who did not answer were contacted by interviews (by telephone). The questionnaire was answered by 1,171 persons, which gave a response rate of 79%.

Attrition analysis

The questionnaire was answered by 83% of the women and 78% of the men. This difference is statistically significant ($p<0.001$). The response rate did not depend on age, but young people from the eastern part of Denmark (Copenhagen and the islands) answered generally to a lesser extent than young unemployed people in the western part of Denmark. There were no statistically significant differences with regard to the duration of previous unemployment.

As mentioned, the Danish sample only includes insured people. In general, it is to be expected that the insured unemployed category comprise 'stronger groups' than non-insured. However, there exist no recent nationwide studies on the composition of insured and non-insured unemployed people and the mobility between these groups. There is a clear need for research and statistics in this area in Denmark.

Scotland

Sample

The sample was selected from the same age groups as in the Nordic countries, but there were different sampling procedures. In the Nordic countries, the sample was collected through the unemployment registers, while in Scotland interviewers were placed in a representative range of unemployment benefit offices throughout the country. All the young people had been unemployed for a minimum of three months at time of first contact. Postal questionnaires were completed six months after sampling, at which point some young people had found jobs, entered schemes or returned to education, while others remained unemployed or were experiencing a further spell of unemployment. The questionnaire was completed by 817 respondents, which gave a response rate of 56%. The sample consisted of 65% men and 35% women, which reflects the actual proportions of men and women unemployed in this age group in Scotland.

Attrition analysis

The attrition consisted of 629 individuals. The attrition analysis could only be based upon gender, area of residence (rural or urban) and length of unemployment, as we did not have access to unemployment register data. There were slightly more men who failed to respond than women, although this was not statistically significant. The length of unemployment did not affect response rates, but there were more non-respondents living in poorer urban areas than in rural areas, although again this was not statistically significant.

Italy

Sample

The survey was carried out from March to June 2000 on a sample of 1,421 youths (aged 18-24) registered as unemployed a year before, living in Campania and Veneto. (Note: the young teenagers, aged 14-17, included in the UN definition of young people, were excluded from the sample). Another stratification criterion was adopted, after the interview quotas had been established, based on gender and place of residence, in such a way that the final sample should be statistically representative of the underlying population in the regions considered. In 1999, the reference period of the survey, the unemployment rate was at 6.5% in central and northern regions and at more than 22% in southern regions. More dramatically, the youth unemployment rate (15-24 years) was 19% in the north and in the centre, but over 56% in the south. The long-term unemployment rate (more than one year) was 3.1% in the centre–north and 14.8% in the south. To mirror this situation, the sample has been stratified, with two thirds of the interviews being concentrated in the south. The two regions considered represent very different labour market contexts, with Campania being one of the highest and Veneto one of the lowest unemployment regions in the country. The sample was selected among individuals registered at the local unemployment office for at least three months at the time when the sampling procedure was carried out, a year before the interview. The main problem arising from this procedure is that jobseekers enrolled in placement registers do not completely overlap with all the unemployed people recorded in the official Labour Force Survey, the so-called *Rilevazione trimestrale delle forze di lavoro* (RTFL). Among other reasons, this depends on the fact that enrolment in the registers is only one of the various criteria requested of those actively seeking a job. In fact, first, it is possible to be registered as unemployed while being employed as a part-time (for less than 20 hours per week) or temporary (less than four months) worker. Moreover, people enrolled in the registers are not always properly qualified as jobseeking unemployed. It is possible to register even if one is not actively seeking employment, as stated in the ILO definition (search activity in the month before the interview and immediate availability to work).

Data were collected by means of direct interviews. Interviewers got in touch with people during a period of four months – from March to June 2000 – through the 'chain rule', exploiting their own direct or indirect acquaintance network and contacts with public or private institutions involved in supporting the analysed population. Interviews were anonymous, but spot checks were carried out, to test the effective submission of the questionnaire. Of those interviews, 1,421 turned out to be valid and complete after verification. They represented 447 of the 500 envisaged in Veneto and 974 of the 1,000 envisaged in Campania.

Attrition analysis

A comparison between registered unemployed in the Labour Force Survey (LFS) and in the YUSE data can be carried out, keeping in mind that the available data refer to young people aged 15-25, living in Italy, rather than aged 18-24, living only in two regions (Campania and Veneto). The period is almost the same: October 1999 in the case of the LFS and the second semester of 1999 in the Youth Unemployment and Social Exclusion Survey (YUSE) case. Another caveat regards the type of question asked in the two questionnaires. The YUSE questionnaire contemplates the following labour market statuses: employment, unemployment, school or university attendance, training, socially useful contacts, unpaid family work, compulsory military service, sickness and other unmentioned status. The LFS contemplates the following alternatives: unemployment; employment; seeking a job, but not actively; not seeking a job, but available to work; not seeking a job and not available to work.

In the YUSE case, it was found that 18% of the sample is unemployed, 36% employed, 44% involved in high secondary or tertiary education and 3% in other activities. In the LFS case, Barbieri and Schever (2001), 35% are unemployed, 11% are employed, 27.6% are not actively seeking a job but are available to work and 26.7% are not participating to the labour market.

Considering the differences existing in the questionnaire, the disparity in the YUSE and LFS shares can be explained as follow: (a) many young people considered as employed in the former dataset are actually involved in informal or occasional activities; (b) those involved in university education are essentially unemployed jobseekers, not available to work or out of the workforce. It should be taken into account that out of 5.6 million people, 900,000 are university students, which corresponds to about 40% of the population aged under 25. Therefore, spreading the university students over the other groups and considering that the employed include workers not considered in the LFS, the distribution of individuals is very similar in the two surveys.

Spain

Population and sample

During 1998, the average number of young people registered as unemployed in Spain was 376,056. Of these, 45.83% had been unemployed for less than three months, and 54.17% were long-term unemployed. The population consisted of young people aged 18-24 who had been registered as unemployed during 1998 for at least three consecutive months. The sample was randomly selected from the database of the INEM (National Employment Institute). The INEM is an organ of the Ministry of Labour that registers additions to and deletions from the list of people making social security contributions. In Spain, unemployed people are not obliged to register with the INEM.

The Spanish sample was selected in February 1999. The data collection process began in February 2000, one year after selection of the sample, and ended in June 2000. During this period, the questionnaire was sent to the selected young people on three occasions.

Attrition analysis

The questionnaire was sent to 5,000 young people, 3,090 (62%) women and 1,910 (38%) men. The final sample was made up of 2,523 young people, 966 men (38,3%) and 1,557 women (61.7%). The response rate obtained was therefore 50.46%. The attrition analysis was limited to gender and level of education, as it was not permitted to use the register information. The response rate did not depend on gender. The questionnaire was answered by 50.6% of men and 50.4% of women.

There were significant differences between the sample and the respondents with regard to level of education (see Table A.1). People without qualification and those with elementary education responded to a smaller extent than the other groups. The percentage of people with secondary-level education was higher among the respondents ($p<0.01$). There were not significant differences between the sample and the respondents with regard to the other educational categories.

Because we did not obtain permission to access the register information, we could not complete the attrition analysis on length of unemployment. Nevertheless, we could obtain an approximate analysis of distortion by comparing

Table A.1: Differences between the sample and the respondents (%)

	Respondents	Sample
Gender		
Male	38.3	38.3
Female	61.7	61.7
Education		
No qualification	1.2	1.9
Primary level	30.0	36.4
Professional education (first degree)	11.8	11.0
Professional education (second degree)	13.9	13.6
Secondary level	15.7	13.3
University diploma	16.3	15.9
University degree	8.6	7.9
	Sample[a]	**Population**
Length of unemployment (months)		
3-6	36.5	36.9
6-12	22.3	26.3
12-24	14.5	20.9
>24	26.0	15.9

Note: [a] Only those currently unemployed for more than three months were included.

the respondents' data with the official statistics for the entire population. As seen in Table A.1, there are no differences between the entire population and the respondents when comparing the percentage of people who had been unemployed for less than six months. However, people with longer periods of unemployment are under-represented among the respondents, with the only exception being of periods longer than 24 months.

Germany

The German sample population comprised young people aged 18-24 at the beginning of a spell of continuous unemployment that lasted for at least 92 days between September 1998 and September 1999 and who were registered at the unemployment registry of the German Federal Employment Services (Bundesanstalt für Arbeit).

A sample of 3,200 young people was drawn in autumn 1999 and 1,918 interviews (a response rate of around 60%) were conducted between March and November 2000.

Data were collected by 80 qualified interviewers supported by a supervisor and using computer-assisted telephone interviews (CATI) conducted by Infas (Institut für angewandte Sozialforschung GmbH), Bonn. A sample of interviews was tape-documented and controlled by the IAB (Institute for Employment Research). Interviewers received study-specific training, in which the IAB research group participated.

Interviews lasted an average of 65.1 minutes. Each participant was informed about the telephone interview by an official letter and received as an incentive a telephone card valued at €6, which had been designed specifically for the study.

The master sample contains information about age, gender, nationality and region of the unemployed. This information was used for selectivity tests. Logistic regression models were estimated, to identify selectivity effects for the group of respondents versus non-respondents. The explained variance for all the calculated models is extremely small, which indicates poor selectivity effects.

Estimates of selectivity effects for CATI participants versus the group of non-respondents (Pseudo R^2 0.008) contained weak significant effects for a small subgroup with missing data and for a small group of the long-term unemployed (aged 26 years plus, meaning that the observed spell of unemployment started long before September 1998).

Estimates of selectivity for CATI participants versus the young unemployed, who intended to participate but did not in fact participate because they were not at home at the time of the interview or because they said they did not have the time to participate. This group was called latent non-participants. Again, the estimated model discriminates poorly (Pseudo R^2 0.005), which means no observable selectivity effects.

France

The French sample used for the YUSE project was extracted from ANPE (Public Employment Service) and UNEDIC (Unemployment Benefit Agency) register data files. As required by the overall design of the YUSE samples in all the countries, the French sample has the following characteristics:

- it consists of young people between the ages of 18 and 24;
- the young people have been unemployed for at least three months between 1 June 1998 and 1 June 1999;
- the sample must be representative by region of residence, level of educational attainment and gender.

As a result, we obtained an initial database to sample from of 25,013 cases and the breakdown by educational attainment is given in Table A.2.

Despite the fact that both the CAP and BEP diploma appear at level V in the French classification system[1], they were kept apart from the rest of level V so that there were enough respondents at all the relevant levels. Both CAP and BEP are very important diplomas in France.

The breakdown by region is given in Table A.3 and by gender in Table A.4.

Table A.2: Initial database, by aggregated level of educational attainment

Level of education				Cumulative	Cumulative
French classification	ISCED	Frequency	%	frequency	%
Missing	Missing	2	0.01	2	0.01
BEP diploma	2	5,151	20.59	5,153	20.60
CAP diploma	2	4,480	17.91	9,633	38.51
Levels I, II and III	5-7	4,938	19.74	14,571	58.25
Level IV (Bac)	3	7,074	28.28	21,645	86.54
Level VI and other V	I and 2	3,368	13.46	25,013	100.00

Table A.3: Initial database, by region of residence

Region	Frequency	%	Cumulative frequency	Cumulative %
Missing	1,956	7.82	1,956	7.82
1. Île de France (Greater Paris)	3,527	14.10	5,483	21.92
2. Unknown	2,190	8.76	7,673	30.68
3. Œst (East)	1,791	7.16	9,464	37.84
4. Loire (Loire Valley)	3,156	12.62	12,620	50.45
5. Bourgogne (Burgundy)	2,032	8.12	14,652	58.58
6. Normandie (Normandy)	2,201	8.80	16,853	67.38
7. Aquitaine	2,459	9.83	19,312	77.21
8. Centre	2,609	10.43	21,921	87.64
9. PACA (Alps and Provence)	3,092	12.36	25,013	100.00

Table A.4: Initial database, by gender

Gender	Frequency	%	Cumulative frequency	Cumulative %
Male	11,130	44.50	11,130	44.50
Female	13,883	55.50	25,013	100.00

Given the budget, a random draw of 4,000 units was carried out. Those 4,000 raw cases yielded 2,001 completed cases, available for the analysis. The survey was carried out from March to May 2000 by a subcontractor (CSA) and conducted by telephone (CAPI). The mean duration of the questionnaire was 29 minutes. Since the survey is retrospective and is not a panel data survey, we were not faced with the usual problem of attrition. However, and for the usual reasons – not at home, moved, refused and so on – there is some kind of non-response (see Table A.5). Finally, the structure of the sample used for the analysis is given in Table A.6.

Table A.5: Respondents and reasons of non-response (%)

Completed cases	51.2
Not at home	8.8
Not at home for the entire survey period	6.3
Moved	5.0
Not applicable	19.2
Refuse to answer (several reasons)	9.5
All	100.0

Table A.6: The final sample, by level of educational attainment

Level of education French classification	ISCED	Frequency	%	Cumulative frequency	Cumulative %
Level VI and other V (without diploma)	0-1	372	18.59	372	18.59
CAP and BEP diploma (V)	2	577	28.84	949	47.43
Level IV (Bac level)	3	595	29.74	1,544	77.16
Levels I, II and III	5-7	400	19.99	1,944	97.15
Other	Other	57	2.85	2,001	100.00

As in the questionnaire, CAP and BEP diplomas are grouped together. As a consequence, we cannot distinguish the two items in Table A.5 either. The structure by level of education is quite different from the structure of the initial database. Since all the other levels of educational attainment are represented in the same proportion in the sample as the initial database, the proportion of individuals holding a CAP or a BEP is less than expected.

The final breakdown of the sample by gender is given in Table A.7.

As a comparison between Table A.4 and Table A.7 shows, the structure by gender is slightly modified in the sample: the proportion of women is only slightly higher in the sample but it does not impact on the quality of the sample.

Table A.7: The final sample, by gender

Gender	Frequency	%	Cumulative Frequency	Cumulative %
Male	844	42.18	844	42.18
Female	1,157	57.82	2,001	100.00

Note

[1] The French social classifications are as follows:

VI	Personnel carrying out jobs that do not require any training beyond the end of compulsory schooling
Va	Personnel holding jobs that presume a short training period of less than one year leading notably to a Vocational Education Certificate or any other certification of the same nature
V	Personnel holding jobs that normally require a training level equivalent to that of the Vocational Studies Certificate (BEP) and the Vocational Certificate (CAP)
IV	Personnel holding supervisory jobs or having a qualification at a level equivalent to that of technical baccalaureate
III	Personnel holding jobs that normally require training at the level of the higher technician's certificate (Bts) or diploma from the university institutes of technology (Iut), at the end of the first cycle of higher education; including Deug
II and I	Personnel holding jobs that require training at a level equal or superior to licence or *Grandes Ecoles*

References

Barbieri, P. and Schever, S. (2001) 'Logici e razionali? Compartamenti strategici dell'offra di Laboro nella tranzizione scuota-lavaro in confiort fra Nord e Sud Italia', Paper presented at AIEL conference, Milan, 16 November.

Julkunen, I. and Malmberg-Heimonen, I. (1998) *The encounter of high unemployment among young people in the Nordic countries*, Report No 188/1998, Helsinki: Tyoministerio.

Index